WHAT SO PROUDLY WE HAILED

Previous Books by Fred J. Cook

THE SECRET RULERS

THE CORRUPTED LAND

THE FBI NOBODY KNOWS

THE WARFARE STATE

A TWO-DOLLAR BET MEANS MURDER

WHAT MANNER OF MEN

THE UNFINISHED STORY OF ALGER HISS

THE PLOT AGAINST THE PATIENT

★★★

WHAT SO PROUDLY WE HAILED

by Fred J. Cook

PRENTICE-HALL, INC.
ENGLEWOOD CLIFFS, N.J.

★★★

*★★★★★★★★★★★★★★★★★★★★★★★★★★★★★★★★★★ CONTENTS

1

TEARS IN THE FABRIC

She was the wife of a long-time country judge, a woman who annually headed the Red Cross drive in her town and devoted herself to charitable causes. She stood in the living room of her well-furnished home and looked about her. Tears, only half-suppressed, filled her eyes. One son, she said, was on his way to Vietnam. Another was finishing college and would soon be draft bait. She was a quiet woman, and she did not wring her hands or wail or complain, but she said: "It makes you wonder sometimes if anything is worthwhile."

In this same year of discontent and bitter disillusionment, another mother in similar circumstances was more angrily outspoken. She and her husband were church-going, conservative people. He was a businessman and a deacon in their church; she was active in women's organizations. She also had a son who was finishing college; already, he had been scheduled to take his Army physical. Over him, too, Vietnam cast its long and sinister shadow.

"This is what you get for living in America today," his mother said, almost savagely.

The revolt of the long-hairs and the draft-card burners had captured the headlines. But gradually there had developed a quieter, deeper and more significant opposition. It came from those middle-class, middle-of-the-road segments of our society who traditionally support the nation's Establishment in its decisions. Even many who normally did not question had begun to do so. Secretary of State Dean Rusk's parrot-squawks—"Munich, Munich, Munich"—did not convince, did not persuade. Many Americans were failing to embrace the patriotic sacrifice demanded of them. They were not loyally resigned to offering their sons' and husbands' lives on the altar of Marshal Ky, our South Vietnamese champion of "freedom" whose idol was Hitler.

Expressed in such rebellions by those not normally rebellious was the trauma of an America struggling to discover its own true identity as it faced the 1968 Presidential year. It was the time for a crucial choice. Whether such a choice could be made given the peculiar structure of American politics, whether there would be any clear-cut delineation of issues, remained to be seen. But the issues were there. They would not go away. And on the question of whether they were met and resolved, or ducked and compromised, could well depend the future viability of American democracy.

Vietnam was the capstone, but not the sum, of our frustrations. In Vietnam we had come to face an ideological negative. Throughout two decades of the Cold War we had pursued this negative with the fanaticism of an outraged Puritan divine at grips with the devil. Anti-communism had

2

been our lodestar, the be-all and end-all of our endeavors. It had led us to support regimes that represented the very antithesis of every democratic ideal—the savage dictatorships of Batista and Trujillo in Cuba and the Dominican Republic; the brutal military oligarchies throughout much of Latin America, in Taiwan, Greece and Turkey. It had led us into the bloody cul-de-sac of Vietnam in support of tyrannical regimes unable to sustain themselves because they did not have the allegiance of their own people.

Vietnam was not the only cause for travail. It was only one in a long litany of misfortunes, most of them linked and interrelated. The long, hot summer of 1967 had gone into history as the worst in the nation's experience—the year when the specter of racial revolution, long brewing, had threatened to tear apart the very fabric of American society. Wave after wave of insensate protest had swept the city streets. Two years earlier the nation had been shocked when Watts, a Negro ghetto of Los Angeles, had erupted to produce the most violent and destructive race riot of our times. In the summer of 1967 Watts seemed almost commonplace. Ghettos across the nation exploded in a frenzy of hate and destruction. Sections of Newark and Detroit stood charred by the emotional firestorm, lone chimneys and blackened walls as stark as those of bomb-gutted Namdinh in North Vietnam thousands of miles away. In Washington, Congress showed every sign of abdicating responsibility. President Lyndon B. Johnson, the architect of the Great Society, stopped using that irrelevant term as additional thousands of American youths were sent to Vietnam.

In such fashion were we paying for our long pursuit of the ideological negative. We have created what John Kenneth Galbraith dubbed "the affluent society"—a society of conspicuous prosperity and consumption with two cars in every garage, two television sets in every home, boats waiting in marinas, and extra telephone lines for the exclusive use of our children. On the surface, viewed from the terraces of the country clubs or the well-tended streets of suburbia, assessed against a background of memory that included the harrowing days of the Great Depression, it seemed to many that America had achieved a virtual millennium. Even if installment payments threatened solvency, even if there was little security beyond the horizon of next week's pay check, this was still the *good* life; look at what we *had*. Euphoric America had been content with its possessions; it had not wanted to think or criticize—or rock the boat. The affluent society meant joys and goodies for everyone. Only a malcontent would presume to suggest that this was not the best of all possible worlds. These had been our complacent assumptions. Then came Newark and Detroit—and Vietnam. And one had to ask: Were these assumptions valid?

A great American had expressed our dilemma in these words:

> In this nation I see tens of millions of [America's] citizens—a substantial part of its whole population—who at this very moment are denied the greater part of what the very lowest standards of today call the necessities of life.
>
> I see millions of families trying to live on incomes so meager that the pall of family disaster hangs over them day by day.
>
> I see millions whose daily lives in city and on farm

continue under conditions labeled indecent by a so-called polite society half a century ago.

I see millions denied education, recreation, and the opportunity to better their lot and the lot of their children.

I see millions lacking the means to buy the products of farm and factory and by their poverty denying work and productiveness to many other millions.

I see one-third of a nation ill-housed, ill-clad, ill-nourished.

If those last words sound familiar, they should. The quotation is from the second inaugural address of Franklin D. Roosevelt in January, 1937. Roosevelt's statement at that time was an accurate summary. Thirty years later it was equally valid.

During those years in which we were creating the affluent society, the gap between the haves and the have-nots had widened into a chasm. Approximately two-thirds of all Americans were enjoying the fruits of affluence, but the remaining third remained very much where they had been in 1937, sunk in the sloughs of poverty and deprivation. Though statistics remained little changed, there was this vital difference between the two periods: In 1937 times had been hard for nearly everyone; in 1967 the good life of the top two-thirds of American society cruelly mocked the enduring hopelessness of the deprived.

It seemed incredible that despite decades of unrivaled prosperity so little actually had changed. Yet statistics clearly showed what had happened. For nearly two years a U.S. Senate subcommittee headed by Sen. Abraham Ribicoff (D., Conn.) had been holding hearings on the

Federal role in urban affairs. Testimony before Ribicoff's committee, based largely on 1960 census figures, showed that some 34–35 million Americans were living in poverty, with family incomes of $3,000 a year or less; another 28 million, who had barely raised their heads above this low-water mark, were suffering severe deprivation. In other words, some 62–63 million Americans out of a population of 180,684,000 in 1960 were still living in circumstances not greatly different from those of the Great Depression days some thirty years earlier.

The prosperity of the 1960's has served only to magnify these trends and intensify the disparity. The prosperous continued to prosper at an accelerated rate, but the condition of those at the bottom of the scale became even more desperate. Census estimates indicated that in 1966 some 13 million American families, more than one-fourth of the total, had incomes of $10,000 or more a year. This compared with 10 million families, or 17 percent, possessing such income in 1961. Clearly, the upper and middle classes of American society had never had it so good. Yet there were millions, approximately one-third of the nation, who remained outcasts in this sea of plenty, and among these millions were many who quite literally were starving to death.

In the South especially, the poverty and suffering—and the callous indifference to them—reminded one more of the brutal serfdom of the Dark Ages in Europe than of the twentieth century in prosperous America. Here was the festering sore that infected so much of the rest of the nation, and any understanding of the cumulative problems

6

and fierce tensions that threatened to overwhelm American society had to begin here at the source—in the South. In April, 1967, a U.S. Senate subcommittee on Manpower, Employment and Poverty, headed by Sen. Joseph S. Clark (D., Pa.) and including Sen. Robert F. Kennedy (D., N.Y.), conducted an on-the-spot investigation of conditions in Mississippi. They came away appalled. Accounts of their shock impelled some of the great news media to take a look. Their reporters were equally appalled.

What the Senators and reporters found was a rich land in which the Negro farmhands, once indispensable cogs in the plantation production line, had become anachronisms in the context of twentieth-century technology. Machines to till the soil, machines to pick the cotton, weed-killing chemicals that supplanted the hoe—all of these tools of the age of science and mechanization had made the Negro superfluous on lands where his ancestors had lived for centuries. He could not get work. He could not earn enough to buy even low-cost Federal food stamps. He hardly ever ate meat, he hardly ever got fresh fruit. He and his children were prey to all the diseases of malnutrition. They were dying at appalling rates.

Individual horror stories abounded. In Holmes County, about 60 miles north of Jackson, Mississippi, Gene Roberts of *The New York Times* encountered Locket Mayze, a 59-year-old Negro left jobless and penniless by the onrush of twentieth-century farm technology. Roberts wrote: "He, his wife and eight children existed, he said, on surplus farm commodities supplied without charge by the Federal government. But the commodities are staple foods, and

7

Mayze's family had eaten fresh meat only once in the last month. That was when a neighbor had given him a hog's head."

Newsweek found Cleosa Henley, a "black ruin of 46," gazing out at soybeans that had supplanted cotton as a money crop on a plantation outside Boligee. Some 200 Negro families had once lived on the plantation and worked the fields. Now only a dozen remained, living in slab-sided, tumble-down shacks. Henley sometimes made $30 a month loading lumber; he had to pay $10 a month rent for his two cardboard-walled rooms. With the rest, he barely managed to scrape up enough for "fatback, rice, grits, meal and greens to keep himself, his wife and seven kids alive," *Newsweek* reported. Even relief food was priced beyond his means. He could buy $98 worth of Federal food stamps for $12—if he could ever get the $12 together all at once. "I just ain't got that kinda money," Henley told the *Newsweek* reporter. "That money is right hard to git."

In the rich, black soil of the Mississippi Delta country, Federal officials estimated there were some 60,000 to 100,000 unemployed farmhands. Robert Sherrill, who toured this region for *The New York Sunday Times Magazine* in the early summer of 1967, gave this account of the sights that met a reporter's eyes virtually everywhere he roamed:

"Choose any shanty: only the number of bodies inside will vary. Here is a mother and six children, residents of Washington County, against the river. Four of the children are asleep on the floor. They sleep most of the day as well as all night. Their lips and legs are covered with scabs and

8

open sores. The youngest has a distended stomach and from it the umbilical knot sticks out like a valve from an innertube. Some days they eat nothing. Most days they have one meal, of cornmeal. . . ."

In Sunflower County, the home of Sen. James O. Eastland, who operates a 5,800-acre plantation there, Sherrill talked to Mrs. Fannie Lou Hamer, a leader of the Mississippi Freedom Democratic Party. Mrs. Hamer, Sherrill wrote, "is a big woman, built out of rings of starch—rice and grits and more grits and flour—held together by bean proteins." Now middle-aged, she had one priceless, precious memory about food. Twice in her life she had eaten turkey. Once she had enjoyed this special treat when comedian Dick Gregory shipped a batch of the birds to Mississippi Negroes, and once she had actually bought a turkey herself, paying for it on the installment plan at 70 cents a week. "Perhaps once a year she eats fruit," Sherrill wrote, "but only if a friend who has moved to the relatively luxurious welfare rolls of the North sends it. She cannot afford it herself."

Such was the condition of the 17.5 million people living in poverty in the Southern states. They were starving, and they were dying prematurely and unnecessarily. A team of investigating physicians for Senator Clark's committee put it this way:

"Malnutrition is not quite what we found. They are suffering from hunger and disease, and directly or indirectly they are dying from them—which is exactly what 'starvation' means."

After examining between 600 and 700 Negro children in Mississippi, one of the investigating team, Dr. Raymond

9

M. Wheeler of Charlotte, North Carolina, declared that what he had seen made him inclined to believe reports that "those who control the state" hoped to eliminate Negroes by driving them out or starving them to death. The suspicion seemed reinforced by the almost positive glee with which plantation owners put the torch to the Negroes' ramshackle cabins once families had pulled up stakes and headed North.

This exodus of the Negro from the South was a major factor in intensifying the pressures of the latter 20th century. Since 1950 America, though it has remained largely unaware of the fact, has witnessed one of the greatest mass migrations of modern times. Into the cities of the North, the Midwest and the West has come a surging and ever-increasing flood of Negro immigrants from the South. This is a migration within the nation that rivals the influx of the Irish and Italians in the 1800's. Mayor Sam Yorty of Los Angeles told Senator Ribicoff's committee that Negroes keep coming into his city in a steady stream that averages 1,000 a month. New York City statistics showed that 837,000 whites and 110,000 nonwhites moved out to the suburbs between 1950 and 1960—and 360,000 non-whites, mostly Negroes from the South, and 367,000 Puerto Ricans moved in. Everything indicates that the tide of migration from the South has increased during the 1960's. And so the pressures in this age of mass society and mass technology have been incalculably intensified.

The cities offered to the Negro little more than a new scene for his suffering and despair. Driven from the plantations of the South by twentieth-century technology, swarming into the cities, the Negro found himself again the vic-

10

tim of a century that has no place for a person without special skills. New technology had driven him from the land, and new technologies denied him a chance in the city. Automation—the onrushing age of cybernation in which machines both think and do—had changed the work patterns of centuries. Within the two decades since the end of World War II, the great bulk of jobs had shifted from the blue-jeans worker to the white-collar class. In the immigrations of the 1800's, new arrivals could find work with pick and shovel. But the migrants of the 1960's, many lacking even the most elementary education and most lacking any skill except the farming skills that were now useless, arrived in the cities and found the doors to jobs closed. They could exist only on the welfare rolls, and these burgeoned in size, contributing to the multiple crises of a wholly unprepared age.

Change had come with cataclysmic swiftness. In two decades centuries-old patterns of life had been altered. America traditionally had been an agrarian economy. Though the industrialization of the nineteenth and early twentieth centuries had begun the change, farmers still constituted 30 percent of the population as late as 1920. By 1962 the population of the nation had nearly doubled, but those left on the farm constituted less than 8 percent of the total, and the number was still shrinking. Both Negro and white farmers, shunted from the land, jammed into the cities and helped to create mushrooming megapolises that characterized the new age. Suddenly, in the mid-1960's, nearly 70 percent of the nation's entire population was living in these great metropolitan areas—the cities and their suburbs—and projections of existing trends showed

11

that by the latter part of the 1970's 80 percent of all Americans would be concentrated in such huge population centers.

This radical shift in population, this herding of great masses of people into relatively small geographical areas, this population explosion unprecedented in our history, overwhelmed every great city in the nation with a plethora of problems with which neither its political nor economic structure could cope. Mass transportation facilities broke down. New, high-speed thruways became clogged and chaotic almost the moment they were opened. Health services were overwhelmed. Antiquated schools were totally inadequate to serve the new masses of students; and, in the suburbs, almost before costly new schools could be finished, the flood tide of pupils, surpassing the most far-out projections, necessitated split sessions. Air and water pollution, caused by this density of population, this concentration of powerful industries, became such serious problems that it was possible that man might in time virtually pollute himself out of existence. Most of these problems transcended city boundaries and city resources. Transportation, air pollution, water pollution were all obviously regional in their scope; they involved, in any given area, a whole complex of towns, cities, counties and states. The old concepts of local government and local resources to meet local needs became archaic and irrelevant to the realities of life in the twentieth century.

In Washington, Senator Ribicoff's committee began early in 1966 to document the nature of these problems and the magnitude of the cities' needs, but in the nation at large it seemed as if not too many people were listening.

Throughout the two decades of the post-World War II era, while these problems had been massing in their overwhelming complexity, America's eyes had been focused largely on foreign devils and foreign crises. The Berlin airlift, Korea, Suez, Cuba, the Bay of Pigs, South Vietnam. The scroll seemed unending, and the eyes of the nation's leaders, its press and its people had been turned outward, with relatively little attention paid to what was happening here at home. And so it remained for one of the nation's more dynamic young Republican leaders to bring into focus the relationship between our absorption in foreign crises and our long-continued neglect of those in our own land.

On August 22, 1966, Mayor John V. Lindsay of New York took the witness stand before Senator Ribicoff's committee in Washington. He pointed out that New York City's budget (which was to soar over $5 billion in 1967) was second in size only to that of the Federal government itself. He emphasized that real estate and businesses were being taxed for all the traffic would bear, that the city had imposed a sales tax and an income tax on top of Federal and state taxes—and still its revenues were totally inadequate to meet the flood tide of multiple and overwhelming needs. Lindsay put his city's problems into focus this way:

> In New York City nearly 2 million people [one out of every four] live in poverty. . . . About 350,-000 [dwelling] units are in buildings built before 1900. We estimate that 800,000 dwelling units, representing over one-fourth of our total housing supply, are substandard and need either replacement or major rehabilitation.
> One in four of our schools is more than 50 years

13

old and is generally located among other scarred and broken buildings.

The condition of many of our 21 municipal hospitals is disgraceful. It is estimated that the city must spend a minimum of $400 million to renovate or rebuild obsolete hospital facilities.

Each day 3.5 million people crowd into the nine square miles of Manhattan south of Central Park. . . . The key to this massive movement is our rapid transit system. But it has responded neither technologically nor geographically to the changing patterns of city life and needs. . . . A program of subway modernization is likely to cost about $4 billion over the next ten years. . . .

After emphasizing again that New York City was almost literally taxing itself to death—and still was unable to cope with problems of such magnitude—Lindsay bluntly told the committee:

The money must come from Federal revenues. Without very large amounts of Federal money, the plain fact is that the crisis in our cities will continue and worsen. This is a malignancy that this great nation cannot afford to ignore.

We figure that over and above what the city now does with its own resources and with Federal and state contributions, over the next ten years in the area of $50 billion would be required to make this city thoroughly livable, with a quality to life and an exciting place to live. This is new money.

This figure startled Senator Kennedy. He obviously considered it preposterous to suppose that the Federal government would spend $5 billion a year for ten years to rehabilitate New York City alone, and he began to cross-examine Mayor Lindsay. But the mayor was not to be shaken. "I say that is a minimum," he told Kennedy.

Returning to New York, the mayor found that his delineation of the magnitude of his city's needs had startled others besides Senator Kennedy. Gabe Pressman, NBC-TV's ubiquitous man-about-town, asked the mayor if he was really serious, and when Lindsay assured him that he was, Pressman asked: "But what would this do to our commitment in Vietnam?"

Here, clearly posed before a large audience for probably the first time, was the real issue of the 1960's. Lindsay met it head-on. He said bluntly that if adequate aid to our cities meant that we would have to cut back on expenditures in Vietnam, that was just too bad, but we would have to do it. It was more important, he felt, to create here the kind of a society the whole world might envy and wish to emulate than it was to fight a questionable war on the mainland of Asia thousands of miles away from our shores.

The theme that popped out in this television interview was to be repeated again and again in the aftermath of the nation-shaking race riots just a year later. That intervening year had been a year of lost opportunity, of continued neglect, of continued inertia; but the sheer thrust of events, the sheer force of the building crisis, had made several elements of the picture more clear. It became obvious that Lindsay had not exaggerated in his estimate of the cities' needs, and it became equally obvious that President Johnson's thesis that we are such a wealthy nation we could

15

have "both guns and butter" was almost 100 percent hogwash.

Mayor Jerome P. Cavanagh of Detroit, the nation's fifth largest city, followed Lindsay to the stand before the Ribicoff committee. Like Lindsay, he emphasized that the financial resources of cities were limited. He said that, in Detroit, he had imposed the first municipal income tax in the nation. "There is a limit to the miracles that local units of government can perform," he said, "and certainly a limit to the resources that we can turn to. We have been preempted out of every field of taxation with two exceptions. One is the local property tax, in which the property taxpayer really bears far too heavy a burden today, and the other is the local income tax. All other excise taxes have been preempted by the State or the Federal government as the case may be."

Cavanagh told the committee that, to solve Detroit's problems, the Federal government would have to contribute ten times as much as it was at present. He estimated that Detroit would need an additional $15 billion in Federal aid in the next ten years, and when Senator Kennedy commented that this seemed a more moderate figure than Lindsay's, Cavanagh set him straight. He pointed out that New York was four times the size of Detroit—and so the requirements were just about the same.

As the Ribicoff committee heard witness after witness, as it probed more deeply into the problem of the blight and decay of the cities, an astronomical figure began to emerge from its calculations. One trillion dollars—$1,000,000,-000,000. That was the sober estimate of the ultimate, ten-year cost of renovating America's cities and making them

16

livable. The senators, most of them former devotees of the "guns and butter" shibboleth, were shocked by the implications of such an enormous sum and began to hunt for ways out. Senator Ribicoff and Senator Kennedy thought that private enterprise could be enlisted to put up most of the money, with Ribicoff suggesting that the investment of $1 in Federal money might stimulate the spending of $5 from the private sector. Even so, even if his optimism should be justified, this would still mean a Federal investment of some $200 billion, or a commitment to spend some $20 billion a year for the next ten years for the rehabilitation of our cities.

Hardly anyone was so naive as to believe that we could or would make such an investment were we to continue to pursue the roles of global policeman and global caretaker that we had taken upon ourselves ever since the end of World War II. These worldwide commitments had seen us pour out $120 billion in foreign aid to almost every nation in the world outside the core centers of Communism. Early in 1967 we had 700,000 troops stationed in 30 countries, and we were furnishing military and economic aid to nearly 100 nations. In addition, we were involved in a full-scale war in South Vietnam—a war that was eating up, as 1967 progressed, between $25 and $30 billion annually.

In the face of commitments so grandiose, President Johnson's "both guns and butter" myth exploded. The President himself, yielding to the demands of Vietnam, wanted to cut down on even the free milk program in the public schools. And instead of the vast additional aid to cities that every expert agreed was essential, retrenchment all along the domestic front became the order of the day.

17

As the urban-racial crisis deepened, President Johnson kept insisting that all would be well if Congress would only pass his programs. Facts told a different story. The President had begun the year, after his party's setback in the Congressional races of 1966, by cutting back on his requests to Congress for domestic spending. In what many interpreted as a political tactic designed to emphasize his fiscal responsibility, he had reduced his requests for Great Society programs to $2.3 billion, though Congress had appropriated $3.9 billion for the previous fiscal year. Higher education proposals were cut by 20 percent, the Appalachia program by $100 million, regional medical programs by nearly $50 million. So it went all along the line. True, Congress in many instances tried to pare even these budgetary requests, but how could anyone suppose it would be otherwise? The entire record of the postwar era told an unvarying story. Whenever a new foreign crisis loomed, military spending soared; and whenever this happened, Congress tried to demonstrate its soberness, its dedication and responsibility by slashing all "nonessential" domestic spending.

The snare and delusion of American policy—a policy that was costing us lives and fortunes we could not afford abroad, a policy that was putting our cities on the rack at home—were neatly capsuled by Senator J. William Fulbright (D., Ark.), chairman of the Senate Foreign Relations Committee and a critic of the war in Vietnam. In a speech on October 14, 1966, Senator Fulbright said:

> The question for Americans today is whether we want our country to be the world's policeman or an

intelligent and humane society whose principal contribution to the outside world has been the power of its example. It is said that we are so rich and strong that we can be the world's policeman and build the Great Society at the same time. Things certainly are not working out that way. The 89th Congress lost interest in the Great Society and became a "war congress." On October 5 I noticed two headlines. One said: "Rise in War Cost Reaches a Peak." The other: "Senate Passes Anti-Poverty Bill: $746 Million Cut."

Such were the priorities that our government, in its infinite wisdom, had established for the American people. The result should have astonished no one, but inevitably, human nature not being attuned to ready recognition of its own folly, it astonished virtually everyone. Senator Ribicoff, sensitive to the plight of the American poor, both white and Negro, had predicted well in advance of the event that the summer of 1967 would be a time of crisis. In early May Senator Kennedy had warned that if a "virtual revolution" was not worked out in the nation's poverty and welfare programs, "the result could be the ripping asunder of the already thin fabric of American life." But few had been listening—or caring. And so the ghettos exploded.

It was, as some described it, almost like the beginning of the second Civil War. America had never seen anything like it. Watts had been an erratic eruption, a one-time thing that could never possibly happen again—or so we had thought. The summer of 1967 destroyed that comfortable delusion. From one end of the nation to the other, cities were wracked by unprecedented violence, the flames

19

of hate and revolt hopping from one to another like sparks in a tinder-dry forest. The streets of commerce became the battlegrounds of race and poverty. Molotov cocktails, hurled indiscriminately, inflamed entire city blocks. Rooftop snipers sprayed bullets at policemen, firemen and National Guardsmen in the streets below.

Newark, New Jersey, witnessed the first major violence of 1967. Almost before Newark had stopped burning, Detroit erupted in a new dimension of violence. Forty-three were killed in Detroit, 2,250 injured, 4,000 arrested; 1,308 fires were set in a 14-square-mile riot area, 3,000 persons were left homeless, some $500 million worth of property was destroyed or damaged. In Detroit, too, the savagery of the streets became visibly integrated. Though the riot began with Negroes in the Negro ghetto, poor whites joined in and looted and burned and pillaged as joyously as their dark-skinned brethren. Local police and the National Guard were powerless before the rampant anarchy, and Army paratroopers were sent in. Before the warfare ended, television viewers were treated to the incredible spectacle of tanks rumbling through battle-strewn streets, their machine guns firing at the rooftops as if in the conquest of some foreign city.

Shock and incredulity swept the nation. Americans, though their country was born in revolution, are a conservative people. Two-thirds of them were comfortably prosperous. Insensate violence like that of the summer of 1967 threatened this majority who felt satisfied and secure. Television pictures of looters carrying away clothing, television sets and refrigerators from ransacked stores; action shots of rifle and submachine gun bullets ricocheting off

20

tenement walls; colored TV pictures of flames engulfing entire blocks of buildings—all of this revolted, angered and dismayed the dominant elements of American society. "What do *they* want?" was the question heard on every side.

Assessments of what "they" wanted, studies into the causes and origins of the riots were undertaken. But even before the smoke of flaming cities had cleared, several things were clear. The mere fact that the riots had happened demonstrated one cardinal fact of fundamental importance to the whole future of American democracy: The responsible Negro leadership was losing its hold on its own people—and its ability to restrain them. Leaders like Dr. Martin Luther King, who had long preached the creed of nonviolence, no longer commanded the respect and allegiance of vast sections of the Negro community. The Stokley Carmichaels and the H. Rap Browns, with their paeans of hate against "Whitey," were lashing their followers on to violence in the conviction that the Negro would be given only what he had the power to take.

This trend, so fateful for the entire future of America, had been spelled out clearly in testimony before the Ribicoff committee months before the explosions of 1967. Testifying about the far less serious 1966 riots in Chicago, Bayard Rustin, executive director of the A. Philip Randolph Institute, told the committee:

> After the rioting in Chicago, a group of young Negroes sitting with Dr. King and me said the following: "You fellows have produced nothing. Dr. King has been here for a year. There has been no accom-

21

modation to him. But when we wanted sprinklers we went out in the street, forgetting your nonviolence and your patience, and we tore up the street, and in 24 hours we had not only the $8 sprinklers we wanted, but we had, in addition to those sprinklers, swimming pools. Now, Dr. King, Daley [Richard J. Daley, mayor of Chicago] hasn't given you a damn thing, but he has given us what we fought for."

This, too, had been the lesson of Watts. The misery of Watts, the needs of Watts, had been ignored for decades; most of Los Angeles had acted as if it was unaware that Watts even existed—until Watts exploded. Then came the investigations and the social service experts, and a few things changed. But not too many. In the summer of 1967 Watts was still seething.

To the young and impetuous, the moral of experience seemed obvious. Ask—and you get nothing. Fight and burn—and you are given. Everyone agreed that those who thought this way represented a minority of the Negro race, but they represented a potent and growing minority. By their actions, of course, they had threatened the integrity of the whole civil rights movement and aroused bitter enmity in society's dominant white majority. The violence of the riots was condemned; yet, when every condemning word had been spoken, there remained a basic truth: Human beings, driven just so far, pressured in hopelessness just so much, will explode. As one rioter said, "We had nothing before; we got nothing now. What do we have to lose?"

The civil rights leadership of the Negro moderates had made great gains on the statute books, but no comparable

22

improvement in the conditions of the Negro's daily life. Under this moderate pressure we had passed civil rights legislation; we had tried, with only indifferent success, to enfranchise the Negro in the South. We had legislated, but not completely perfected, the integration of school systems; we had made gestures toward the elimination of job discrimination. All of these had seemed at the time like tremendous advances—and they would have been if they had taken place 50 years earlier. Then there might have been time to build a whole and compatible American society, competent to deal with the new pressures of the latter twentieth century. But change had come too late, and the affluent society spiraled along on its merry way, widening the gap between the upper and lower segments of our society, increasing the sense of bitterness and frustration among both Negroes and poor whites. As Joseph Alsop wrote in his nationally syndicated column, it seemed as if the civil rights movement had produced "hardly more than two tangible results to its credit—urban riots and desegregated men's rooms."

Some of our more perceptive public leaders recognized that such unnatural violence did not take place in a vacuum, that the wild words of a few agitators could never have launched such upheavals unless they had been like sparks shot into a tinderbox. Gov. Nelson A. Rockefeller of New York, commenting on the Newark riot, said that first, of course, law and order would have to be restored, but that then there would have to be "a national commitment at tremendous cost" to correct the conditions that had made the riots possible. People must understand, he said, that when you live in a tenement and are awakened in the

23

night by the screams of your child, whose face has just been gnawed by a rat, you do not feel very kindly disposed toward the world. Either we are going to correct such conditions, he said, or we are in for trouble that will "tear apart the fabric of American life."

Whitney M. Young, Jr., a moderate civil rights leader, drew the inevitable comparison between our persistent neglect of the deprived one-third and our willingness to squander bounteous billions for military projects and the grandiose flexing of our national muscles. Here we were, he said, spending a bare $2 billion a year to care for some 34–35 million poor, but we thought nothing of allocating $3 billion a year to land a man on the moon (a project that will cost $30 billion or more overall), and we were pouring out $25–30 billion a year to fight a war in Vietnam. Seeing all this, Young said, "people get cynical" and lose faith in law and order and the purposes of society.

The lopsidedness of a system that could allocate profligate billions to the military for foreign adventures—and that at the same time pinched pennies for virtually every domestic project—drew the ironic fire of David Brinkley on one NBC-TV broadcast. Commenting on President Johnson's plan to raise personal income taxes to finance the war in Vietnam, Brinkley wondered in his wry way what happened to all the money we were already raising. Perhaps the best way to understand it, he said, was this: In 1966 the personal income taxes paid by all Americans came to some $62 billion—and the Pentagon spent more than $70 billion. In other words, every penny of all the income taxes paid by all Americans was swallowed up by the

24

Pentagon, and in addition the Pentagon got some $8 billion more from other Federal revenues.

Such was the face of America as it approached the Presidential campaign of 1968. The 1967 revolt of the ghettos had at least focused attention on the neglect and decay of our cities—and on their astronomical needs if the increasingly urban life of the latter 20th century was to be made bearable for man. And so a pivotal issue had been drawn, the issue on which the future course of American life would depend: we could continue on our reckless course of global interventionism at the expense of all else—or we could give a new priority to our national resources; we could build here the Great Society we were capable of creating. But we could do this only if we were determined to put America first.

Would the politicians of the land seize the issue? Probably no great political party ever had a greater opportunity than that offered the Republicans as the 1968 campaign drew near. The Democrats were boxed into the futility of policy represented by Vietnam. They would not be able to extricate themselves from this Asian quagmire without producing something that could be labeled "a victory"—and North Vietnam and the Communist world were not about to let them have such a victory. Even the eternal optimists of the Pentagon were conceding privately that we were mired in a stalemate that could continue for years and would cost us infinitely more blood and resources.

Here were all the elements of golden opportunity for the Republican Party. The irony lay, of course, in the fact that President Johnson and the Democratic leadership had been

25

the ones to perceive the possibilities of the Great Society; it had been left to the Democrats since the days of Franklin Roosevelt to fight the battles for domestic reform and domestic improvement. The Republican Party, dominated by a rural primitivism, had been wedded to a McKinley-like laissez-faire philosophy that belonged back in the early days of the nineteenth century. It had fought against the prospect of domestic expenditures, and it had often played the role of unconscionable demagogue in foreign affairs. Its policy line, epitomized so well by the late Senator Joe McCarthy, had been to accuse the opposition of softness and treason; and, even in the light of the immensely unpopular war in Vietnam, its tendency had been to try to out-hawk the Democratic hawks.

There were, fortunately, other voices in the party belonging to men more attuned to the realities of the age in which they lived. Mayor Lindsay in New York was an example. Governor Rockefeller of New York, though he tended to be a hawk in foreign policy, understood domestic needs, and Senators such as Jacob Javits (N.Y.), Charles Percy (Ill.) and Mark O. Hatfield (Oreg.) were ready for some revised thinking. These men saw the need to redistribute our national resources—to send back to the cities and states large slices of Federal revenues, the only fiscal pool in the nation large enough to cope with the overriding demands of a shifting urban population. If such men and their thinking could prevail, the Republican party had the opportunity to put together a new constituency that might rule for decades as had the one Franklin Roosevelt organized for the Democrats in 1932. But it was by no means certain that a party that had demonstrated in 1964 its infinite capacity for committing hara-kiri before a national audience could be lured into accepting the responsibilities of the twentieth century—and the nation's need for a legitimate, viable choice.

This, then, was the picture:

The Democrats were helplessly imprisoned in the folly of Vietnam, the first foreign war in which American youths had been sent to die by Presidential fiat. So entangled, despite the acuity of their domestic vision, the Democrats seemed helpless to break out of the rigid molds cast by twenty years of Cold War thinking; they were incapable of charting, or at least of implementing, great new domestic courses.

The Republicans, if they could rid themselves of their own heavy cargoes of myths and illusions, were not so handicapped. The very great probability existed that they could make peace in Vietnam as the Democrats could not. They would be free to accept, as President Eisenhower had in Korea, the kind of settlement a Democratic administration, to save its political face and avoid charges of sell-out, would be compelled to spurn. And if Vietnam could once be settled, a modern and enlightened Republican administration could give American policy the new priorities and the new directions it so much needed. In doing so, it could build for the party an urban base and a minority following missing since the time of F.D.R.

The basis for this new constituency clearly existed in a nation ever more urban, composed of an ever younger and better educated population, confronted with new problems vast in their magnitude, largely in revolt against foreign interventionism and not wedded to the stale myths and pre-

27

sumptions of the Cold War. It might be more tempting to play the role of demagogue as the Republican Party had done before, to shout that President Johnson had let down our boys in Vietnam, to proclaim that what we needed at home was not more help for the ghettos but stiffer laws and more guns. If that was to be the Republican choice, disaster for the nation both abroad and at home could well lie ahead, for the election of 1968 would be as meaningless to the American people as the farcical plebiscite of 1967 had been to the citizens of South Vietnam. The American people deserved a better opportunity from their democracy than that. But if they were to get it, sharp changes—changes in old attitudes and in the adoption of new—would have to be the first order of the day.

2

THE GOOD GUYS AND THE BAD

One of the absurd myths of our time—but one that has been all-pervasive—is the notion that policy is divisible; that foreign policy is a separate and sacred thing, bearing no relation to domestic policy; that, in the words so commonly used to describe it, "politics stops at the water's edge" and all good Americans must rally patriotically around the flag, however idiotic the cause to which the flag has been committed. It should have been obvious that there can be only one policy, a national policy, an American policy, and that foreign affairs are but one arm of what should be an integrated whole. If one arm is permitted to dominate the whole, if it is removed from the realm of debate and reason, the whole of American democracy is suborned and perverted.

In the latter part of 1965 Sen. John Stennis (D., Miss.), usually considered one of the best-informed men in Congress on military affairs, declared with apparent calm that the Vietnam war would go on and on—and that American

29

children now in kindergarten would grow up to fight and die in the jungles of Vietnam.

Such a prediction, it would seem, should have touched off a barrage of questions. Was the Senator mad? If he was not, were our policy-makers mad? And, if they were, were we a nation of idiots to sit still and take it?

Months later, the answers to all three propositions seemed fairly clear. By that time, events had demonstrated that there was nothing wrong with Senator Stennis' wits. Many persons had considered him an alarmist when, in an earlier forecast, he had estimated we would have to send 400,000 troops into Vietnam. But by August, 1967, we had some 475,000 there; President Johnson had committed us to send 50,000 more; and no one seemed very certain that the steady escalation would be halted short of the military's goal of at least 600,000 men. By August, 1967, in Washington and in Saigon, American officials on every level except the very highest, where responsibility lay, were acknowledging privately that we were in a stalemate, and R. W. Apple, Jr., was reporting for *The New York Times* from Saigon: "Victory is not close at hand. It may be beyond reach. It is clearly unlikely in the next year or even the next two years, and American officers talk somberly about fighting here for decades."

The roots of the Vietnam war are buried deep in American experiences in two world wars. In World War I Woodrow Wilson's blunder in snubbing the Republicans when he went to Paris to write the peace and set up the League of Nations led to the repudiation of the league and the Republican marriage to an impossible isolationism in a shrinking world. Our withdrawal from the affairs of mankind served only to encourage the depredations of Mussolini and Hitler and Tojo; and, in the end, we paid the price for our head-in-the-sand actions in the blood-letting of World War II. The shock of Pearl Harbor, the subsequent engagement of our fighting men on widely scattered, worldwide fronts, blew the isolationism of the American Firsters into ideological discard. It became clear to all but the most stubborn that America could no longer isolate herself behind her oceans and that, like it or not, she must assume a leading role in world affairs. Thus was laid one cornerstone of what was to become the bipartisan foreign policy.

The other cornerstone was fashioned by Franklin D. Roosevelt. As Assistant Secretary of the Navy in the Wilson administration, he had observed at close hand all of the evils that had flowed from Wilson's tactical blunder, and he was determined that this bit of history should never repeat itself. And so, even before our involvement in World War II, he had drawn into his cabinet such distinguished Republicans as Frank Knox and Henry L. Stimson; and in the Senate he began to woo Arthur Vandenberg, a Michigan Republican and a power on the Senate Foreign Relations Committee. Vandenberg had been an ardent Midwest isolationist, but he recognized the realities of the times. The war was clear proof of the follies of isolationism, and if similar tragedies were to be prevented in the future, America would obviously have to play a leading role in trying to prevent them. Thus Vandenberg became an internationalist. He cooperated with the war and peace aims of the Democratic administration, and Roose-

31

velt named him to the American delegation that went to San Francisco to set up the United Nations. In this pattern was charted the course of the future. Foreign policy would be perfected as always in the executive branch, but now, in private consultations and military-like policy briefings, the opposition party—the one potential source of effective criticism—would be drawn into the formulation of programs that would emerge into the light of day as united efforts, virtually immune to real dissection and debate.

There can be no question that the original intent of the bipartisan policy was good. It was needed to prevent a repetition of the debacle that had followed World War I. But danger lay in the possibility that, if it became a fixture, vital decisions would increasingly be made by a small, inner coterie and would be presented to Congress and the American people as virtual *fait accomplis*. In that case the people through their elected representatives in Congress would have less and less to say about their own destiny; they would be imprisoned in the choices made for them in private conclaves dominated by the President, his State Department advisers and his military experts.

The first major step along what was to become this well-traveled highway was taken on March 12, 1947, when President Harry S Truman proclaimed the Truman Doctrine. The seeds of Vietnam and our far-flung global commitments are to be found in this epochal event, with its built-in misconceptions of today's world. The core of the Truman Doctrine was a rigid ideological fixation that pictured the planet Earth as divided into two armed, inimical camps, one labeled "Communist," the other "The Free World." In all previous recorded history the world had never so precisely aligned itself into legions of black and white; there had always been innumerable ideological variations and mixtures, always shades of gray, and common sense said there always would be. But common sense was not a strong virtue of the high military advisers who dominated the inner councils of the Truman administration. By instinct and by life-long training, these men liked to draw rigid battle lines; they thought in terms of "the enemy" and "our side"; they did not perceive political nuances that, in reality, so often altered the picture and changed the equations of force.

This militaristic domination of our foreign policy was self-evident in the events that led to the promulgation of the Truman Doctrine. In late February, 1947, the British informed us that they were soon going to have to withdraw their expeditionary force from Greece, where Communist guerrillas were battling an established, but corrupt, royalist regime. If Greece fell, Turkey, guarding the Straits of the Dardanelles, might also fall, and Russia would bestride the Middle East. This was the power prospect, posed in hard terms of military strategy and quite divorced from the ideological hoopla with which we were soon to invest it.

One of the great virtues of Americans—and a correspondingly great and confusing weakness—is their native and naive aversion to power politics. We will pursue a moral delusion with utter fanaticism, whether it is to make the world safe for democracy or to save it from communism, but we shy away from acting as nations have acted through the ages on principles of hard, calculated self-interest. We somehow have to be different—and, presumably, better. And so we have to deceive ourselves about

33

the nobility of our purposes before we launch vast and perilous undertakings. If the delusion happens to coincide with our true national interests, the policy works; but the danger, of course, always exists that we will end up pursuing the delusion for the delusion's sake, at the expense of our national interests.

All these elements were woven into the Greek-Turkish crisis. The situation, serious enough if viewed in the hard, practical terms of a critical shift in the world balance of power, underwent an apocalyptic transmutation at the hands of Truman and his hard-line advisers, Secretary of State Dean Acheson and Fleet Admiral William D. Leahy, the President's personal chief of staff. The rationale went like this: Never since the days of Rome and Carthage had world power been so polarized; the Soviet Union, modern reincarnation of the evil of Carthage, was hell-bent on world conquest, and only one nation was strong enough to thwart her evil designs—America. This was Armageddon, and we must battle for the Lord.

Such was the spirit in which President Truman asked Congress for $400 million in aid to Greece and Turkey. His speech bristled with militant phrases. Time and again he emphasized what we *must* do. He painted a horrendous picture of the foreign devils we were pitted against; conveniently, he offered no analysis of the nobility of the regimes we were supporting. The American public could only assume, naturally since we were supporting them, that they must be clad in angel's robes.

In Greece, Truman proclaimed, "a militant minority, exploiting human want and misery, was able to create political chaos which, until now, has made economic re-

34

covery impossible." The Greek government could not cope with the "terroristic activities of several thousand armed men, led by communists." The United Nations was powerless to help. So it evolved upon us "to help free people to maintain their free institutions and their national integrity against aggressive movements that seek to impose upon them totalitarian regimes." The clincher came in this sentence: *"It must be the policy of the United States to support free peoples who are resisting attempted subjugation by armed minorities or by outside pressure."* (Italics added.)

Here, clearly expressed though it was little appreciated at the time, was the rationale for global interventionism. If we were going to resist "subjugation by armed minorities" within a country, we were going to be against the very kind of revolutions in which our own nation was born. We were going to be against any revolution anywhere unless we happened to agree with its ideological purpose. Since we had already ruled out the United Nations as a force of any consequence in such matters, it was obvious that we— and we alone—would decide when an internal upheaval in a foreign country called for rigorous suppression. And we were already casting the mantle of righteousness over the regimes we blessed in such instances; they were our partners in "the free world."

Thus was the word "freedom" stretched to cover a gallery of some of the world's most precious rogues. Some three weeks before Truman proclaimed his doctrine, Stewart Alsop had cabled from Athens a scathing description of the Greek regime we were about to support. The chief characteristic of the Greek government, he wrote, seemed to be "its total impotence," and most Greek politicians, he

35

said, had "no higher ambition than to taste the profitable delights of a free economy at American expense." The situation in Turkey was even more unsavory, so much so that Truman played down the Turkish aspect in advancing his joint-aid program. Yet it was such regimes, so whitewashed, that were increasingly to become our partners in "the free world," with their lone virtue their aversion to "the menace."

It was this misconception of the nature and perils of communism that lay at the heart of the Truman Doctrine; it was this, essentially, that would plunge us two decades later into the pit of Vietnam. For Truman and his military advisers, who set the tone of the nation's thinking in those years, viewed Russian communism as a monolithic force intent on conquering the world and bringing all peoples under the heel of one demoniac ideology. In essence, they accepted as valid Karl Marx's pipe dream of a worldwide brotherhood of the proletariat. But it is obvious now—and it was obvious then to more astute statesmen—that Communism is not a unified menace; that it cannot, any more than democracy, join all of its adherents in a common crusade. The intense nationalism of even very small nations, the self-interest of very large ones, are forces that splinter the Communist world just as they do the world outside the Marxist orbit.

Even in the late 1940's, there were those who perceived the fallacy of the Rome-and-Carthage analogy that underlay the Truman Doctrine. George F. Kennan, who has been generally credited with drafting the first proposals for the containment of Russian power in Europe, had no delusions about Russian intent. From our embassy in Mos-

36

cow he had sent repeated warnings that we must beware. But the rigidities of the Truman Doctrine alarmed him. In Washington at the time the doctrine was being drafted, he saw an advance copy of it; and according to Joseph M. Jones, the State Department expert who did most of the spadework, Kennan objected strongly to "the portraying of two opposing ways of life and the open-end commitment to aid free peoples."

Supreme Court Justice William O. Douglas, who had been a strong contender for the Vice Presidential nomination in 1944 when Truman was selected, was also alarmed. Unlike Truman, he was a world traveler, with contacts in many lands, and during the Korean War he passed along to the White House a warning that was ignored—that the Chinese Army would enter the conflict if we invaded North Korea. Douglas, in a recent interview, disclosed how he attempted to convince President Truman that the Russian and Chinese Communists were not one happy band of brothers. From his contacts with Red Chinese leaders in the 1940's, Douglas said, he became convinced that they wanted to remain independent of Russia and that, indeed, eventual conflict between China and Russia was inevitable. On a visit to the White House he tried to tell Truman this, he said, and he mentioned that his views were shared by Jawaharlal Nehru, then Prime Minister of India. Truman contemptuously dismissed Nehru as "a Communist," Justice Douglas said. He added: "Truman had no understanding of foreign affairs. He would walk over to the globe and give me a grade-school lesson in history, pointing out to me who were the good guys and who were the bad guys."

The good guys and the bad guys! We Americans have

37

this naive tendency to reduce infinitely complex international situations to the "good guy–bad guy" simplicities of a Wild West shoot-down. We seem incapable of understanding that some guys in the world are neither particularly good nor particularly bad. We seem incapable of appreciating that many of them, liking neither our hard line nor the Communists' hard line, would simply like to get on with their own private affairs and say "a pox on both your houses." The extent of our alienation from such a commonsense understanding of the nature of men and nations perhaps was best exemplified during the administration of President Eisenhower when his Secretary of State, John Foster Dulles, verbally banished into outer darkness all neutralists the world over, proclaiming the novel doctrine that anyone who was not for us was against us. The neutralism he was denouncing was the very course America herself had followed in all the years of her history down to World War I.

Since this sharp division of the world in our minds into good and evil flies in the face of human experience, it naturally becomes necessary to examine the bases for such a wholesale and persistent national delusion. It would have been impossible for Truman and his advisers to brainwash an entire nation unless the nation itself had been already thinking, or had been predisposed to think, along similar lines. Not only do Americans by nature have this tendency to invest their international policies with trappings of moral crusades but in this particular instance, as the beneficiaries of a capitalist system that had been good to them, they had an almost Pavlovic fear and detestation of communism. Communism represented the other pole, the antithesis of their good life, and so it was easy for them to see it as one monolithic demon threatening everything they held dear.

This feeling was especially virulent in the immediate postwar era. Disillusionment had set in. Americans wanted peace and a stable order in the world, but there was no peace and no stability. Stalin's grim legions kept all that they had conquered in Eastern and Central Europe, and Communist intrigues threatened to undermine the tottering, war-torn democracies of Western Europe. Elsewhere, the world was swept by tides of revolution as native peoples struggled to throw off the centuries-old yoke of colonialism, and at the heart of many of these rebellions were Communist leaders trained in Moscow. Americans, looking out at such scenes of chaos from their own secure and prosperous nation, could hardly help but feel that everything had gone wrong again, just after they had spent such blood and treasure to set matters right.

This mood in the nation was tailor-made for acceptance of demagogic Republican shouts that we had been sold out at Yalta, that we had been betrayed by our leaders, that the Roosevelt-Truman era represented "twenty years of treason." The sellout-treason thesis got its first trial run in the Congressional campaigns of 1946—and it worked. Republicans made great gains, and many of the newly elected men were those who had ridden to victory on rabid anti-Communistic slogans. When, therefore, Truman promulgated his doctrine calling for virtually a worldwide quarantine of Communism, he had little serious opposition. The Republican Congress had set up a great outcry about cutting Federal expenditures and reducing the size of the

Federal bureaucracy, but obviously, having been elected on the platform that it had, it was not going to label itself softer on communism than the man in the White House. So the $400 million in aid to Greece and Turkey was voted; so Congress soon found itself committed to the Marshall Plan to rebuild the economies of Western Europe. And all this was done with little examination of the basic thesis of the Truman Doctrine, with little appreciation of the scope of the global game we had begun.

It was enough that we were against Communism. For this we would vote almost any amount of money, and in the nation at large, though there were some grumblings, there was little effective protest. A major reason for this apathetic acceptance of a global role that conflicted with America's centuries-old tradition of noninvolvement and isolationism may be found in the simple fact that the new policy assuaged both the psychotic fears and the monetary self-interest of the most powerful elements of the American Establishment. Coming to grips with the twentieth century had been a traumatic experience for these powerful forces. The Russian Revolution initially had shaken them to their foundations and aroused in them the paranoid fear that the same thing might happen here—a fear that led to the wild Bolshevik witch hunt of 1919–1920. The false era of prosperity in the 1920's had dampened this fear, and besides, at that time, communism seemed pretty well contained in Russia, where it was obviously having its own troubles.

A comfortable rationalization developed in business circles that communism could never be made to work, that eventually it would collapse of its own weight. But hardly had we begun to accept this article of faith when two disturbing things happened. First, the Great Depression made it seem for a time as if *our* system were collapsing of its own weight, and secondly the heroic resistance of the Russian people in World War II and the incredible overthrow of the invincible Nazi Army at Stalingrad seemed to indicate that the devil's system *had* worked. If seismographs could record psychic shocks, and if they had been tuned in on the American business community at the time, they would almost certainly have gone into a wild, frenzied dance. The ghosts of our post-World War I frenzy returned to haunt us, and we envisioned a rampant communism engulfing the world.

Tied in with these apprehensions was a Bourbon-like resistance among wealthy and influential Americans to any further change and experimentation at home. The Rooseveltian reforms, so badly needed to combat the worst effects of the Depression, had injected government and its regulations into once-sacred fields. Minimum wages had been established; the 40-hour week had been legislated and overtime payments made mandatory. The shock, the fury, the sheer outrage of business knew no bounds. Newspaper publishers were especially incensed. They could no longer work reporters 60 hours a week at $20–$30 a week, with no overtime. In their rebellion, many of them became active in organizing right-wing organizations that aped, in patent admiration, many of the techniques of Joseph Goebbels, Hitler's propaganda chief, who had been adept at painting all opposition with a communistic tar brush. Publishers such as the late Roy Howard, the little Caesar of the Scripps-Howard chain of newspapers, devoted years of

41

persistent effort to the exaggeration of every aspect of the Communist menace and the endeavor to show that Democratic liberals were little more than camouflaged Communists. There is no precise way to gauge the impact of such innuendoes, constantly repeated in bold headlines, but common sense and all we know about human psychology say that the brainwashing must have been tremendous. In the end, of course, the result of these journalistic endeavors, backed up by the wild charges of Republican demagogues, frustrated by their party's long banishment from the White House, was the era of McCarthy.

By this time, in the early 1950's, the package all tied neatly together. The Cold War was producing its spinoff of unrivaled prosperity at home. The billions spent for foreign economic aid stimulated purchases of machinery and equipment in the American marketplace. The annual military budget soared to $40 billion—and kept going up. This meant enormous profits for a dozen or so of the greatest corporations in the land. It meant bustling factories and steady employment for hundreds of thousands of workers. It meant that multiplied effects from such an enormous subsidization of the American economy were felt by virtually every gas station and supermarket in the land. You could not name a state, in many states you could not name a county, where current prosperity was not intimately tied to the long-maintained Cold War boom. We had created "the warfare state," and any threatened cutback in military expenditures brought cries of agony and outrage from the boondocks to Washington.

All this was accomplished—and to many this was the incomparable beauty of it—without rocking the domestic

42

boat. During the regimes of Mussolini and Hitler, the American press had often pointed out that when a dictator gets in trouble domestically he turns to foreign adventures and foreign conquests, using the country's flag to effectively throttle opposition. Though America was not under the heel of a dictator, it had a democracy that could be manipulated by tight, interlocking controls at the top, with business and the press and the pulpit uniting their forces and with labor quiescent. Through the long decades of the Cold War, the effect of this manipulation was not so very different from that created by a dictator's foreign opportunism. A never-ending series of foreign crises demanded all our attention, and we had little to spare for what was happening at home. With each crisis came an excuse to boost to a still higher plateau the military budget on which so much of American prosperity now depended; and each time the military got more money, the legislators who almost fell over themselves to vote it became appropriately horrified at the prospect of mounting fiscal deficits and decreed that all other spending must be cut to the bone—"nonessential," domestic spending, of course.

The pattern was repeated endlessly; the refrain was always the same. All that ever differed was the particular incident that triggered the speeches. In 1961, after President Kennedy's reaction to what he termed Khrushchev's ultimatum at Vienna regarding the status of Berlin, National Guard and reservist units were called to active duty and the Pentagon's budget was boosted to more than $50 billion, a new all-time high. Almost without a dissenting voice, Senators and Congressmen applauded military spendings—and then cut back on every other proposal in

43

sight. Medicare and aid-to-education moldered in Congressional pigeonholes, the Peace Corps budget was slashed 25 percent, appropriations for international education exchanges were cut 15 percent, and the U.S. Arms Control and Disarmament Agency was almost starved to death on what *The New York Times* called "a caretaker's budget of $2 million."

This was a crisis that turned out to be not much of a crisis after all (the reservists never did find anything much for themselves to do after they got to camp), but it had had its effect; it had boosted Pentagon spending to a new plateau, and it would never drop back to a mere $40 billion again. What the whole misadventure showed was how easily we could become exercised about foreign devils, how willingly we could pour out our billions to combat them—and how blissfully unaware we could remain of far more serious matters at home. For in 1961, when we became so exercised about the fate of Berlin, there were some eight million rats infesting the tenements of New York City biting sleeping babies in the night—and no one very much cared. Thousands of Negroes were already being automated into discard on Southern plantations and were crowding the city ghettos; some three-quarters of them, thanks to the quality of the Southern education to which they had been exposed, were functionally illiterate and unemployable. But nobody cared. Pollution gathered in thick, smothering smog over many of our cities, carrying with it cancer-inducing agents and sending to premature graves some persons with defective hearts. But nobody cared. Our harbors and rivers were polluted, their shellfish poisonous to human consumption; commuter railways and subways serving the new 70 percent urban population creaked toward collapse; water systems to supply our urban millions were drying up or proving inadequate to meet the demands of a suddenly shifted, massed population. But no one cared.

3

THE POLITICS OF SELF-DESTRUCTION

If politics does not serve the real interests of a nation and its people, there inevitably comes a time when a solution will be sought in more desperate recourses. Our own Civil War a century ago stands testament to that. America, as the Presidential campaign of 1968 approached, had not yet come again to this tragic pass; it still had time, there was still a chance. But our politics had become dangerously irresponsible. For two decades the political oratory had been increasingly demagogic and increasingly deceitful.

The erosion of public confidence had been frightening. In November, 1967, in a special Gallup poll conducted for the National Broadcasting Company, the question was asked: Do you believe that political leaders are telling the truth or do they say anything they think will get them elected? Seven Americans out of ten opted for the latter proposition, expressing a complete cynicism about the honesty of political dialogue. This represented an issue even more fateful for the nation than Vietnam and exploding ghettos.

Such complete disillusionment posed a clear threat to the continuance of a viable democracy. Yet how could it be otherwise? The nation was engaged in the most unpopular war in its history. And at each step along the way, virtually nothing that we had been told about this most unpopular of wars had turned out to be true.

We had been assured time and again that the war was all but won; but events continued to prove that it was anything but over. We had been told that the war was going so well that we could look forward to bringing the boys home by Christmastime, 1965; but in 1967, instead of coming, the boys were going—another 50,000 of them on top of the 475,000 who had already gone. And though we had been told that our young men were being sacrificed in a noble cause because we were helping a people passionately committed to freedom, the weekly casualty lists regularly showed that far more of *our* men were dying for *their* freedom than their own, which seemed to cast some doubt on the degree of South Vietnamese dedication.

We had been told that we must stand firm in South Vietnam because we must honor our commitments; but the nature of our commitment to South Vietnam was anything but clear, and the events of 1967 demonstrated that, by honoring this commitment with an all-out war, we were virtually compelled to dishonor all others. When the Arab states attacked Israel, a nation to which our commitment was far more binding than any we had ever had with South Vietnam, we were so tied down in a land war in Asia that we could do little more than send Israel our good wishes. It

47

became quite obvious that even a nation so rich and powerful as the United States could honor only one major commitment at a time. Even we could not do *everything,* and the Israeli-Vietnam dichotomy exposed the hollowness of our global pretensions.

In Washington, Stewart Alsop said there was "an erosion of confidence that you can almost smell." Nothing was going right—and nothing was what we had been told it would be. For twenty years we had been sending military equipment to countries throughout the world; we had been told that this was necessary to help "free peoples" fight communism. The Arabs had fought the Israelis, in part at least, with arms and armor we had supplied. The same thing had happened earlier when Pakistan and India had had their border skirmishes. Each side had blasted away at the other with arms given by America to protect "the free world." Neil Sheehan of *The New York Times* looked into the manner in which peace-loving America had armed the world in the delusion that such arms, once dispensed, would be used only to fight the communist devil. He found that from 1949 to June, 1966, we had been responsible for scattering $46.3 billion worth of armaments around the globe. Of this total, $30.2 billion had been outright gifts, mostly to militaristic regimes that had no one to fight but their own people.

We had been told for two decades that we must pour out these billions upon billions in arms and economic aid to build and protect "the free way of life" in the rest of the world. But events kept on asking: Who is free? In Greece, where we had started the whole business with the Truman Doctrine, a new military junta picked the summer

of 1967 to seize power, and in one of its first acts it pro-
scribed Melina Mercouri, the actress, whose father had
committed the offense of trying to make his countrymen
aware of the virtues of democracy. Later, the Federal
Bureau of Investigation disclosed it had uncovered a plot
against Miss Mercouri's life, and she was placed under
police guard. Even in New York City she was not safe from
the plots of our "friends" in "the free world."

The incident was only one of many that exposed the
shabby rhetoric on which we had based national policy.
The essence of our trouble was that we had found no way
to make democracy a viable, exportable ideal. But we
could not acknowledge this. We waved the banner of righteousness and lofty purpose—and played footsie with military dictators, decadent regimes and fascist rogues. The
rewards of such trafficking got a telling exposure in the
United Nations. The Soviet Union charged into the U.N.,
backing up the Arab states after the Israeli debacle and
demanding that Israel be censured and punished. In the
voting showdown, our fascist partners in what we envisioned as our holy crusade against communism ganged
up on us almost to a man and sided with our communist
enemy. Drew Pearson tallied up the scorecard this way:

> *Spain*—The United States came to Generalissimo
> Franco's rescue with large amounts of cash when he
> was in jeopardy and has kept dumping in military cash
> to a total of about $3 billion. Spain voted with Mos-
> cow.
> *Greece*—That country was the recipient of about
> $3 billion under the Truman Doctrine, to preserve

democracy and persuade Greece to avoid Russia. Now in the hands of a military dictatorship, Greece voted on the side of Russia.

Turkey—Another recipient of Truman aid that received nearly $10 billion in military aid to bolster the Turkish Army. It voted with Russia.

Pakistan—This is another military dictatorship which has not held an election for years. The U.S. has plowed $4 billion into Pakistan to support the dictatorship. It voted for Moscow.

The list seemed to write its own moral. It seemed to say that a national policy based on rhetoric in defiance of truth is doomed to disaster.

Fanatics of the right and left, though they superficially seem poles apart and make fierce noises at each other, are really kindred and ruthless spirits who will climb into bed together whenever expediency suits them (witness the Hitler-Stalin Pact). We should have learned that the community of man cannot be simply divided into two ideological camps, communist and noncommunist. But we had persisted in our pursuit of the demon, in our refusal to recognize that there were different brands of communism in the world, that nationalism and national self-interest are powerful forces determining the reactions of communist states to one another; and, in attempting to rally the world to combat a monolithic myth of our own creation, we had ignored the reality of the military and fascistic dictatorships that by our gifts of billions and arms we had helped to impose on the peoples of foreign lands. Not only was it impossible to trust such dictators on any issue of principle, but by siding with them and supporting them and helping

50

to keep them in power, we were making ourselves heartily detested throughout great areas of the world. All of this, it would seem, should have been obvious. But our highest officials continued to mouth the same old refrains. Foreign exchange students coming to this country in the summer of 1967 were being briefed by apparently intelligent and capable spokesmen of the State Department, and they were coming away shaking their heads in incredulity at having been fed the same old line: There was only one issue in the world, communism versus anticommunism, and this irreconcilable ideological conflict was all that mattered.

Complete was the divorce of official minds from basic reality. It was little wonder that seven out of ten Americans had lost all faith in the honesty of political dialogue, for the conflict between truth and pretense in our policies could no longer be obscured.

Vietnam was a barrel of eels into which no sane man would have thrust his hands short of sheer necessity. For America there was no such necessity, but we plunged in anyway of our own free and eager will.

Throughout centuries of history Vietnam had been a divided, war-torn land. Periodically the Chinese had invaded, sometimes conquering and sometimes being repulsed. It is a point of some historical significance that the great Vietnamese heroes even today are those who defeated the Chinese or lost their lives trying. Even when the Chinese were apparently victorious, their rule in time degenerated into a technicality, observed by token payments of fealty to Peking that cloaked the virtual independence of Vietnam.

Vietnam, however, was never for any length of time one united country. It was a land divided by the rivalries of competing royal families, warring sects and deeply felt religious differences. At one time a wall 18 feet high and 11 miles long was built across the waist of the country, dividing Vietnam at the 18th parallel very much as the Geneva accords of 1954 were to split it into North and South. The disagreements among the Vietnamese kept the country in continual turmoil, and this lack of unity played into the hands of the French when, in the mid-nineteenth century, they began to take greedy, imperial bites out of the tragic land.

The French completed their conquests by 1883 and set up on the Southeast Asian peninsula the colonial empire known as French Indo-China. The guerrilla warfare of today has its antecedents in that event. The Vietnamese revolt against the French began on August 25, 1883, and it never really stopped. As Harrison Salisbury of *The New York Times* discovered during his visit to North Vietnam in late 1966, the Vietnamese view the present war as just another chapter in their old, old struggle to throw off the yoke of colonialism. For more than three-quarters of a century they had fought against the French, against the Japanese who supplanted the French in World War II, and then against the French again when the French returned and tried to reestablish their colonial empire. The war against the Americans, in North Vietnamese eyes, was only an extension of the war against the French, and Salisbury learned that many North Vietnamese "found it extremely hard to tell where the war against the French ended and that against the Americans began."

52

There was good reason for this confusion. We had crept into the war on such stealthy little cat feet that we sometimes had difficulty ourselves defining just where and when we took the first step. Jean Lacouture, the French journalist and correspondent for *Le Monde,* writing from the vantage point of twenty years' experience in Vietnam, has put it this way in his *Vietnam: Between Two Truces:*

> The internationalization of the war occurred in two ways, and at two different times; it actually began in the first days of 1950, on the occasion of the arrival of Mao Tse-tung's advance units at the Vietnamese frontier, and it developed further on the occasion of General de Lattre de Tassigny's trip to Washington in September, 1951. At that time official French quarters defined their new war aims and had them accepted in Washington; these aims had now become a "crusade" against communism, establishing Vietnam as the "barrier in Southeast Asia." From then on France presented itself as the sentinel of the "free world," burdened with the tasks of preventing the "Red tide" from engulfing Southern Asia. . . .

The French were singing us our theme song, and we were so in love with the tune that we promptly forgot all the traditional principles of American democracy. As a people who had fought eight long and bloody years to strike off the chains of colonialism, we had always been opposed to the imperialistic designs of great powers; we had championed the self-determination of peoples; we had cast ourselves in the role of guardian angel of the oppressed. These were some of the noblest American ideals, imprac-

53

tical at times in given situations, but expressions of altruism and high purpose that contrasted vividly with power politics. These ideals were forgotten. In our alarm we could not see beyond the wart on the end of our nose, the wart of a growing communism.

So motivated, the Truman Administration broke with the heritage of the past and threw our power and our billions behind the imperialistic drive of the French to subjugate the Vietnamese. It was an initial wrong decision, putting us on the wrong side in a bad cause, and it was persistence in this initial error that was to bring us steadily to the ultimate impasse that is the reward of folly implacably pursued.

Even with our help, even with the aid of copious quantities of war matériel and money, the French could not build the buffer against communism that they had promised and we had sought. On May 7, 1954, French military ambitions collapsed in the debacle of Dien Bien Phu, and it became obvious that though the French still retained strong forces in the country, they could no longer hope to defeat the now-triumphant Vietminh, led by a new national Vietnamese hero, Ho Chi Minh.

Ho was a passionate Vietnamese nationalist. He had tried to get the Allies, when they were writing the World War I peace treaty at Versailles, to recognize Vietnamese independence. Failing in that, he had spent a long lifetime intriguing and conspiring to one end—the freedom of the Vietnamese people. All of this might not have mattered so much to us, but Ho, in our eyes, had committed the one unforgivable sin: He was a Communist.

When Japanese power collapsed after Hiroshima and

54

Nagasaki, Ho returned to Vietnam from China, where he had spent most of the war years in prison. The French had practically no forces in the North, and Ho quickly established his own independent government. Ironically, as Harrison Salisbury has pointed out, the Declaration of Independence that he proclaimed for the Democratic Republic of Vietnam began as a direct paraphrase of our own.

> All men are created equal. They are endowed by their Creator with certain inalienable rights, among these are Life, Liberty and the pursuit of Happiness.
> This immortal statement was made in the Declaration of Independence of the United States of America in 1776. In a broader sense this means all the peoples of the earth are equal from birth, all the peoples have a right to live, to be happy and free. . . .

Twice Ho and the Vietminh believed they had won their war and their independence—and twice they had been double-crossed. The first pact that was violated was the one concluded between Ho and the French in 1946. In this the French recognized the independence of the North Vietnamese as part of a French Southeast Asia Federation. The French government, however, repudiated the agreement by bombarding Haiphong and slaughtering thousands of Vietnamese in November, 1946—an action that led to all-out war with the Vietminh and to Dien Bien Phu.

That victory could and should have settled things in Vietnam, but it did not. At the Geneva conference of 1954, which coincided with the fall of Dien Bien Phu, a formula was worked out to insure peace. Ho and his regime in the North were recognized, and the country was tentatively

55

divided into two parts, North and South, with the proviso that elections would be held within two years to decide on the unification and leadership of Vietnam. Neither the South Vietnamese nor the United States signed the Geneva agreements, but we "took note of them" and indicated we would abide by them—a half-pledge that, as events were to show, we had no intention of honoring.

The anticommunist monkey on our back was still ruling our policy. The alarm that had led us to underwrite the French effort to reestablish hegemony over Southeast Asia increased with the debacle of Dien Bien Phu. The American military, who had exercised a Circe-like influence over foreign policy since the end of World War II, clamored for all-out intervention. The strong military pressure on President Eisenhower built up to the point where it seemed almost a foregone conclusion we would enter the war, and Vice President Richard M. Nixon even leaked the word that we were about to commit troops to the battle. The leak backfired. A storm of public and Congressional protest blew the partially formed, interventionist plans into limbo. President Eisenhower, always reluctant to take strong action, then practiced this negative virtue, and by so doing he saved us at the time from the folly the military was proposing.

But the tragedy was that he did not save us completely. By one of those compromises for which he was famous, he agreed to let us see what we could do by dipping our fingers just a little bit into the Vietnamese stew.

The French Army still had forces grouped around Saigon, the beautiful city that had been the center of French power and culture in the South. The Vietminh had

had less power here; and, with the Geneva accords, thousands of them emigrated to the North, while some 850,000 Catholics moved from the North into the South, reinforcing the strong Catholic minority in South Vietnam. It was a situation made to order for meddling—and we meddled. We became beguiled by the possibility of establishing a democratic regime in the South, walling off Ho's Communists in the rockier, more industralized North and cutting them off from their main source of sustenance, the rice from the rich Mekong Delta rice bowl. It did not matter greatly to our planners, apparently, that the South Vietnamese had never really known democracy, that the traditions and forms for it did not exist. We, in our beneficence, would give it to them, backed by our billions and our arms. We even had their leader all picked out for them.

He was Ngo Dinh Diem, an intellectual ascetic, an almost monkish recluse. Diem was a man much respected for his character, and he had been a committed and lifelong, if not very effectual, nationalist. As a young man he had served the French in various administrative capacities, but he had broken with them when he saw that the French were not disposed ever to grant the Vietnamese a larger measure of self-government. He had then spent years in futile conspiracies trying to undermine the French hold on Vietnam, and he had been forced finally to flee the country. He had spent four years in exile in the United States, living in seclusion in Catholic retreats in New York and New Jersey.

Diem was a fanatical anti-Communist, and this probably had much to do with rallying strong support for him among the Catholic hierarchy in this country. The late

Francis Cardinal Spellman of New York became one of his enthusiastic backers, and *Ramparts* magazine, the liberal exposé organ founded by Catholic laymen, has made a strong case for the proposition that it was Catholic support, represented by Cardinal Spellman and Joseph P. Kennedy, that helped persuade many national leaders, both in Congress and the executive branch, that Diem was the ideal man to establish a democratic, anticommunist regime in South Vietnam.

Several previous offers to return to South Vietnam in a position of power had been made to Diem, but he had turned them all down, feeling that there were strings attached and he could not be his own man. However, in June, 1954, a month before the signing of the Geneva agreements, Diem changed his stand and agreed to return to South Vietnam to serve as Premier in the tottering regime of Bao Dai. There can be little doubt that he went with our blessing and with the support of the "military advisers" and Central Intelligence Agency operatives whom Eisenhower permitted the war hawks to send into the country.

From the first, certain elements of this ticklish equation should have been obvious. The clearest of all clear facts was that we were starting a risky and dangerous game with a personality handicap. Ho Chi Minh was a national hero in all Vietnam. It was inconceivable to us, because he was a Communist. But it was true. He was the one who had engineered the successful revolt against the French, who had capped years of struggle by Communists and non-Communists alike with the glorious triumph of Dien Bien Phu. Diem, on the other hand, had long been in exile. He had borne no part in the successful, patriotic struggle; and

58

though he was highly regarded in intellectual circles in Saigon where he was known, his contacts with the people he had come to rule had been limited. If he were ever to succeed, he would have to cultivate a popular following; he would have to build a rapport with the people. Perhaps someone possessing a Kennedy-like charisma could have done it, but Diem was an introvert, not an extrovert; he was a thinker and recluse, not an out-going politician.

The tip-off came the very day of Diem's arrival in South Vietnam. Robert Shaplen, a *New Yorker* writer who has specialized in covering the Far East ever since he headed the *Newsweek* Far Eastern bureau from 1945 to 1947, told the story of Diem's arrival as related to him by Col. Edward G. Lansdale. Colonel Lansdale was the American counter-insurgency expert who had worked a small miracle over-coming the Communists in the Philippines, and he had been sent to Saigon to see if he could not work a second and larger miracle there. As he recalled the event for Shaplen, a huge crowd had turned out to welcome Diem. It was not, he thought, so much that the Vietnamese were fired up by a passionate enthusiasm for Diem, but rather that they were joyous over what appeared to be the end of the long war and they were curious to see what the new strong man looked like. Diem's plane was hours late in arriving, but the people waited. Finally Diem appeared, preceded by a motorcycle escort, sirens blaring. As Lansdale later recalled it: "Diem's car, a big black sedan, shot by at about sixty miles an hour and nobody even saw him."

One could almost feel the thud of the letdown. It was a symbolic beginning.

Diem never did establish any close ties with his own

59

people, and before many years had passed he had succeeded in alienating them almost completely. He showed initial strength by subduing the gangster sects that, with French connivance, had controlled the rackets of Saigon and had almost grabbed authority over the police department. But he became more and more withdrawn, more and more suspicious, ever more inclined to rule by police state methods rather than by democratic means. His Svengali and Rasputin was his brother, Ngo Dinh Nhu, who became head of the powerful secret police force organized on the Japanese wartime model. Nhu fed Diem a constant stream of frightening rumors, gossip and suspicions until Diem finally would trust virtually nobody outside his own family; he refused to degelate any power or authority, handling the most trivial matters himself, down to the granting of passports; and he played one general off against another and rotated them in commands in such a manner that none, he hoped, could ever gain such a secure grip on power as to challenge his authority. In such fashion we brought the glories of democracy to South Vietnam.

A so-called election was held in October, 1955, but it was so rigged that it was a stench even in the nostrils of the most insensitive. With Nhu's secret police intimidating all opposition, Diem was proclaimed the winner over Bao Dai by the unbelievable vote of 5,722,000 to 63,000. So sanctified, the Diem regime became even more harsh in its repressions. The elections of 1956 under the stipulations of the Geneva agreement were never held. And for one very good reason. As President Eisenhower himself later acknowledged and as State Department representatives have conceded since, there was little question in anyone's mind that the people of South Vietnam, if given any kind of a free choice, would have voted for Ho Chi Minh, their national hero. This admission, made by American officials with the greatest reluctance, is a most humiliating one. What it says is that America, the great champion of free elections and the democratic process, had not dared to insist upon its principles and had not had the principle to get out of the whole mess when its puppet became a dictator.

Up to this time there had been little overt opposition to Diem. The Vietminh cadres that remained in South Vietnam had remained aloof, evidently waiting for the promised 1956 elections, hoping that the Geneva agreements would be implemented. When it became clear that Diem had no intention of carrying out the Geneva accords, when in addition he abolished traditional elections in the villages, the propaganda campaign against his regime began and quickly took root among a people who were being daily more alienated by his autocratic methods and police-state repressions.

Even today, more than a decade later, there is an obdurate refusal to recognize the simple truth of what happened in South Vietnam—events which, of course, are the basis for any rational understanding of the war in which we are involved. According to the fairy tale that Dean Rusk insists upon repeating, the trouble all began when Ho Chi Minh's aggressive communist forces infiltrated peaceful South Vietnam in a "war of national liberation." Peace can come at any moment, Rusk assured us, that those evil demons from the North "stop doing what they are doing." A mountain of evidence, the almost unanimous accord of the world's best authorities, writers and correspondents on South Vietnam, contradicts him.

The best experts on Vietnam—men like the late Bernard Fall, Shaplen and Lacouture—all agree that the first stirrings of revolt in the countryside occurred in 1957, and that 1958 saw the resumption of guerrilla warfare and the spread of terroristic tactics. "By 1958," Shaplen writes, "the Vietminh had fully resumed its campaign of terror in the countryside, kidnaping government officials and threatening villagers who in any way cooperated with the government. . . . By the end of 1958, the Vietcong had increased its political and military offensive in South Vietnam to the point where security in the countryside had become a serious problem and the government was in trouble. . . . By the end of 1959, the Communists controlled about a third of the countryside, and they had already managed to create important bases in secluded forest areas in the delta and in the highlands.

As Lacouture emphasizes, the trouble was not invasion from the North, but rebellion in the South as the result of the harshness of Diem's policies. He writes:

> Soon the Ngo family's "witch-hunting" policy no longer left open to the growing numbers of its opponents any alternatives other than prison, exile, or the guerrilla forces. Soon future President Suu was in jail, all the former government chiefs were in exile, and many people who wanted primarily to escape the pursuit of Diem's police or Nhu's "Republican Youth" were in the guerrilla forces. . . .
>
> During 1959 the regime's situation in the South

62

changed decisively. It was then that the only attempt at a democratic election, made at the request of Washington, proved embarrassing: Dr. Phan Quang Dan, a notorious anti-communist, was trumphantly elected in Saigon over the official candidate. This choice was later invalidated. At that very time, as we have seen, new legislation promulgated in Saigon opened the great period of the "witch hunt": four persons out of five became suspects and liable to imprisonment if not execution. War generally entails extraordinary legislation; one can say here that extraordinary legislation entailed war. The Marxist organizations hardly took the first steps. But, taken by the throat, they counterattacked.

To all of this there has now been added irrefutable documentation. George McT. Kahin, a professor of government at Cornell University and director of the Southeast Asia program there, and John W. Lewis, an associate professor of government at Cornell, have produced a series of monitorings of Hanoi broadcasts *made in Saigon* and circulated privately among leading figures of the Diem regime. These show that, in 1958, there came into existence a clandestine radio station using the name of the National Liberation Front and calling for resistance to Diem. The monitorings reveal that, in 1958 and 1959, Hanoi regularly *attacked* these broadcasts, charging they were American-sponsored! It was not until September, 1960, that Hanoi gave its support to the National Liberation Front, and even then the aid was only a trickle. "Contrary to United States policy assumptions," Kahin and Lewis write, "all available evidence shows that the revival of the civil

63

war in the South in 1958 was undertaken by Southerners at their own—not Hanoi's—initiation . . . *not as a consequence of any dictate from Hanoi but contrary to Hanoi's injunctions."* (Italics added.)

The rationale we have used for pursuing the war in Vietnam with napalm, rockets, defoliation chemicals and a bomb tonnage surpassing that of World War II in Europe is that we are fighting to protect a poor people struggling for their freedom against cruel, evil and unprovoked aggression from the North. Knock out that prop and we stand exposed as a nation using false pretenses to justify a ruthless and aggressive war of its own. Yet it is to this that Kahin's and Lewis's evidence, reinforcing so much else, brings us. And there is one additional, but inescapable, humiliation. If Kahin and Lewis could obtain those damning monitorings of Hanoi broadcasts, it stands to reason that they could hardly have been a secret all these years to the State Department.

Such, then, was the situation that John F. Kennedy inherited when he became President in 1961. Here was an intellectual, idealistic and politically sensitive President; yet it was he who was to increase the American commitment in Vietnam until it became a pit for Lyndon Johnson to fall into. Many factors entered into this wrong judgment, not the least of which was the overweening influence of the military in political and diplomatic affairs.

When Kennedy took office the situation in neighboring Laos seemed much more critical than that in South Vietnam, and the military's recommendation was the only one the military is ever inclined to make—the application of all-out force. The Joint Chiefs of Staff and most other

64

advisers, Theodore C. Sorensen later wrote, "appeared to favor the landing of American troops in Thailand, South Vietnam and the government-held portions of the Laotian panhandle. If that did not produce a cease-fire, they recommended an air attack on the Pathet Lao positions and tactical nuclear weapons on the ground. If North Vietnamese or Chinese then moved in, their homelands would be bombed. If massive Red troops were then mobilized, nuclear bombings would be threatened and, if necessary, carried out. If the Soviets intervened, we should 'be prepared to accept the possibility of general war.' "

The calmness with which supposedly sane men could advocate such a chain reaction leading to World War III is enough to send cold chills up and down the spine. It would be difficult to imagine a more damning indictment of the fanatic, short-sighted military mind than this, and it is a devastating thought that it is precisely this type of mentality that has consistently forced Lyndon Johnson to perpetrate ever greater follies. Fortunately, at this time, it was Kennedy who was in power, and his was a more perceptive mind than Johnson's. Besides, he had been badly scorched in the first days of his administration when he had accepted the military's word as gospel in the Bay of Pigs invasion fiasco, and so he studied the Vietnamese situation with some caution.

First, he sent Lyndon Johnson, then Vice President, on a tour of Southeast Asia, an expedition during which Johnson exhibited in embryo the traits that were later to mar his Presidency. In Saigon Johnson became so carried away with his own rhetoric that he hailed Diem as the Winston Churchill of Southeast Asia, a libel on Churchill if there

65

ever was one. Then, on his return, he submitted a report recommending "a major effort to help these countries defend themselves." If we did not do this, he said, we would have to "throw in the towel in the area and pull back our defense to San Francisco and a 'Fortress America' concept. More important, we would say to the world in this case that we don't live up to our treaties and stand by our friends. This is not my concept." Here was the kind of mind that could see no alternative between waging a major land war on the continent of Asia and putting San Francisco into the front-line trenches. Still Kennedy hesitated.

He decided to send another investigative team to South Vietnam to tell him what the situation really was, but unfortunately the composition of the team he picked virtually predetermined the kind of report he would receive. The President's new eyes in Vietnam were to be Gen. Maxwell D. Taylor and Walt Rostow, a White House foreign policy planner with a hard-line bent. Arthur M. Schlesinger, Jr., then a White House aide, later noted that no one went along from the State Department and commented that this "expressed a conscious decision" by Rusk to turn the Vietnamese problem over to the Secretary of Defense "because the military aspects seemed to him most urgent." But the effect was "to color future thinking about Vietnam in both Saigon and Washington with the avowed assumption that Vietnam was primarily a military rather than a political problem."

This cart-before-the-horse emphasis was to be at the root of our future troubles. It should have been obvious by this time that a civil war like that in South Vietnam could not

66

be won without a whole-hearted commitment by the people on "our side"; and it should have been obvious that, in Diem, we were dealing with an Oriental despot, not the leader of a democracy—with a despot whose effect on his own people was to commit more and more of them to the Vietcong. The Taylor-Rostow report recognized Diem's failings, but in essence rationalized them away. With the military mind's predilection for seeing force as the solution to all problems, it argued that we could win this test of nerve with communism if we would just beef up Diem with more aid, more arms and more good sound American advice. Taylor already was toying with the idea of sending in an American military force of some 10,000 men for "defensive" combat operations around vital airfields and supply depots, and he and Rostow plainly implied that it might be necessary to take more drastic measures if the infiltration from the North could not be stopped.

The pit plainly yawned, yet Kennedy decided to tiptoe along the brink. His motivation had little to do with Vietnam. According to James Reston, the veteran Washington columnist and an associate editor of *The New York Times,* the greater Kennedy commitment to Vietnam was another unfortunate by-product of Kennedy's overreaction to his encounter with Khrushchev at Vienna. Khrushchev, completely misunderstanding the stuff of which Kennedys are made, had tried to bully the young President, evidently reasoning upon the basis of the Bay of Pigs evidence that he was dealing with a weakling. President Kennedy himself later told Reston, the columnist said, that he thought Khrushchev had decided "anybody who was stupid enough

67

to get involved in that situation was immature, and any-body who didn't see it all the way through was timid and therefore could be bluffed."

Kennedy told Reston it was therefore necessary to take steps to make U.S. power "credible" to the Russians. This was the reasoning behind his "crisis" speech on Berlin, the ridiculous call-up of National Guard units, the dispatch of the Rainbow Division to Germany, the increase in the military budget—and the intensification of the war in Vietnam. Our commitment to Vietnam was stepped up, Reston said, because President Kennedy "wanted to prove a diplomatic point, not a military point." And, the columnist added, "That, I think, is where we began to go off the track."

It was the beginning of the trend to steady escalation. Under Eisenhower we had had some 1,400 "advisers" in Vietnam. Kennedy raised the number to some 15,500 men, poured in matériel and money and helicopters, and gave the effort status by appointing a high-ranking military man, Gen. Paul Harkins, as commander of the American military mission. All was futile. Diem refused to listen. He resented every suggestion made to him; he balked at reform; he continued his police-state, repressive, rule-by-conspiracy tactics. The Vietnamese people, sickened by it all, became steadily more alienated.

But this was not clear in Washington. Diem's government fed our embassy in Saigon glowing reports of progress in the countryside through the so-called "strategic hamlet" program designed to win over the peasants. The war, these reports insisted, was going so beautifully that it could not go any better. And we believed it all. A simple

68

run-down of a succession of official statements shows how completely and disastrously the minds that were deciding our destiny were divorced from reality.

• A Senate committee concluded in 1960 "on the basis of the assurance of the head of the military aid mission in Vietnam, that the U.S. Military Assistance Advisory Group (MAAG) can be phased out of Vietnam in the foreseeable future."

• In the winter of 1960–1961, a State-Defense Department counterinsurgency plan proposed extensive military and social reforms in Vietnam—and predicted we could win in 18 months.

• Former Defense Secretary Robert S. McNamara, after his first tour of Vietnam in 1962, declared: "Every quantitative measurement we have shows we're winning this war."

• Maxwell Taylor, returning for a fresh look in late 1962, a year after his first visit, saw "a great national movement" rising to destroy the Vietcong.

Believing it all, President Kennedy told Congress in his 1963 State of the Union message: "The spearpoint of aggression has been blunted in South Vietnam."

In the spring of 1963 American officials reported 30,000 casualties had been inflicted on the Vietcong in 1962—double the number of all Vietcong supposed to have been in existence at the beginning of the year. Secretary McNamara announced: "We have turned the corner in Vietnam"; and General Harkins proclaimed the war would be won "within a year."

As late as April 22, 1963, Dean Rusk in a speech in New York claimed "morale in the countryside has begun

69

to rise" and "the Vietnamese are on their way to success."
None of it was true.

All the time our officials were seeing and proclaiming
victory, defeat and disaster were the realities. President
Kennedy might have realized the truth if he had only believed what he read in the newspapers. The American press
does not always cover itself with glory, but Vietnam has
to be judged one of its finest hours. Consistently, over a
period of years, some of the best reporters modern American journalism has produced had been trying to bring home
the truth to the American people and American officials
through dispatches from Saigon. Homer Bigart of *The
Times* had set a standard that was to be carried on by
David Halberstam, who later won a Pulitzer Prize. Malcolm W. Browne of the Associated Press, Charles Mohr
of *Time,* and François Sully of *Newsweek* all wrote clear-
eyed dispatches, sometimes at the risk of repudiation by
their own conservative-oriented managements back home.

Halberstam, Browne and the others went out into the
countryside and saw for themselves. At the very moment
when Kennedy was being told by all his official sources that
we were doing so well it would be almost impossible to do
better, Halberstam was reporting on the disenchantment of
the peasants, the graft and corruption of the Diem regime,
and the disinclination of the South Vietnamese army to
fight. He told in his newspaper dispatches and later in his
book, so appropriately titled *The Making of a Quagmire,*
how Vietnamese commanders were censured by Diem if
they incurred heavy battle losses; how, as a consequence,
even when they had the Vietcong trapped, they would leave
an escape route open so that the Vietcong could slip away

70

and they would not have to suffer heavy casualties. Then, of course, the official communiqués would trumpet a great "victory," the shattering defeat of the Vietcong, the great valor of the South Vietnamese. But none of it had happened.

Reading the day-by-day flow of Halberstam dispatches, Kennedy sizzled. He finally telephoned *The Times* and tried to get Halberstam recalled from Vietnam, but *The Times,* to its credit, refused to yield to the Presidential pressure. It was certainly one of Kennedy's less admirable actions; he would have done much better to question his own sources. For in South Vietnam, then as now, events had a disconcerting way of giving the plain lie to official delusions.

The moment of truth for Kennedy began in early May, 1963. At that time Diem and Nhu began a campaign of repression against the Buddhists, who only comprised some 80 percent of the population of South Vietnam. When Diem refused to let the Buddhists display their flags on Buddha's 2,587th birthday, a large crowd gathered in Hue to protest, and Diem's troops fired into the demonstrators, killing and wounding indiscriminately. A wave of indignation swept South Vietnam. Soon Americans were shocked at the horrifying pictures that appeared on page one of their newspapers—photos of Buddhist priests in acts of self-immolation, turning their gasoline-drenched bodies into blazing pyres on the public streets of Saigon. For a nation like ours with a tradition of religious liberty, it was a shattering moment.

Worse was to come. At the beginning of September, 1963, the Diem regime, unrepentant, sent Nhu's secret

71

police out to sack and loot and burn the Buddhist pagodas. It was an act of savagery, capping all other acts, that demonstrated vividly just what a glorious "free world" we were bringing to Vietnam. Kennedy was both shocked and angered. At one of his last press conferences, in September, 1963, he denounced the persecution of the Buddhists, said bluntly that Diem had lost touch with his people, and warned that the Diem regime would have to reform. Then he added a clear and explicit guideline which, if it had been followed, might have averted future tragedies. He said:

"In the final analysis, it is their war. They are the ones who have to win or lose it. We can help them, we can give them equipment, we can send our men out there as advisers, but they have to win it, the people of Vietnam." (Italics added.)

Three months later, Diem, Nhu and Kennedy were all dead. In Saigon an Army coup overthrew the Diem regime, and Diem and Nhu were assassinated. In Dallas, Kennedy himself was killed. And Lyndon Johnson was President.

Now, if ever, was the time to cut our losses and call it quits in South Vietnam. The fall of Diem was followed by months of political chaos. Coup followed coup, and premiers changed virtually overnight. It became clear that South Vietnam had no stable government and that it lacked any leader of the stature needed to unify the country and inspire the people. In this vacuum only the Vietcong, reluctantly admitted even by our own officials to be the only cohesive political force in the nation, could be expected to win. If we were not prepared to accept a victory by the Vietcong and probably the unification of all Vietnam under

72

Ho Chi Minh, then it could no longer be, in Kennedy's words, "their" war; if a puppet government was to rule in South Vietnam without real support from the people, we would have to prop it up; and the war, if it was to be "won," whatever that meant, would have to become eventually "our" war—the very kind of a war Kennedy had always dreaded, pitting American troops against Asians on the Asian mainland.

But Kennedy was gone and Lyndon Johnson was quite a different type of man. He was a man with limited knowledge of foreign affairs, and he was, by both experience and temperament, a man oriented to think in military terms. He had served in both the House and Senate on military committees; he had been a Navy officer during World War II; he had been chairman of the Senate Preparedness Committee and of the Space Committee, and he had been a member of the appropriations subcommittee for the armed services. For years some of his closest contacts on the Hill had been with generals and admirals sent to sell him their bill of goods, and so he was accustomed to thinking in their terms. It was a fateful combination of circumstances. And it soon bore its inevitable fruit.

On November 27, 1963, only five days after the assassination of President Kennedy, the new President and his Cabinet held a "crisis" session on South Vietnam. It was to be nearly four more years before some details of this session would leak out in a little-noticed speech by Bill D. Moyers, a key LBJ aide and confidant in the early days. According to Moyers, this first "full-scale meeting devoted to Vietnam" was "a gloomy session." It should be noted that, right up to the moment of Kennedy's murder, Mc-

Namara, Maxwell Taylor and other administration spokesmen had still been issuing the rosiest of forecasts about the situation in Vietnam; some of them had even been predicting early dates when we would be bringing the boys home. But the real low-down as given to Johnson was the exact reverse of these public pronouncements. McNamara called the Vietnam situation "disturbing," according to Moyers, and said that the Vietcong "had made far greater progress in the last six months than had been realized." The picture was this: "Unless the current trend could be reversed in 60 to 90 days . . . a Communist-controlled state was practically inevitable."

Moyers said that, after the meeting, Johnson talked privately to an official who had been dealing with the Vietnamese problem for two years and asked him if the situation was really so serious. "Yes," the man said, "only I feel even more pessimistic. There are far more reasons to be pessimistic than optimistic."

It was at this meeting in the very first days of his administration, Moyers indicated, that Johnson decided to do whatever might be necessary to "keep our commitments" in South Vietnam. Everything depended, of course, on just what the President should decide those commitments were. Presidents Eisenhower and Kennedy had both considered that we were obligated only to help the Vietnamese help themselves; Eisenhower explicitly—and Kennedy implicitly in his press conference statement and remarks he dropped to his aides—repudiated the idea that we should make Vietnam "our war." Only Lyndon Johnson would decide to do that. But the American people, who would have to pay the piper, were not being let in on Lyndon Johnson's

74

thoughts. The new President occupied himself with turning off lights in the White House and vowing with great fanfare to keep the Federal budget under $100 billion, all at a time when the looming demands and costs of his Vietnam Policy made this patently impossible.

In the offing, of course, there was an election to be won; and Lyndon Johnson, whatever his private resolutions, was going to win that election by smothering the dove of peace in a Texas bear hug. His opponent, Sen. Barry Goldwater, was divinely fashioned for the Johnson purpose. Poor Barry could hardly speak without suggesting that we should get into the Vietnamese war with both feet; that we should bomb North Vietnam; that we should even take nuclear weapons, if necessary, and blast apart the rain forests along the infiltration routes. Such suggestions horrified Lyndon Johnson, and he gave the voters a clear choice between sober responsibility and rash irresponsibility; between voting for LBJ, the man of peace, or Barry Goldwater, the war hawk. And the American people, in the only national referendum that has ever been vouchsafed them, voted overwhelmingly for peace. Here is some of the LBJ campaign rhetoric that helped the voters make up their minds:

September 25, 1964—"There are those who say you ought to go north and drop bombs and try to wipe out the supply lines. . . . We don't want our American boys to do the fighting for Asian boys. We don't want to get involved in a nation with 700 million people and get tied down in a land war in Asia. . . ."

75

September 28, 1964—"So we are not going north and we are not going south; we are going to try to continue to get them to save their own freedom with their own men, with our leadership, and our officer direction, and such equipment we can furnish them."

October 21, 1964—". . . we are not about to send American boys 9,000 or 10,000 miles away from home to do what Asian boys ought to be doing for themselves. . . ." *

There was more, much more, all in the same vein, all assuring the American people that LBJ was not going to do precisely what in a few short months LBJ was going to do. The tip-off had come, though it was not recognized at the time, weeks before those glowing disclaimers of intent were uttered. The occasion was the still-mysterious Tonkin Gulf incident.

On July 31, 1964, South Vietnamese PT boats attacked two North Vietnamese islands in the Tonkin Gulf about three miles off the mainland. Subsequent investigation by the Senate Foreign Relations Committee showed that U.S. officials in Saigon knew all about the foray, but nobody bothered to notify the 7th Fleet. So on the night of August 4, when the U.S. destroyer *Maddox* went cruising through the Tonkin Gulf in the same area, North Vietnamese PT

---

* In all of these speeches the President always contrived to leave himself a tiny escape hatch. Woven into his talks were such qualifying phrases as "at this time" or "we do not *now* contemplate" taking drastic action. But there can be little question that the intent was to assure the public we would not get into a major land war in Asia, and this was the way the public took it.

boats fired some shots. Two nights later the *Maddox* and the destroyer *Joy* were fired on again. Just why the destroyers were at the scene of action in the first place, just who fired the first shots, just how what happened did happen, all this has never been thoroughly explained to this day. Apparently the only damage done was the shattering of a searchlight on the *Maddox,* but from the fuss and fury you would have thought that the *Maine* had been sunk all over again in Havana harbor.

The 7th Fleet bombed the North Vietnamese PT boat bases, and back in Washington Lyndon Johnson erupted like the leader of a Texas posse about to hang of bunch of cattle rustlers. He whipped out a resolution that gave him full authority to do anything he wanted. Tom Wicker, chief of *The New York Times'* Washington bureau, who said that his source was the highest, was later to write that Lyndon Johnson had been carrying the Tonkin Gulf resolution around in his pocket "for weeks" before the Tonkin Gulf incident happened, waiting for the first excuse to spring it on Congress. Events were to demonstrate the trickery of the whole exercise.

Ostensibly, the resolution was a simple response to the Tonkin Gulf affront, but it was so imprecisely worded that it could be interpreted—and later was—as an open-ended grant of power to the President. The resolution empowered the President to take all necessary steps to "repel any armed attack against the forces of the United States," and it also gave him full authority "to prevent further aggression." *The Nation* and a few other journals warned that there might be a hidden joker in this sweeping language, but in Washington Congress felt certain it was just responding

77

patriotically to the Tonkin Gulf incident. Senator Fulbright, chairman of the Senate Foreign Relations Committee, received the resolution immediately and shepherded the measure through the Senate with little debate. He has conceded many times since that he made a mistake, but has said he felt certain at the moment that the resolution was intended to apply *only* to the Tonkin Gulf affair—that it was not, in effect, a carte blanche grant of authority to the President to make war.

Yet, in testimony before Fulbright's committee on August 17, 1967, Under Secretary of State Nicholas deB. Katzenbach argued in loud and arrogant tones that the Gulf of Tonkin resolution was in effect virtually a declaration of war. "What could a declaration of war have done that would have given the President more authority and a clearer voice of the Congress than that did?" he demanded. The Senators almost to a man, Democrats and Republicans alike, were appalled—and angered.

"This is the wildest testimony I ever heard," one Senator told *The New York Times*. "There is no limit to what he says the President could do. There is only one thing to do— take it to the country."

Such was the situation in which our once-great democracy found itself, its most vital power abdicated into the hands of one man. He had hardly been able to wait to use the broad authority he had tricked out of Congress. The victor in November, 1964, by one of the greatest landslides in history, he had been in office barely a month when he did what he had explicitly told the people he would not do. He began the bombing of North Vietnam in retaliation for an attack by the Vietcong on U.S. installations at

78

Pleiku. That was the beginning. It was, we were assured, a limited and "measured" response forced upon us by altered circumstances, but our "measured" response swiftly became insensate. We rained upon tiny North Vietnam a load of bombs surpassing that with which we had blasted Nazi Germany in World War II. We razed whole cities to the ground, as Harrison Salisbury and other American reporters discovered when they visited North Vietnam at the end of 1966; we bombed schools and hospitals; we burned children and the aged—and sometimes our own soldiers by mistake—with napalm; we scattered antipersonnel bombs indiscriminately around the North Vietnamese countryside. And that was not the end. More thousands of young Americans were being sent to fight and die in Vietnam; our bombers were unleashed on targets just ten miles from the Chinese border—and this meant that, at jet speeds, miscalculation by a few seconds could trigger "the incident" that would plunge us into war with China.

"What I cannot understand," said a perplexed young American mother in the summer of 1967, "is why *our* Vietnamese don't fight like *their* Vietnamese."

A simple question. And the answer, too, was simple. *Their* Vietnamese were passionately committed to a cause in which they believed; *our* Vietnamese had nothing for which to fight. *Their* Vietnamese believed they were fighting for the freedom of their country against an imperialistic foreign invader; *our* Vietnamese, after more than a decade and a half of our efforts, could only see that they were being asked to die for the perpetuation of corrupt regimes in Saigon.

79

The North Vietnamese rallied around the wisp-like figure of their great national hero, Ho Chi Minh, architect of their victory over the French. *Our* Vietnamese were being asked to sacrifice themselves to the cause of Marshal Ky, a flamboyant fly-boy who had fought for the French against his own people. In fact, in the entire South Vietnamese Army only two officers with the rank of lieutenant colonel or higher had battled in their people's cause against the French. We had been asking for reforms in the countryside for years; they had been pledged again and again— but, except for words, little had been done. The Ky regime seemed more intent upon garnering the loot that comes from governing than ameliorating the lot of its people. In this summer of 1967 R. W. Apple, Jr., of *The New York Times* was writing: "The corruption—the sense of a diseased society—is most pervasive in Saigon. Many of the stories that float through the city's cafes are no doubt false; but in a sense that does not matter because most of the people believe them." And he quoted an American official, a veteran of five years' work in the provinces, as summing it all up this way: "Nobody considers the Vietcong Robin Hood any more. But the Government and the Army are still the Sheriff of Nottingham, and you'll never sell that."

That, however, was precisely what we were trying to sell. Back in Washington, as the stench rose about the rigged South Vietnamese elections, President Johnson was comparing Marshal Ky and his military junta with our founding fathers, implying that they were the spiritual heirs of George Washington.

To the minds of our so-called leaders only the delusions

80

were real. President Johnson, Dean Rusk, Maxwell Taylor continued to talk about "the people of South Vietnam" who were struggling for their freedom against a cruel aggressor, and to listen to them you would think that all the people of South Vietnam, except for a few dissidents who were in the Vietcong, were united in a common purpose. General Taylor, for example, in his book *Responsibility and Response,* suggested that we should prepare ourselves to answer more Vietnam-type fire alarms all around the world, and he kept talking about those 16 million South Vietnamese who were struggling to be free. There was not the slightest intimation of the one most vital fact in the whole issue—that the majority of the South Vietnamese simply were *not* on our side.

There was some discrepancy about population statistics in the war-torn country (after all, we were reducing the population every day), but the best independent assessments all tended to one conclusion: The people of South Vietnam were not with us. Indeed, a huge percentage, possibly a majority, were actively opposed to us. Harrison Salisbury reported that the best estimates of the situation he could obtain showed that the National Liberation Front, in spite of all our efforts and in a year when we had been told again how magnificently "our side" was doing, had actually *gained* ground in South Vietnam in 1966 and ruled more territory at the end of the year than it had at the beginning. It claimed to control some districts even in Saigon itself (R. W. Apple, Jr., later was to report that some Saigon bars catering to U.S. servicemen were making protection payments to the Vietcong), and out in the

81

countryside the NLF insisted it ruled areas inhabited by ten million persons, compared to four million under the Ky government.

Even official U.S. data on the loyalty of the countryside was decidedly disquieting. In August, 1967, *The New York Times* reproduced our own official breakdown of the situation in the hamlets. This showed a total hamlet population of 13,432,800. It contended, perhaps hopefully, that 7.4 million of these lived in hamlets either under the "partial" control of the Saigon government or "government-leaning." The hard figures, dealing with who actually controlled what, painted a far more disillusioning picture. These showed that the Saigon government had "total control" over only 168 hamlets with a population of 489,300; the Vietcong, on the other hand—and this we admitted—had "total control" of 3,978 hamlets with a population of 2,923,200.

Even in the "total control" areas of the Saigon government, the disenchantment was so strong you could almost smell it. In December, 1966, the Columbia Broadcasting System got the Opinion Research Council to conduct a public-opinion poll in South Vietnam. The pollsters obviously could not go into areas controlled by the Vietcong; they could sample the sentiment only of those supposedly on "our side." Indeed, they had to abandon plans to check in 14 of 55 districts, including one in Saigon itself, because they were "not totally secure." The results, then, must be considered the *most* favorable we could possibly get in South Vietnam, yet they were hardly of a nature to bring joy to the dedicated warriors in the Pentagon and the White House:

- Asked whether their lives were better than they had been the year before the poll was taken, only 25 percent of the South Vietnamese felt that there had been some improvements; *48 percent said things were worse.*
- One person out of five whose native village had been damaged or destroyed in the fighting openly blamed the Americans.
- Fifty-two percent could *not* say that they felt Red China was *more* warlike than the United States.
- *Only 39 percent said the Americans should go on fighting in South Vietnam.*
- Forty-six percent said we should stop the bombing and burning, and 63 percent said we should devote more attention to negotiations.
- Only 7 percent thought we should increase the bombing of the North, which we did during 1967 anyway; only 4 percent thought we should invade North Vietnam.
- *Asked what they wanted for their country, 81 percent said "peace"; only 4 percent said "victory over communism."* (All italics added.)

This was a picture of a dedicated people battling with us for freedom against the hordes of evil? Only official minds chained to their own past errors and delusions could ignore such evidence. Reporters could not.

In Saigon Stewart Alsop sat down for a pulse-feeling session with eight bright young student leaders from Saigon University. He quoted a young Buddhist as saying: "Among the intellectuals in the city, like those in this room, it is understood that the presence of the Americans is a necessary evil. But among the simple people, the peasants in the countryside, the Americans are of course hated and

83

feared by 90 percent—by all those who do not work for them, or profit from them in some way." Alsop found that this apparently was not an extreme statement. "As the talk proceeded," he wrote, "one thing became abundantly clear. Not one of those eight young men—not even the Catholics —felt any sense of commitment to the war against the Communists in their own country."

To such a dead end had the long pursuit of an ideological negative brought us. The best that could be said for us was that we were "a necessary evil"—and no one but ourselves felt our commitment, felt *any* commitment at all. The evidence was clear, but in Washington President Johnson still saw himself as Horatio at the Bridge.

Vietnam was not enough. He was going to extend the blessings of our "free world" to all of Asia. In a number of speeches in 1966, he and high administration spokesmen began to expand on the envisioned glories of the Johnson "Asian Doctrine." The President himself touched it all off in a speech in which he trumpeted "the determination of the United States to meet our obligations in Asia as a Pacific power." Vice President Hubert H. Humphrey, expanding on the glories of the "Johnson Doctrine," saw it as "a pledge to ourselves and our posterity to defeat aggression, to defeat social misery, to build viable, free political institutions, and to achieve peace. . . ." These were "great commitments," said Humphrey, and he added: "I think there is a tremendous new opening here for realizing the dream of the Great Society in the great area of Asia, not just here at home."

The events of 1967 were to suggest that we might better begin by turning the Great Society into a reality instead of

84

"a dream" at home. But it was evident that we were hell-bent on solving the world's problems first. No mere "Asian Doctrine" was enough for Dean Rusk. In testimony before the Senate Preparedness Investigating Committee, he declared we needed no written treaty, no commitment of any kind, to spring to arms to combat what we considered aggression. "No would-be aggressor should suppose that the absence of a defense treaty, Congressional declaration or U.S. military presence grants immunity to aggression," he declared.

He made it clear that we would act unilaterally anywhere and everywhere that we in our infinite wisdom might decide the need had arisen. Not just Senator Fulbright, but even Sen. Richard B. Russell (D., Ga.), long the stalwart champion of the military, was shocked by the visions conjured up by Rusk's testimony. With Russell's encouragement, Senator Fulbright started hearings to find out just where and how, in what places of the world and how many places, we were committed; and the State Department, in furnishing him with a 71-page list, included two after-dinner toasts of President Johnson. These toasts, one to the King of Thailand, the other to the President of Israel, were evidently considered solemn commitments, obligating the power and presitge of America.

With the ghettos of America exploding and even Joseph Alsop writing that his war-hawk's plummage was drooping, President Johnson asked Congress to impose a 10 percent surcharge on all individual and corporate income taxes to raise an extra $7.4 billion. The reason? Not the costs of his phantom "Great Society," but the costs of the war in Vietnam.

Budget Director Charles L. Schultze told Congress that, of a $44 billion budget increase in 1966, $29.7 billion had gone to the Pentagon—and all but $3.8 billion of this had been eaten up by the war in Vietnam. For all domestic problems there had been a mere $5.6 billion increase, and it was estimated that even this sum might be cut back $1.5 billion. If such savings could be realized, Schultze boasted, non-Vietnam spending would constitute only 14 percent of the nation's total output, compared with 16 percent in fiscal 1964 and 16.5 percent under Eisenhower.

A summary of our spending priorities during the entire two decades of the Cold War was even more devastating. Since 1946 we had spent over $1.578 billion through our regular national budget. More than $904 billion, or 57.29 percent, had gone for military purposes. Less than $96 billion, a mere 6.08 percent, had been allotted to "social functions," a term that included expenditures for education, health, labor and welfare programs, housing and community development.

The imbalance was clear. We were spending for all of the incredibly costly implements of modern war, but not to meet the needs of our own people. The Great Society had become The Sick Society in Senator Fulbright's words.

4

RATS—AND OTHER ESTABLISHMENTS

"New York is a sprawling, voracious monster of a city. It covers 315 square miles; it is crammed with some eight million people. At least a million, a full eighth of its total population, live in packed squalor, six and ten to a room, in slum tenements whose mere existence is a nauseous stench on the air—tenements so rat-infested that, on an average, one hundred persons a year are badly chewed and, so far this year, two have actually been gnawed to death. Symbolically, perhaps, there are in New York more rats than people—an estimated nine million of them."

It was nearly ten years ago that I wrote those words in the opening paragraph of a special issue of *The Nation* magazine, entitled "The Shame of New York." The conditions that I described had existed then for years—and they continued to exist. Though my revelations raised quite a storm at the time, and though the late New York *Herald Tribune* subsequently spent more than a year (in a series of almost daily articles) documenting facet by facet the crisis of the city, nothing much changed; nothing much was done. No effort at all commensurate with the magnitude of the thronging problems was undertaken. Nearly ten years later, Mayor Lindsay was to tell the Ribicoff committee that two million persons, a quarter of all New Yorkers, were living in poverty, and the rats were almost as numerous—an estimated eight million of them still at large, an average of one rodent for every person.

All that had happened in the intervening years was that rats had become the subject of bucolic humor—in the Congress of the United States, at least.

In the early summer of 1967, with the ghettos of America already erupting in the first tremors of the earthquake to come, congressmen practically laughed themselves silly at the idea that something should be done about the rats infesting our cities and taking nips out of sleeping tenement children. President Johnson had asked Congress to appropriate $40 million, to be parceled out to the cities on a matching-fund basis during the next two years, for a campaign to exterminate rats. The request touched off one of the most hilarious, rib-tickling scenes Congress had enjoyed in a long time.

Rep. H. R. Gross (R., Iowa) set the intellectual tone for the discussion when he announced that he was opposed to "a rat corps" which, he said, would probably be presided over by "a high commissioner of rats." Gales of laughter.

Rep. James A. Haley (D., Fla.) also had a witticism to contribute. "Mr. Speaker," he said, "I wonder sometimes if some of our distinguished committees that bring before us a monstrosity such as this would take into consideration the fact that we have a lot of cat-lovers in the nation, and why not just buy some cats and turn them loose on the rats. . . ."

The cat-rat idea appealed to the mentality of Rep. Samuel L. Devine (R., Ohio). He commented that "one of our most respected colleagues tells me he has about 23 cats in and around his barns" who could be enlisted in a volunteer cat-rat war. "These feline rat-catchers are most effective, particularly since they are led by a highly respected tomcat called Cotton who has earned a most enviable reputation in the rat-catching department."

The brilliance of this repartee was almost convulsing the House, but it remained for Rep. Joel T. Broyhill (R., Va.) to make the sally to end all sallies. He envisioned the emergence, if the bill was passed, of "a bunch of new bureaucrats on rats" and "a great demand for a lot of rat patronage." He concluded: "I think the rat smart thing for us to do is to vote down this rat bill rat now."

There was more, much more. The House of Representatives had not had such a merry time in years. Rep. Martha W. Griffiths (D., Mich.) and a few others tried to point out that this was not quite so hilarious a matter as their chortling colleagues seemed to think. The best available health department statistics showed that Americans suffered as many as 14,000 rat bites a year (New York City averages from 500 to 600 annually, and authorities are convinced many go unreported); rats do an estimated $1 billion worth of damage a year to food and goods; and rat bites help to spread rabies and other diseases. Real funny facts. Representative Griffiths thought that since the House had just voted a $75 billion defense appropriation bill almost without a murmur of dissent, it might at least find it in its heart to invest $40 million in a two-year campaign to get rid of rats. Rep. William G. Bray (R., Ind.), taking his stand on lofty principle, proclaimed that he supposed all who voted against the rat-control bill would be "accused of being for rats and against people," but nevertheless the bill must be defeated "to keep our government from being financially ruined. . . ." Nobody bothered to explain how $40 million would financially ruin the government when $75 billion would not—but then nobody had to. Everybody in Congress by this time understands these matters. With Congress still convulsed by its own humor, the rat-control measure was soundly defeated by a vote of 207 to 176, and the fiscal soundness of the nation was assured. Rats, haw, haw! *

The Congressmen had hardly stopped having their fun when Detroit exploded.

It was, perhaps, only a minor incident. The rat-control measure sponsored by President Jonhson certainly was not a piece of major legislation like a housing bill or an education bill. But perhaps it was all the more significant for just this reason. It was a humane measure, designed to combat

---

* As James Reston later wrote in *The New York Times,* "The public reaction to that act of insensitivity was too sharp for even this Congress to ignore." The rat-control measure was called up again in the House on September 19, 1967, and it passed without a chuckle. An analysis of the vote showed heavy switching among Republicans who represented urban or suburban districts, leading to the speculation that they had heard in no uncertain tones from their constituents. Forty-two Republicans who had voted against the rat bill in July voted for it in September, as it passed the House 277 to 173.

living conditions that are a lasting reproach and disgrace in our cities. It required, in money terms, only a pittance compared to the vast amounts being squandered on the Vietnam war. Yet the only response such a proposal could evoke in the House of Representatives of the United States was an outbreak of raucous humor.

Probably no single incident highlights more clearly the schizophrenia of our politics. Congress is divorced from reality. A majority of its members have shown that they still think in terms of a rural primitivism; that they have no conception of the needs and pressures of the twentieth-century mass society in which 70 percent of us live.

There has grown up in this nation a deeply rooted system by which rural boroughs control the destinies of a 70 percent urban people. Time and again in Presidential elections since 1932—the only forums in which the national will is expressed—the American voters have underwritten broad liberal programs designed, even if sometimes imperfectly, to meet some of the needs of the present century. And time and again this express will of the people has been thwarted in Congress. The liberal domestic proposals of Harry S. Truman, which evidently had sufficient appeal in 1948 to result in one of the biggest upsets in history, were swiftly throttled by a Congressional cabal, and some of them, like Medicare, did not surface successfully until nearly twenty years later. The liberal platform of John F. Kennedy was similarly smothered for three years until a combination of circumstances—the wave of national remorse and guilt over the tragedy in Dallas and the arm-twisting of a Lyndon Johnson determined to be elected President in his own right—popped the cork of the

91

Congressional bottleneck and loosed, momentarily, a flood of progressive legislation.

Then came Vietnam and the emphasis on war rather than a "Great Society." With the Democratic setback in the Congressional elections of 1966, Congress returned to its old obstructionist ways. It was not by chance that the vaudevillians who staged their slapstick in the House to defeat the rat-control bill were almost without exception the products of Southern or rural constituencies. For it is this Southern-rural coalition that has controlled the machinery of Congress for most of the last thirty years, ever since it was formed in 1938. Its rule is the rule of a minority—a minority that has been able to capture the levers of Congressional power and that has set its face flintily against change.

To both partners in this combine, change is anathema. The Southern Democrats, racists in politics, intent on denying the Negro equality and depriving him of the ballot with which he might threaten their white rule, fight desperately to preserve the status quo. This means to them States' Rights; it means a battle to whittle down and restrain Federal power in all things, for the Federal government threatens to enforce the idea that all men, regardless of color, are entitled to equal rights, privileges and opportunities. The rural-based Republicans are hardly less paranoid. The big-city Democratic machines are their traditional enemies, and the Republicans fight to build up their rural vote to maintain counteracting bases of power. In New York it is the "upstate" vote that is relied upon to offset the tide of Democratic ballots from New York City; in Illinois it is the rural "downstate" vote that must over-

92

come the margins established in Cook County. The necessities of political life, then, have given the Republican Party in many states an anticity image in an age when the city and the problems of the city are paramount. When the party has had long-term control of state governments, as it has in New York, for example, the inimical city has been grossly discriminated against in the distribution of state-aid funds; the rural areas, where the party's strength is concentrated, have been inordinately favored. The rural Republicans and the Southern Democrats become then, as a result of the exigencies of politics as they see them, increasingly dissociated from the real world of our times. Both are intent upon maintaining their power undisturbed, and this community of interests helps to forge their blood brotherhood in Congress—a brotherhood in which party labels become irrelevant.

One tragedy is that the vital interests of this brotherhood are based upon the conditions and concepts of a nineteenth-century, agrarian world that has little in common with the mass-society, urban world of our times. And the second tragedy is that this cross-partyline polarization of interests and outlook has enabled forces representing distinct minorities of the American people to capture autocratic control of the intricate, internal mechanism of Congress in defiance of all of the precepts of American democracy.

There is an old saying among Americans that we win every war and then lose the peace. We have usually applied this expression to our disillusionment over the aftermaths of World Wars I and II, but it is equally applicable to our own Civil War, concluded slightly more than a century ago. The underlying causes for which that war was fought —the freeing of the Negro slaves and the denial of States' Rights—became ultimately lost in the peace. The nation, it is true, was welded together in an enduring union, but the basic issues remained, modified only in degree, to become root causes of some of the major ills and problems of our time. The war technically freed the Negro slaves, but the great bulk of them remained chained like serfs to the land, perpetually in debt and servitude to their white landlords, existing in a misery little changed from the miseries of their past. The Negro technically had become an American citizen with all the rights and privileges of an American, including the right to vote; but, in actuality, down to the present day, the Thirteenth, Fourteenth and Fifteenth amendments passed to guarantee him these rights have remained little more than scraps of paper.

The racial sickness of the South remained uncured, and a century of obdurate battle in denial of the very issues over which the Civil War had been fought served only to prolong and intensify the heritage of hate and rebellion that would become the critical issue and the burden of our time. This denial of change and reform resulted largely from the creation of a one-party system in the South. The Democratic Party became and remained the white man's party, and Republican resistance was ineffectual; indeed, at times, actually nonexistent. This meant that any Democratic candidate who captured his party's nomination was virtually assured of election to the House or Senate of the United States. It was a delightful state of affairs, made to order for trafficking by wealthy and backward interests wishing to influence national legislation. Wealthy oilmen,

94

determined to protect the 27½ percent depletion allowance and the other tax privileges that so favor them and fleece the average American, could pour their money into Southern politics, betting on a sure thing. Their sure-shot bets in the South produced a marvelous, extra dividend: In a one-party system, their Senator Claghorns could be returned to Congress again and again, for term after term.

So seniority was built up, and *seniority is the fuel on which Congress runs.* The work of Congress depends upon its committees. A modern and progressive President such as the late John F. Kennedy may see the needs of the nation and draft legislation designed to cope with the worst of them; but, when his proposals go to Congress, they are channeled to the appropriate committees for study, for hearings, for action. Until the committees act, Congress cannot act; and if the committees do not act at all, Congress usually cannot act at all. *The committee system, then, is ideally designed for forces that would hold back the pace of change, and seniority is the name of the game.* The key committees holding life-and-death power over the most vital issues are stacked with veteran members of the House and Senate, with members who mainly represent parochial and minority interests. One of the classic ironies of our politics lies in the simple fact that the South, which after all lost the Civil War, has succeeded on most occasions in dominating the legislative functions of Congress through the one-party, seniority system.

It is a domination that could hardly have been achieved and maintained without the obliging cooperation of rural-based Republicans, who are supposed in popular mythology to hate Democrats as cats hate dogs, but who really do

95

not. For the North, like the South, has its one-party districts. Until very recently it was a historic event for the Democrats to elect a U.S. Senator from the Midwestern farm belt, and even today, in most of these states, it remains a decidedly uphill struggle. In the lower house there are any number of Congressional districts, gerrymandered by rural-controlled state legislatures, that have voted Republican with an almost religious faith since Lincoln's time. Congressmen and Senators elected from such Northern districts built up seniority just as did their Southern cohorts; they joined their Southern blood-brothers on the powerful key committees; and the combination represented, whether the Republican or the Democratic party technically controlled Congress, a continuing rural and parochial predominance in national legislative affairs, one increasingly at variance with the needs of a 70 percent urban nation.

All of this, of course, did not just happen by accident. Accident doubtless played its part in the regional situations that provided the basis for inter-party collaboration. However, beginning in Franklin Roosevelt's second term, the coalition became a deliberate, functioning collaboration, with key functionaries of both parties in Congress conferring and mapping a mutual course of action. There resulted what has been called the Senate Establishment or, in broader terms, what Prof. James MacGregor Burns has labeled the Congressional Party. Leaders of this inner coterie were perfectly well aware of what they were doing, and they sometimes even let the voters in on the secret. The late Sen. Olin Johnston (D., S.C.), one of the veteran wheelhorses in the upper house, once declared bluntly,

96

"The South cannot afford the luxurious expense of two-partyism." And he spelled out the reason. "The last strength of States' Rights," he said, "is vested in the powers of your representatives in Washington whom you have elected, and reelected, and reelected. Their seniority is the source of your strength and power in Washington to preserve our States' Rights."

When Kennedy was elected in 1960 he faced the future with idealism and hope, and a sense that a new era in political power was being born. In his inaugural address he proclaimed: "Let the word go forth from this time and place, to friend and foe alike, that the torch has been passed to a new generation of Americans—born in this century, tempered by war, disciplined by a hard and bitter peace, proud of our ancient heritage." Kennedy's great appeal, like that of his brother Robert today, was to the legions of youth, to change and progress, to the striking off of old shackles, to the opening of closed doors of the mind and the thorough airing by new winds. In his vision of a new generation coming to power, JFK expressed a reality of American life, for America is becoming, thanks to the high birth rates of the war and postwar eras, predominantly a young nation. In 1966 half of its population was less than 26 years old, and by 1972 more than half of all Americans old enough to vote will be under 32. The emphasis, then, as Kennedy so clearly perceived, should have been on the leadership of "a new generation"; but, as he quickly discovered, the behemoths of the old order sat like a group of walruses, ivory tusks agleam, across the pathway of his legislation through the committees of Congress. Here was a popular young Democratic President whose party controlled both houses of Congress by wide margins. But, for the more than three years of his abbreviated term, his program remained almost completely bogged down in the Congressional quagmire of the coalition.

The situation became so intolerable that in 1963 Senator Clark of Pennsylvania, flying in the face of sacred Senate precedent, led a rebellion on the floor and exposed in a series of speeches the mechanics of what he called the conservative Senate Establishment. Describing this fight, foredoomed to failure, he later wrote:

> . . . Though the Senate has been shaken by wars, deaths, the electorate, and other calamities, those in it dedicated to the preservation of the status quo in economic and property rights and to the past in human rights—that bipartisan conservative coalition which I have called the "Senate Establishment"—have still not given way to the new generation. . . .
>
> . . . I believe that the Senate has become archaic, outmoded, obsolete as a meaningful democratic institution. If the Senate is to perform its constitutional role in the twentieth century, it must be changed to meet the needs of the twentieth century, and made capable of responding to the problems of the twentieth century. . . .
>
> . . . The Senate Establishment is, in a word, the bulwark against democracy in the Senate, majority rule in the legislative branch of the government, and the will of the American people as expressed in national Presidential elections. These are, perhaps, strong words. But I strongly believe them to be true.

What especially incensed Clark and other Senators who joined in his protest, notably Sen. Paul L. Douglas of Illinois and Sen. William Proxmire of Wisconsin, was that the Democratic Party to which they all belonged had won great victories in the industrial states of the North and Upper Midwest, beginning in 1958 and continuing through the elections of 1960 and 1962. However, these gains, so notable for the party, giving its membership in the Senate a predominantly liberal cast, had not been reflected in control and influence in Crongress. There the bipartisan coalition retained its stranglehold on the committee system and packed the committees with controlling margins of conservative members drawn from the Southern-rural backwaters of the nation.

Clark first concentrated his fire on the makeup of the Democratic steering committee, the key cog in the party's machinery in the Senate because it had the power to determine assignments to the functioning legislative committees. The Senate in 1963 had 67 Democratic Senators to only 33 Republicans. Clark felt that 45 of the Democrats could usually be counted as liberals on important issues, but giving the conservative wing of the party the benefit of every possible doubt, he found that it could not muster more than 27 Senators, all but a few from the South. The Democratic steering committee at the time was composed of 15 Senators. Of these, nine were from the conservative bloc, only six from the liberal faction. In other words, a conservative contingent that represented at the utmost no more than 40 percent of the Democratic voting strength in the Senate controlled two-thirds of the seats on the vital steering committee.

With stalwarts of the old order exercising this ironclad control over the steering committee, it was little wonder that a curious game of hanky-panky was played out in the appointments of Democrats to serve on major committees of the Senate. Clark's analysis showed that the seniority rule, so sacred when it worked in favor of the Establishment and the vehicle by which it had secured its vise-like grip on the Senate's mechanism, was blithely scuttled when liberal Democrats, who had built up seniority, sought favorable committee assignments. Though the Democrats from the South represented a decided minority within their own party, they continued to control both the membership and, even more important, the chairmanship of key committees.

Clark's most devastating analysis concerned what happened to nonfreshmen Democratic Senators (in other words, those who had seniority) who voted for cloture and what happened to those who voted against it. Cloture means the shutting off of debate on any given issue so that a vote can be taken. Under Senate rules it can be imposed only by a vote of two-thirds of the membership, a provision that plays into the hands of the bipartisan coalition. Liberals had endeavored to change the rules so that cloture might be imposed by a mere majority vote, but the Southern Democratic bloc and their rural Republican allies had fought fiercely and successfully against such tampering with the sacred Senate rules. The issue was vitally important to the racists of the South, for as long as cloture could not be imposed, they could filibuster so long and tie up other essential business of the Senate so long that no meaningful civil rights legislation could be passed. The success of the South in preventing cloture was one exam-

100

ple of the manner in which the minority tail wagged the majority dog in the Senate. And the revenge that was then exacted upon the liberal majority by the oligarchic Southern minority in control of the Democratic steering committee was a second and even more vivid example of the far-reaching influence of a tail-wagging-dog state of affairs.

Twenty-two nonfreshmen senators with seniority rights had sought new committee assignments. Clark's staff prepared this breakdown of what happened to them:

"Eight nonfreshman Senators (Bartlett, Byrd, Cannon, Hayden, Jordan, McGee, Smathers, Thurmond) who opposed rules change submitted eligible bids for new committee assignments. Seven of them (88 percent) got new assignments. Six (75 percent) got the assignments that represented their first choice (only Thurmond was disappointed).

"Fourteen nonfreshman Senators who favored rules change applied for new committee assignments. Five (36 percent) got new assignments (Mansfield, Hart, Pell, Young, Clark); *only one Senator* (7 percent) of the group (Mansfield) got the committee that was his first choice."

As Clark emphasized, among the Southern contingent opposing the cloture-rule change, three-quarters were rewarded with the committee assignment of their preference; among the liberals who voted to change the rules, only one —Sen. Mike Mansfield, the majority leader—got the committee assignment he wanted. Could the lesson of who holds power and how it is wielded be more clearly demonstrated than this?

By the time the steering committee had finished its work, again and again bypassing the requests of liberal senators whose seniority entitled them to the assignments they

101

wanted, the standing committees of the Senate had been so thoroughly stacked that the conservative coalition held in its hands the power of absolute veto. There were at this time just 23 Southern Democratic Senators from the states of the old Confederacy, plus Oklahoma and Arkansas. This Southern bloc comprised a mere 34 percent of the 67-man Democratic Senatorial membership. But this is how that 34 percent minority positioned itself on the half-dozen most important committees of the Senate:

• Of the 18 Democrats on the powerful Appropriations Committee, nine (50 percent) came from the South.

• Five out of 12 members of the Armed Services Committee (42 percent) came from the South.

• Six of the 11 members on the Finance Committee (55 percent) came from the South. It was in this committee, one of the most important of the Senate, that Kennedy's Medicare proposal dropped out of sight as if a manhole cover had been lifted and it had been shoved through the opening.

• Five out of 12 party members on the Foreign Relations Committee (42 percent) came from the South.

• On the steering committee, seven out of 15 members (47 percent) were from the South, and the old guard grip here had been solidified by beefing up the Southern contingent with a couple of other hard-line conservatives from other sections.

• On the Policy Committee, three out of nine (33 percent) came from the South. This was the only committee on which Southern representation was in line with the number of seats that Southerners held in the Senate.

The intent of the Senate Establishment, or the Club as

it is sometimes called, was nakedly obvious in some of its other maneuverings. Since Democrats outnumbered Republicans in the Senate by 67 to 33 as a result of the 1962 elections, sacred Senate precedent decreed that they should have at least a 2-to-1 edge in the composition of committees. To reflect the altered situation, the size of some of the key committees could have been increased and new Senators added to them, as had been done at times in the past; but this would have meant that *some liberal Senators* should be appointed, thus diluting the coalition's control. So, in some instances, the Establishment decided to keep things very much as they had been.

This decision led to a couple of revealing stratagems. The Appropriations Committee, since it holds the purse strings, is obviously a most important and sensitive cog in the Senate machinery. The Establishment's decision to keep the committee at 27 members, with an 18-to-9 ratio, meant that one Republican Senator already on the committee would have to be bumped off. It was just a coincidence, of course, that the Republican with the least seniority—and so the one elected to walk the plank—was Jacob Javits of New York, a liberal. The bumping of Javits stimulated curiosity, and research uncovered one curious fact. The State of New York is the financial center of the nation; yet, from the earliest days of the Republic down to 1963, only *five* New Yorkers had sat on the Senate Appropriations Committee. And the Establishment, by its decision, had just cut short the tenure of the last of these.

Even more interesting was the intrigue over the composition of the Finance Committee. Here, in Senator Clark's phrase, "the battle raged, with bloodshed on all sides."

103

The Finance Committee, under the long-time dominance of the arch-conservative Harry Byrd of Virginia, held in its hands two of the most important measures Kennedy had sent to the Senate. One was Medicare; the second, tax reform.

Kennedy had been genuinely shocked, as Arthur Schlesinger tells us, by the discovery that some $40 billion in taxes annually dodged the Federal tax collector through loopholes deliberately written into the tax laws by Congress. The most unconscionable of these, the 27½ percent oil depletion allowance and other equally remunerative dodges created especially for the oil industry, had resulted in the creation of a favored class of millionaires and billionaires. This aristocracy of intrigue and influence battened off the special tax privileges that they and they alone could enjoy; and, by so doing, they transferred the tax burden to the backs of the working men and the American middle class. Even the Vietnam war could be financed without a tax increase—indeed, with a tax *decrease* for the average American—if the special privileges of these rich leeches could ever be revoked. Kennedy had tried to revoke them. He had proposed what became known as "a Spartan tax plan" to eliminate some of the worst inequities and give the average American citizen a fair shake. But nothing could have been further from the minds and intent of the oligarchs of the Senate.

To preserve this system of privilege in the face of the increasingly liberal composition of the Senate, the Establishment decreed that the size of the Finance Committee would not be changed. It remained at a ratio of 11 Democrats to 6 Republicans. In other words the Democrats, who held 67 percent of the seats in the Senate, did not even have a 2-to-1 edge on this vital committee; and since six of the seats they did hold were in the hands of conservative Southerners, the coalition's stranglehold on the committee was maintained unshaken. Under this setup, Medicare remained buried in a committee pigeonhole, and conscience became an unknown word in writing our tax laws.

In backing up Senator Clark in his attack on the Establishment, Senator Douglas added some new dimensions to the picture of the Senate's power structure. He called attention to the manner in which Southerners monopolized committee chairmanships. This was extremely important. The chairman of a Senate committee is, in most instances, a virtual czar over what happens to legislation referred to his body. It is he who decides whether hearings shall be held, when they shall be held, how long they shall last. It is a simple matter for a chairman to "hear" to death a bill he does not like; in other words, to drag out the hearings on it to such inordinate length that time runs out and there is no opportunity to bring it to a vote on the floor before the Congressional session closes. Committee chairmen have other great powers. They can appoint subcommittee chairmen, who may also gather about them an investigative staff and hold hearings, exercising additional influence on the course of legislation and national affairs. In the light of all this, therefore, it has to be considered extremely significant that, in the Senate in 1963, 10 of the 14 chairmen of principal committees came from the Southern states and 2 more from the Southwestern states. Only 2 came from the liberal wing of the party, which held two-thirds of the party's strength in the Senate.

Senator Douglas drew an analogy between the dominance of the Southern minority in Congress today and that which it had exerted in the years prior to the Civil War. He said that at that time, too, "The southern Democrats controlled the political organization of the party in the Senate and the House. They insisted on a rigid control of the party in their interest, and they drove out of the Democratic Party some of its fine spirits, perhaps its best spirits, in the North. . . . They found their way into the Republican Party. And for the following 52 years, the Democratic Party remained out of power, with the exception of the two administrations of Grover Cleveland.

"I am not suggesting that the situation today is precisely analogous. I am not suggesting that our southern friends wish to eliminate the 13th amendment and to restore slavery. I can say, however, that in the main they are determined to ignore the 14th and 15th amendments to the Constitution. . . . Dominant white opinion in the South is not willing to give the Negro those basic rights over which the Civil War was fought and won."

There had developed as a result what Douglas called "an intolerable situation." The Democratic Party, he said, won its Presidential elections in the great industrial states. It won them "on platforms which are believed in by the voters and which pledge to carry out legislative programs which will be in the interests of the great masses of the American people; namely, the wage earners, the small farmers, the white-collar workers, the small businessman, the housewives and the consumers." Then Congress convenes—and the machinery of the House and Senate is largely "in the hands of those who fundamentally do not believe in the

106

program by which the Presidential election was won and for which the great mass of voters of the country cast their ballots." The repetitive result of campaigns won and pledges unfulfilled was making voters cynical. Indeed, Douglas speculated, perhaps this was one of the Machiavellian purposes of the coalition. In his more "sardonic moments," he said, he wondered whether this repeated strangulation of the party's program in Congress was "a part of the plan—to discredit the party, to defeat the Senators from the North and the Senators from the West who otherwise might threaten the supremacy of the bipartisan alliance. . . ."

In such fashion had the American political system become imprisoned in the hands of men separated from the mainstream of American life and pursuing their own private, regional and selfish interests.

This four-day 1963 Senate discussion has been cited at length here for two reasons: It is the fullest exposure we have from inside the system itself of just how the system works, and it is this same system that is working out our destinies today—a system that is the captive of the same men and forces, divorced now as then from the realities of modern urban life.

Those moments of fun and frolic in which the House had laughed itself silly while it voted down President Johnson's rat-control measure had happened naturally, inevitably, because this is the kind of leadership we still have in the House. The Southern-rural coalition still dominates the committees of the House and Senate and runs the affairs of the nation with little appreciation of the most basic problems of modern urban life.

In the House in 1967, 15 of the 20 chairmen of standing committees came from small towns or rural areas. Only two, Rep. Emanuel Celler of New York and Rep. William L. Dawson of Chicago, came from large cities. The South had only about one-fifth of the U.S. population, but Southerners headed 11 of the 20 committees of the House; if the border states were included, 14 of the 20.

The same disproportion was manifest in the Senate. Only 2 of the 16 committee chairmen came from the cities —and not very big cities at that. Sen. Mike Monroney comes from Oklahoma City; Sen. Lister Hill is from Montgomery, Alabama. Again the South maintained its committee dominance. Nine of the 16 committees were chaired by Southerners; 11 out of 16 if the border states were included.

In age, as in all else, the committee leaderships were of a sort that almost precluded any real rapport with a nation decidedly youthful in its population. Though the median age of all American citizens was 28, that of the House and Senate committee chairmen was 67. Granted that there must always be a certain disparity here since Senators cannot be elected until they are thirty and so the Senate will usually be composed of predominantly older men, still there seems little justification for so wide a gap as expressed in the rule of many committees by the extremely elderly. Seven of the 16 Senate chairmen were 70 or over; one was 90. Six of the 20 House chairmen were 70 or over; two were 80.

The issues that seemed important to this kind of ancient leadership could hardly be expected to be those that mattered most to the nation at large. Where vigor and vision

108

were needed, where the hour cried for the "new generation" leadership that President Kennedy had proclaimed,
we were saddled with the whimsies of aging men, mourn-
ing the lost glories and better world of their youth. It was
little wonder that a Congress so led and so oriented could
find nothing but humor in a proposal to spend $40 million
in a two-year campaign to rid our cities of rats—and at the
same time could see nothing incongruous in voting far
more abundant millions to combat every fancied kind of
rural menace.

Ever hear of Bangs disease? It causes abortions in cows
and hogs and can be passed on to people as undulant fever.
It is undeniably a health hazard, but hardly more so than
rabies and other diseases that can be transmitted by rats.
Yet a House that could laugh out of existence a rat-control
bill that would have cost only $20 million a year could turn
around and blithely spend $21.5 million, plus another
$250,000 for research, to compensate farmers who have
had to butcher their animals in the Bangs-disease control
program.

Then there were the weed contracts. Nobody loves
weeds, but few persons have any idea just how dedicated
Congressmen are on the weed-war front. Some $26.9 mil-
lion a year of the taxpayers' money is passed out to the
states, state universities and research stations to combat
weeds. Another $2.7 million is spent on experimentation.
Another $3.2 million goes to eliminate witchweed, a para-
sitic growth that destroys corn crops in some Southern
states. No doubt about it: In the minds of the present Congressional leadership, weeds are a far more serious matter
than rats.

109

Then, of course, there is the water hyacinth menace. Water hyacinths grow in such profusion in the South that they sometimes choke channels and waterways. They foul boat propellers. Sometimes fish cannot live in the clogged waters. As anyone can plainly see, this is the kind of crisis situation that a proud nation like ours cannot endure—and so Congress spends another $6.7 million a year to try to control the water hyacinth.

Caught in the disarray of their party over Vietnam, squeezed in the implacable vise of the myopic Establishment, liberal Democrats from the northern cities have to go back to their constituents not having been able to produce in Washington, facing the prospect of probable defeat. One such Congressman, blocked from getting the kind of action his district needed and wanted, shook his fist and raged as he denounced the leadership of his party. Younger Democratic Congressmen insisted that the seniority system was being used more rigorously than ever to entrench the older, Southern clique in the seats of power at the expense of newer members with fresh ideas.

"I would be in a better position if I were a freshman Republican," a second-term Democrat told *The New York Times*. "They have their differences too, but they stick together when it's important, and they give their new members something to do, put them in key positions and let them share in policy. With us, the boll weevils [the Southerners] get everything."

Congress can neither function nor deal adequately with modern problems unless the archaic grip of the Southern minority can be wrenched from the throttle. This is a deed

110

of self-amputation that the Democratic Party has not been able to perform.

This suggests that if Congress is to be brought abreast of the times the Republicans will have to do it. But for the Republicans to perform this feat they themselves must be brought into the twentieth century. So far they have shown only an eagerness to seek refuge in the nineteenth, and their party, the favored instrument of big business ever since the days of Mark Hanna and McKinley, has based its strength paradoxically on rural one-party districts that it has been able to manipulate and control. *If* it could change, *if* it could be induced to act responsibly in the national interest as it has rarely done in the last twenty years, *if* it could have the vision to follow the lead of men like Mayor Lindsay of New York, then there would be a great opportunity to build for itself an enduring urban base.

This is asking a lot of Republicans. It is asking that they change. It is asking that they foreswear their own role in the bipartisan coalition; that they put the interests of the nation above the immediate and petty advanage to be gained from Congressional infighting. If America is ever to emerge into the Great Society, there must be new priorities that will put America and America's vital interests first. Such priorities, as long as the Democratic Party remains tied to the coattails of Lyndon Johnson and the Southern coalitionists, can only be established by an opposition party not chained to past error and bankrupt policies.

5

Since the mind of man changes more slowly than the world he creates, there exists in our time a generational gap as enormous as the credibility gap President Johnson has succeeded in achieving. The difference of viewpoint between generations has been, of course, an enduring fact of human existence from the beginnings of recorded time, but it is doubtful if this gap ever before has yawned into the wide chasm that exists today. The mere fact that a young nation with a median age of 28 is being directed in Congressional committees by chairmen with a median age of 67 represents a significant, but in reality a lesser, dimension of the overall problem. The transcendent factor, the element that has widened the dimensions of the traditional gap into a gulf, is that this ancient and sometimes senile leadership exists in the jet-age era, in an era in which change has been piled upon change with a rapidity that challenges the perception of even the most agile mind.

It is not just that the House and Senate committees are

112

stacked with men who are old and whose mental processes in many cases are atrophying. Men born in the last century, men whose formative years and early adult lives were spent in the first two decades of this century, were molded in their ways and their thinking by the life of centuries past, rather than the life of the century present. They were brought up in a world closer to the world of our Revolutionary forebears of the eighteenth century than the world that exists today, the world with which they have to try to deal.

These men, of course, were no fools in their time. They know that color television is here. They travel on jet planes across the continent. They see the cluttered thruways. The externals of change are as visible to their eyes as to the eyes of others, yet almost inevitably the mind lags; it fails to comprehend the less obvious elements of change, the magnitude of the technological upheaval that, in the short span of 20 years, has rendered archaic all the worlds of our past and has presented us with a new world with massive problems unlike any we have faced before.

Some perspective may be gained from reminiscence. I belong to the generation now in its fifties, born in those years just before the First World War. The world that I knew as a child was so utterly different from the world of today that my children, when I talk of it, sometimes look at the old man with the kind of glance that says: Is he for real?

As it happened, I was born and grew up in the little coastal town of Point Pleasant, New Jersey. In those days it was a common sight to see two-masted and three-masted schooners beating up the coast from the Carolinas with deckloads of pine. The road that ran past our house was graveled, but it stopped a few hundred yards beyond, petering out into a sand trace that ran between bayberry and beach plum bushes. A horse-and-wagon from the market in town delivered groceries; the Acme and the A&P with their chain-store techniques had not yet eliminated the local merchant. The iceman tonged blocks of ice into the icebox that sat in the kitchen, with a pan underneath to catch the water as it trickled down—a pan that would overflow, especially in hot weather, if someone forgot to empty it in time.

The telephone was still a novelty. There were only a couple in our neighborhood, and when one had to use the phone one ran across the street to a neighbor's house, turned the crank on the old-fashioned box and gave the operator a number. Cars were even scarcer than telephones. There were only two in the whole neighborhood that I can remember, a Model-T Ford and an Overland. When friends who had a car came to visit in the summer, it was an event to plan a trip to Asbury Park ten miles away. The roads were bad and bumpy, especially if we had had summer rains; the car could "speed" up to 25 miles an hour, maybe 30; and we wondered whether we could get to Asbury Park and back without mishap.

Few houses had central heating or plumbing; few had electricity. We had progressed from the candles of colonial days to kerosense lamps that often smoked if the wick was not trimmed properly. In winter we closed off most of the house and lived in a couple of rooms, the kitchen that was kept comfortable by the big iron kitchen range on which my mother cooked and the front living room that had a potbellied stove whose plates used to glow red when the fire was hot inside.

The 1920's saw the beginning of change. Houses were wired for electricity; everybody had central heating and plumbing, and outhouses, a feature of the American landscape for centuries, disappeared. My father, who had ridden a bicycle back and forth to work all the years of his life, bought a car and learned to drive. Radio arrived. I can still remember listening to the 1924 Democratic National Convention in Madison Square Garden, a group of us clustered around our two-tube radio set, sitting close together so that we could detach one earphone from each headset and pass it over to a neighbor.

The Twenties wrought great changes; modern life began. Living through the decade was much like learning to walk. The country was developing, altering, but the break with the past was not yet complete. Radio was the marvel of the day; there was no television. Buses and trucks had begun to cut into the railroads' monopoly; trading schooners vanished from the seas, to be seen no more. Cars became plentiful, and the two-lane concrete road was the epitome of progress. Thruways had yet to be designed in the imaginative brains of engineers. The airplane was a curiosity for the country fair grounds; hardly anyone actually traveled by air, and most persons thought that when air travel came in a big way, if it ever did, the dirigible, not the plane, would be its vehicle. These were big changes in the patterns of life to be wrought in a few short years, but they were still partial in nature, not total. And then it all stopped.

There came the crash of 1929 and the Great Depression.

115

Hard times affected almost everyone. And the hard times yielded only to war. Between the two, the Depression and the war, the onward surge of this century of technology was slowed, and great numbers of people lived, as their fore-fathers had lived for generations before them, close to the land. Though my father worked long hours in a hardware store, we had always grown a great part of our own food—nearly all the white and sweet potatoes we would use in a year, our own strawberries, tomatoes, carrots, beets, peas, beans, cabbages and corn. There was a cherry tree in the backyard, a couple of huge old apple trees, a grape arbor, pear and peach trees. Mother spent much of the summer canning, and the shelves in the cellar always bulged with canned vegetables and fruit, jellies and preserves. And always, of course, there were chickens and eggs from our own chicken yard. Such was the way life was lived. It was the custom. No matter what happened, no matter how hard the winter, one could always be sure of one thing: There would be food in the house.

The Second World War gave these patterns, which had already begun to fade, a new lease on life. Food was scarce and rationed, and it became the fashion of the day to grow Victory Gardens and to can again. On the industrial front, the nation's domestic features remained unchanged; all energies, all goods, all the resources of science had to be concentrated on winning the war. But with the winning of that war, with the coming of peace, the change was dra-matically completed. A spate of new products and new techniques, the onset of automation, the burgeoning of megapolises—all of these sweeping and revolutionary changes were packed into the brief span of some 20 years; the world of today was created.

The portents had been there for years, but depression and war had slowed the march of events. As far back as 1933, a group of Mississippi Delta farmers had watched in amazement as a strange new mechanical device picked in an hour as much cotton as a field hand could pluck in a week. This first successful demonstration of a cotton-picking machine horrified the more perceptive who saw the magnitude of the changes that would come with its adoption and widespread use. One newspaper editor suggested that the contraption should be dumped in a nearby creek, and a civic group correctly saw a "heavy menace hanging over the Negroes of the South."

It was not until well after the end of World War II, however, that this menace became a reality. Machinery was acquired slowly. As late as 1953, Mississippi farmers picked only 14 percent of the cotton crop by machines. In 1966 more than 90 percent of the crop was picked by machines.

The impact on the Southern Negro population cannot be overestimated. Economically speaking, the Negro became obsolete. Where once it had required 165 man-hours to tend an acre of cotton during the growing season, mechanization and chemical weed killers had reduced this figure by 1966 to less than 35 hours. The peak work season that had given the Negro 120 days of labor in the 1950's dropped to less than 50 days in 1966. Under such conditions, the Negro had only two choices: starvation or emigration. Many thousands made the inevitable decision and left the South.

What was happening in the South was symptomatic of the change taking place across the length and breadth of rural America. In the cherry country of Michigan, New

117

York and Pennsylvania, mechanical tree shakers came into use. One machine did the work of 80 hand-pickers, and costs were cut from $60 to $20 a ton. Mechanical loaders baled and stored hay and corn silage in a matter of hours—a job that, 15 years before, would have required days upon days of manual labor.

Under such pressures there took place the massive population shifts that lie at the root of the present urban crisis. There was the influx of both Negroes and poor whites from farm to city, and the abandonment of the city for the mushrooming suburbs by the middle class that had been its backbone. The city itself became increasingly the habitat of two disparate classes: the ghetto poor (both Negro and white) and the rich, or at least the decidedly well-to-do, who could afford to live in costly, exclusive high-rise apartments. Around the perimeter of the city spread rings of bedroom suburbs occupied by the white-collar, middle-class working and professional force. The cities and their satellite suburbs virtually merged into one another in continuous strips of grim and grimy factories, cluttered business centers, and suburban sleeping quarters. By 1966 the new megapolises had become the dominant fact of American life, and the extent to which they had is probably best expressed in this one graphic statistic:

MORE THAN HALF THE POPULATION OF THE ENTIRE NATION IS CROWDED INTO JUST ONE PERCENT OF THE LAND SPACE.

This unprecedented herding of the populace into a confined area produced new problems unlike any America had ever experienced before. So complete, so abrupt, so sudden was the departure from the past that Americans, mircocosms in this world of change, had difficulty in appreciating the extent of that change and the totality of its effect upon their lives. They could see to a degree what was happening, but they lived for the most part from day to day, immersed in the immediacy of personal problems, and they tended to accept the world that technology had created for them. And there was little national leadership of a quality able to enlighten them. The eyes of the nation's leaders were focused almost exclusively on the foreign menace we had created in large part from our own fears and prejudices. The face of "the enemy" wore the mask of every man's pet detestation; but the enemies that the new urban world was creating for us were a nebulous sort, the result of situations, of underlying forces, of impersonal technology. They could not be pictured in human terms. They lacked the impact that comes from dramatization, but their evil potential threatened our society more fundamentally than did the dramatized foreign demon.

One day in the late summer of 1967 I made a trip into New York. The sunshine was bright along the Jersey coast when I left, but as I passed through the continuous factory belt of North Jersey—the oil refineries, the chemical companies, the metal processing plants that extend in an almost unbroken chain from the Amboys through Newark and Jersey City to the threshold of New York—the rays of the sun began to filter down, struggling through a dense and yellowish haze. From the streets of Greenwich Village the tall tower and spire of the Empire State Building, New York's distinctive landmark, almost disappeared behind the yellow curtain, looming up only in dark, dim outline like the Tower of London in a pea-soup fog. Here was the

119

visual evidence of an ever-present phenomenon of modern urban life—air pollution.

"Air pollution," we say—and shrug. Does it really matter? Well, if you do not care how long you live or how painfully you die, of course it does not matter. But if you would like to be able to count on a normal life span, if you would like to see your children and your children's children have *their* chance for normal life, it means everything.

A scientific analysis of New York's atmosphere has shown that the average street-strolling New Yorker takes into his lungs toxic materials that are the equivalent of smoking 38 cigarettes a day. This average New Yorker is breathing in sulphur fumes which, combined with moisture and oxygen in the air, can turn into droplets of sulphuric acid. He is breathing in cancer-inducing hydrocarbons. He is breathing in whiffs of deadly carbon monoxide, nitrogen oxides, aldehydes and other compounds. He does not in normal circumstances get enough of any of these lethal compounds to keel over on the spot like a bludgeoned ox. But, day after day, he is drawing into his lungs with the air he breathes a toxic clutter that is helping by minute and imperceptible degrees to shorten his own life. Statistics show it.

Staten Island is a relatively small hump of land sitting almost athwart the entrance to New York harbor and located much closer to the Jersey shore than the city of New York, of which it is a part. The northern and western shores of Staten Island are much closer to that foul-smelling oil refinery-chemical strip of North Jersey than the central and southern portions, and it is along the north shore, in

120

addition, that population is most heavily concentrated. Still one would hardly expect that there would be any great variation in health statistics in such a comparatively circumscribed area. But there is. A study financed by the U.S. Public Health Service and made public in January, 1967, showed that deaths from lung cancer occurred much more frequently in the heavily polluted northern section of the island. For white males 45 and older, the northern rate was 55.4 per 100,000, compared to 40.2 in the central and southern regions. For white females, the rate was 8.2 in the north—and just half of that, 4.1, in the rest of the island.

Other studies have produced similar results. Much has sometimes been made of the fact that there does not seem to be a great disparity in lung cancer rates among smokers in urban and nonurban areas. But what about *nonsmokers?* Comparative studies show that lung cancer rates among nonsmokers in urban areas run *eleven times higher* than they do in the countryside. In one five-year Los Angeles laboratory experiment, a group of mice exposed to the day-by-day Los Angeles air developed one-and-a-half times as many lung cancers as did a set of mice breathing clean air.

Air pollution is a similar boon to that other great killer of modern man, heart disease. In 1957 a U.S. Public Health Service team studied mortality from coronary heart disease among white persons between 45 and 64 in 163 metropolitan areas, then compared the statistics with those obtained in nonmetropolitan counties. They concluded that "death rates for coronary heart disease among white persons aged 45–64 varied directly with the degree of urbanization for both males and females. In metropolitan counties with

121

center cities, coronary heart disease rates were 37 percent higher for males and 46 percent higher for females than in nonmetropolitan counties." In Chicago a study of cardiovascular disease made for the Chicago Board of Health showed much higher death rates in the city than in rural sections of Illinois. The Chicago rate was 25 percent higher for males between 25 and 34; 100 percent higher in the middle-aged 35–54 bracket; and *nearly 300 percent higher in the 55–64 age group!*

While the tensions and pace of city life may account for some of this disparity, there can be no question that air pollution is a major factor. This has been demonstrated every time a mass of stagnant, polluted air hangs for days over a great city. The most startling episode of this kind occurred in London in early December, 1952, when a heavy fog lay unmoving over the city for four days. Chemicals trapped in the smog reacted upon one another, forming new compounds. Acids so created dissolved the nylon stickings of women in the streets. For persons with heart and respiratory problems, the effect was fatal. When the smog lifted and London counted its toll, statistics showed that more than 4,000 persons had been killed by the polluted air. Mortality figures for the very young, those 4 to 52 weeks old, and for the very old, those 75 and older, ran 300 percent above normal.

Similar episodes in the small Pennsylvania manufacturing city of Donora and in New York City itself have dramatized the lethal effects of air pollution in periods of siege when heavy, unmoving masses of smog close in over a city and hang there for days. Less visible is the insidious toll resulting from the daily inhalation of minute particles

122

of toxic compounds, but life-expectancy studies, comparing rural and urban statistics, have indicated again and again that the city dweller, both male and female, sacrifices on the average a good two years of life compared to his country cousin.*

The befouling of the air we breathe is matched by the incredible contamination of the waters we use.

On a trip to Washington, D.C., in the spring of 1967, my wife and I took an afternoon drive along the Potomac to Mount Vernon. It had rained heavily a few days earlier, and the Potomac was roiled and mud-yellow. It also stank with a stench that was unmistakable—the odor of a sewer. How, indeed, could it be otherwise? For the Potomac is today little more than an open, running sewer for the capital city of Washington and the satellite cities and towns of the Washington metropolitan complex. Tests have shown that some 14 feet of sewage sludge now line the Potomac's bottom.

What is true of the once-beautiful Potomac applies to virtually every river, lake and pond that verges even remotely upon one of our great metropolitan areas. The Hudson River, originally one of the most beautiful and majestic in the nation, is one long channel of filth; the

---

* A careful scientific study of a three-day smog that smothered New York City at Thanksgiving time, 1966, showed that air pollution caused the deaths of 168 persons. Dr. Leonard Greenburg, chairman of the Department of Environmental and Preventive Medicine at the Albert Einstein College of Medicine, directed the study. He emphasized that the 168 deaths were just those that could be directly attributed to the smog's effect, but he added that lung damage suffered during the period would probably be a contributing factor in New York deaths for years to come.

123

Connecticut, the longest river in New England, flows with a coat of contaminating scum; the great Mississippi has become so polluted that, in 1963, an estimated five million fish expired; and the Great Lakes have become little more than cesspools for the great industrial cities of the Midwest.

The menace to health can hardly be exaggerated. Not only do shellfish in contaminated waters become a principal source of hepatitis, one of our fastest growing ailments, but in many areas the filth poured into entire watersheds, only partially purified, comes running out in the home every time a faucet is turned to take a drink. It is one of the ironies of our urban life that we so blithely and unthinkingly pollute the very waters that we then turn around and drink. The city of Rensselaer, New York, for example, has thought nothing for years of dumping its raw sewage into the Hudson—and then drawing its drinking water from the same river little more than a stone's throw from its sewage outfalls. Many towns along the Hudson similarly rely upon this badly contaminated river for the water that they drink. The dangers implicit in such reliance were illustrated in an incident that occurred in the summer of 1964. A group of children saw a watermelon floating in the Hudson, fished it out, ate it—and promptly came down with typhoid fever.

The pollution of our rivers is matched, if indeed it is not surpassed, by that of the Great Lakes, those huge freshwater inland seas. A river, with its scouring currents, does at least sweep some of the filth that is dumped into it out into the bays and oceans, but in a lake the contamination is trapped—and stays. For 50 years Lake Michigan, that great and exceptionally deep lake, has been polluted by the wastes dumped into it by the cities and towns along its shores and by the effluent from 15 major and 35 minor industries. Though some of these industrial wastes are today subjected to partial treatment, three giant steel companies and three big oil refineries still discharge *7.2 billion gallons of waste each day into the Calumet River,* which flows into Lake Michigan. So polluted has Lake Michigan become by this deluge of wastes that one Public Health Service engineer estimates "it would take over 200 years for the pollution now in Lake Michigan to be removed." So lethal are the waters that, in 1963, 10,000 gulls and loons died along the southern and western shores of the lake; and two of Milwaukee's four beaches have had to be closed permanently, the other two intermittently, since 1959. Yet four million Americans, 60 percent of all those in the area, depend upon the Great Lakes for their drinking water—a water whose filth often clogs the water intakes.

To cite such facts is only to sketch the dimensions of the air and water pollution problems that are the inevitable by-products of a heavily concentrated urban civilization. We can see in our everyday lives, if we look, some of the more obvious and dire effects that our way of life is producing, but the long-range potentials, the problems that are building for our children and their children, are little short of horrendous. This is so because the capacity of the earth and its atmosphere to absorb the contamination of man is by no means infinite. We live, we survive, in a relatively thin blanket of oxygen that extends only about 2,000 feet above the earth's surface. What will happen in coming centuries if the pollution from our increasingly more

125

potent urban civilization goes unchecked and contaminates much of this life-sustaining blanket? Will man smother, or sicken and die, in the debris-filled atmosphere he has created? The possibility is real enough to haunt far-visioned scientists. Water is a similar problem. We depend greatly on the resources of the subterranean reservoirs far down in the earth, but these, too, can in time become contaminated—indeed, in some instances already are contaminated —because the layers of soil above them have become so saturated with wastes that they can absorb no more. So massive is this daily barrage of pollution that it has been suggested we should call America "the effluent society." Best estimates show that the nation spews out 133 million tons of aerial garbage each year, and *each day* 173 billion gallons of sewage and industrial wastes go gushing into American rivers.

The costs in human terms are such that the very future of man is menaced. Surgeon General William H. Stewart told a U.S. Senate subcommittee that studies show clear links between pollution and cancer, the common cold, emphysema and chronic bronchitis. New York City has been told that its very existence is threatened. "I don't know if you can continue to survive if you create conditions where you are going to dissolve in your own filth," an Interior Department spokesman warned at one pollution conference. Mayor Lindsay's Task Force on Air Pollution has estimated that the city could become "uninhabitable within a decade" if its air is not cleansed. And, on a broader scale, scientists are convinced that the continued existence of the human species on this planet is at stake. "There is no doubt that we are exploiting the Earth the way a parasite exploits

126

its host," Dr. Harold G. Cassidy, a Yale University chemist, told the American Institute of Biological Sciences. And he added: "But if our host, the Earth, is killed, we have nowhere else to go."

Such are the portents. It is clear that if the human species is not to become as extinct as the dinosaur, drastic and swift remedial action must be taken. To say this, as President Johnson most eloquently has said it, is a far cry, however, from doing something about it. For the problems involved are so infinite in their complexity and so fantastic in their costs that they mock the relatively puny efforts we have made so far to atone for the indifference of decades.

None of these problems can be localized; all are clearly national in their scope. New York City, which has the dirtiest air in America according to the Public Health Service, is located at the eastern terminus of a 3,000-mile jet stream that flows across the continent. The city must contend not just with its own filth, but with the effusions from the New Jersey factory belt and with particles of pollution from all of the cities stretching across the breadth of the land to Los Angeles. If New York City's air is to be purified, the air of the nation must be purified. Water pollution presents problems of similarly awesome scope. There is obviously little to be gained from the installation of the most modern purification systems in individual industrial or municipal plants if plants and cities 10 miles or 100 miles upstream continue to dump raw wastes into the water. New York State has voted a billion-dollar bond issue to clean up pollution in the Hudson, which lies almost entirely within its borders. But how do you clean up the pollution of Lake Michigan or the Mississippi? Just to ask the ques-

127

tion is to conjure up a vivid idea of the dimensions of the problem. To make the Mississippi run sweet and pure again, you would have to eliminate the pollution of the Missouri and the Ohio and *their* tributaries since all flow into the father of rivers. This is obviously a staggering task that involves half of the states of the nation.

Only the most stringent and uniform national codes, which we have been slow to adopt and which have been opposed by short-sighted legislators with rural orientations, can help to meet the crisis of the hour. But such codes, if and when adopted, raise a second mountainous barrier to accomplishment. The costs will be astronomical. So far we have spent billions upon billions of dollars for the flag-waving project aimed at putting the first man on the moon by 1970; at the same time we have been dribbling out insignificant millions for projects that might make our own earth more livable. The priorities clearly need to be reversed or, if we have money enough both for space and domestic needs once shorn of the incubus of Vietnam, equal attention should be given to the earth and the space race. The absolute necessity of such a reordering of our priorities is shown by a simple glance at the best estimates of cost. These estimates for cleaning up our air and water by the year 2000 range up to $400 billion; and even the most conservative estimate of $275 billion would mean that $8.3 billion a year would have to be funneled into the antipollution campaign, an allotment that does not stand a chance while we are in Vietnam.

Tied in with the pollution problem, especially the air pollution phase of it, is the whole question of urban transportation. It is one of the great ironies of our time that as

128

our population has become more concentrated, as urbanization has increased, we have placed our major reliance upon the automobile, a vehicle best suited to covering long rural distances and one that produces intolerable pollution and congestion in our cities. Many of our cities (Los Angeles is a prime example and New York is not far behind) are now almost literally strangling to death in a glut of freeways and a daily chaos of bumper-to-bumper traffic. The only solution is to bring our mass transit facilities into the latter part of the twentieth century; but this solution, so obvious, so eloquently advocated by experts like New York's Traffic Commissioner Henry Barnes, has not as yet even been attempted. Indeed, almost every step that we have taken has been a step backward until we have reached a point when the horse-and-buggy era of the Gay Nineties seems to have had distinct advantages.

This is not a figure of speech. Some years ago the Pennsylvania Railroad ran a demonstration train from the Jersey shore into downtown New York. A veteran Wall Street commuter who had been riding the line for 50 years whipped out a 1903 timetable and began to compare the running times in that era and those in the modern jet age. In the old days, of course, since local transportation was poor, trains had to stop every few miles to pick up passengers. Since then many local stations have been eliminated, and more are being dropped all the time. Still it took an hour-and-a-half to an hour-and-three-quarters to make the 40–50-mile commuting run to New York, a time matched by the best expresses of the early 1900's. And much comfort and convenience had gone. Diesels had replaced the old and dirty coal-burning engines, but many of the coaches were still pre-World War I vintage and the roadbed, according to trainmen, was so poorly maintained that speed limits had to be fixed on certain sections, precluding a faster running time to New York. All that had happened as the century progressed was that rail travel had retrogressed to the point at which it became a national scandal.

Perhaps we were paying then, and are continuing to pay, for the atrophying of the human brain once its owner is blessed with a monopoly. One thing is certain: The railroads in America died from the executive suite down. Faced with a new age, faced with the competition of car and bus in short-haul situations and that of the jet plane in longer travel, the railroads clung to their turn-of-the-century patterns; they refused to change. All their managements could see, as they began to lose passengers, was that services must be cut back to balance the books. It apparently never occurred to most of them to fight, to modernize to meet competition. The deterioration was steady and obvious to anyone who began commuting to New York even as recently as the end of World War II. Fewer trains ran from year to year as the drive sharpened to save money by cutbacks; maintenance became so bad that you would walk into a train at night and find all the lights out (they would not work), or with the thermometer standing near zero outside there would be no heat. I recall one Pennsylvania train I rode that completed its run with a lantern hung on the snout of the locomotive. The headlight had gone out and there was not an extra bulb handy. Under these conditions, passengers fled from the railroads as from the plague; and the more they fled, the happier short-sighted managements

130

became. Passenger service never did pay anyway, they argued, and they appealed to public utility commissions to cut out passenger service altogether and let them just run the freights that paid. In most cases the public utility commissions, being more accustomed to serving the utilities than the public, went along with this economic logic, and passenger trains on many historic lines simply stopped running.*

The result is idiocy. As early as 6:30 or 7 in the morning on the Garden State Parkway, the New Jersey Turnpike and other major arteries throughout the nation, there are modern driven men, either alone or in car pools, fighting their daily before-breakfast battle at speeds of 60 to 70 miles an hour, just to get to work. One of these characters stands out vividly in my mind, although he was not so very different from hundreds of others. But on the particular morning I encountered him he was driving a big high-powered car, hunched forward as if he had a demon on his back, hands gripping the wheel, face grim and determined as if he were about to crash through for a touchdown for

---

* An example was the abandonment of the Erie-Lackawanna's famed "Phoebe Snow" express from New York to Buffalo. William R. Wright, a veteran with 15 years of experience in the rail passenger field, outlined in *The Nation* on February 27, 1967, the series of steps by which railroad management deliberately made the "Phoebe Snow" so unprofitable that it could be abandoned. These included *adding* two hours to the running time to Buffalo; abandoning the convenient Main Street terminal in Buffalo for "a tin shanty in the East Buffalo freight yards"; and cutting off the dining car in mid-afternoon so that hungry passengers arriving in Buffalo at 8 P.M. could not get food. Such tactics bled the "Phoebe Snow" to death; rail management showed phenomenal losses—and the New York Public Utility Commission acceded to the elimination of the famous flier.

131

Yale from the five-yard line. He almost sheared off my front fender cutting in, almost clipped the car in front of me cutting back—and then he was gone, lost in the herd of hurtling steel and gaseous exhausts.

In New York City itself there is always day-long pandemonium. It hardly matters what time you take to the streets; rush hour or nonrush hour, the incredible never-ending, never-clearing glut of cars is there. Traffic, construction work, bridges, narrow double-parked crosstown streets make walking almost as fast as driving. Pick out a pedestrian on the sidewalk who seems to be going in your direction. Time and again, he will catch up to you, pass you, go ahead of you while you curse and battle the lights, the cars, all the other frustrated human beings.

It does not have to be this way. We Americans like to think that we are the first in everything, that we are the world's very best—especially in all things mechanical and scientific. The plain truth is that we are not. The full truth is even worse than that. The reality is that in our two decades of preoccupation with the Cold War and foreign crises like Vietnam we have been surpassed by other nations, smaller and poorer nations that have intelligently devoted their energies to the solution of their own problems.

Japan has built the New Tokaido Line, the fastest and most modern railroad in the world. It connects Tokyo and Osaka, 320 miles apart, an axis that is to Japan very much what the Boston-Washington corridor is to America. The Tokaido is literally an entirely new railroad from roadbed to rolling stock, constructed between 1959 and 1964 at a cost of $1.5 billion. Now 76 trains a day, each with a passenger capacity of 1,000, flit over this line at speeds of 125

132

miles per hour (they have been clocked up to 160 m.p.h., and the super-expresses, making just two stops, average 101 miles per hour for the entire Tokyo-Osaka run). They are competitive with the airlines in time because, in Japan as everywhere, it takes almost as long to get from an air terminal into a city as it does to make the city-to-city flight; the rail fares are cheaper, and the accommodations luxurious. So popular is the Tokaido that it has cut into air travel to such an extent that All-Nippon Airways has been forced to cancel some of its Tokyo-Osaka flights.

Some years ago a journalist friend of mine came back from Japan in a state of shock. He had ridden the New Tokaido from Tokyo to Osaka—and then had returned to riding our own slow, dirty and uncomfortable commuter railroads. The contrast stunned him. He kept talking for days about the Tokaido—its quiet, its comfort, its seemingly effortless speed. Its air conditioning was quiet and effective. It had reclining seats with footrests that popped out, enabling passengers to ride in airliner comfort. A streamlined blue-and-white train, the Tokaido departed from its own exclusive terminal in Tokyo; it moved smoothly with a low, electrical whine, gathered speed quickly and was soon hurtling along the tracks with only a faint rumble of the wheels and virtually no pitching or swaying to indicate its high speed. As in airliners a young, seductive-voiced stewardess spoke over a high-quality public address system, informing the passengers of the train's speed and progress.

Even the more ordinary trains on the New Tokaido Line generate high speeds and whisk swarms of travelers in and out of Tokyo in a comfort and convenience unknown in

133

America. Japan is now planning a *new* New Tokaido Line with cruising speeds up to 160 miles per hour—and Japan is by no means alone. In Europe, country after country puts American rail travel to shame. France has its Mistral; Italy its Settebello; Germany its Blauer Enzian; Russia its Aurora. All are high-speed, luxury trains that demonstrate vividly what *can* be done.

In America we have made only the most tentative gestures toward bringing our railroads into the latter half of the twentieth century. In May, 1967, the Pennsylvania Railroad tested an experimental train, built with Federal aid, on 22-mile-long trial runs between New Brunswick and Trenton, New Jersey. The train attained a maximum speed of 156 miles an hour in a performance that was billed as a preview of what will become regular New York to Washington service, cutting travel time on the 212-mile strip to about three hours.

But for the immediate future, if not indeed the foreseeable future, we appear doomed to live with our archaic and dwindling commuter lines, our overburdened and inadequate city rapid transit services, and all the inevitable glut, noise, fumes and frustration of a nation possessed by the automobile and dedicated to its use in every inappropriate situation. Both the rail lines feeding into our cities and the rapid transit facilities inside them have been neglected for 30 years, and the chaos and pollution of the streets is the inevitable result.

New York City's subway system is the most extensive in the nation, yet it is poorly adapted to modern needs. The city's first subway line was opened in 1904; its last in 1932. Since that time it has expanded some platforms, bought a

134

few newer coaches built much on the model of the old ones (it did not get its first air-conditioned subway cars until the summer of 1967), and it has raised its rates from a nickel to 20 cents. Everything else has stood still. As far back as 1951, New York City voters approved a $500 million bond issue to build a new subway—a much-needed Second Avenue subway on the East Side, one of the most rapidly improving sections of the city with new office and apartment buildings springing up all along Second and Third Avenues. The money was borrowed—and then spent for other purposes. To this day the Second Avenue subway, with its envisioned connecting links to other systems and a new tunnel under the East River to Queens, remains an unfulfilled dream. It is now being planned for again, part of the package included in a huge state transportation bond issue Governor Rockefeller persuaded the voters to approve in the November, 1967, general election.

New York's problems and inadequacies are matched in every other great city in the nation. The Joint Economic Committee of Congress made an exhaustive study of our urban needs in 1966, coming to the conclusion, like Senator Ribicoff, that we would need to spend a colossal one trillion dollars in the next decade. In making its projections the committee estimated that, by 1980, 75 percent of our population would be concentrated in only 2 percent of our land area. It envisioned the growth of 40 urban complexes of over one million population each, with an overall total of 140 million residents. It estimated that urban transit lines (this, it must be emphasized, does *not* include rail lines feeding into the cities) would require an expenditure of $10.9 billion from 1966 to 1975. Even this estimate was

135

probably conservative. Mayor Lindsay had put New York's needs alone at $4 billion, but the Congressional estimate put it at $2.5 billion. The discrepancy is probably explained by the fact that the Federal figures were based primarily not on any ideal of improvement but on projects already authorized or planned, awaiting only funds.

Even within these limitations, the city-by-city estimates involved such huge sums of money that they give a vivid idea of the scope of the problem. Here is the run-down: Atlanta, $329 million; Baltimore, $531 million; Boston, $590 million; Chicago, $930 million; Cleveland, $60 million; Los Angeles, $900 million; Philadelphia, $506 million; San Francisco, $1.2 billion; Seattle, $111 million; Washington, D.C., $950 million.

The impact of transportation on the quality of life in what threatens to become a world of urban monstrosities has been demonstrated on occasion by paradox. There have been a few instances in recent years when New York City has been blitzed by blizzards so severe that all street traffic has been halted and drivers have been ordered to keep their cars out of the city except for absolutely essential missions. Infallibly, such weather disasters have proved a boon in disguise. The city suddenly becomes a quiet, peaceful, livable place. The air clears before high winds from the west, and New Yorkers take deep breaths, appreciating perhaps for the first time in months or years what relatively pure air smells like, how invigorating it can be. These brief spells of quietude and cleanliness imposed by nature do not last long; the streets are quickly cleared, and with their clearing pandemonium returns. But the hiatus is enough to make New Yorkers wonder sometimes what life could be like in the city *if.* . . .

Speculation is neither unnatural nor ridiculous. It takes freak disasters of nature to show us what we are missing— and what we are suffering—in our urban lives. The statistics that reinforce experience's impressions build a startling picture. Thousands of cars stopping and starting, smoking and fuming on congested city streets, throw out into the air a long list of dangerous and potentially lethal compounds. For every thousand gallons of gasoline consumed, these substances are spewed into the air: 3,200 pounds of carbon monoxide; 200–400 pounds of organic vapors (cancer-inducing hydrocarbons); 20–75 pounds of oxides of nitrogen, intrinsically more lethal than the hydrocarbons; 18 pounds of aldehydes; 17 pounds of sulphur compounds; 2 pounds of organic acids; 2 pounds of ammonia; and 0.3 pounds of solids such as zinc, metallic oxides and carbons.

In some cities the automobile is the major source of air pollution. It has been estimated that about two-thirds of Los Angeles' smog, for example, is caused by emissions from the wild melee of automobiles engaged in the daily rat race on the tangle of thruways. Purification devices are now being installed in new-model cars with great fanfare, but what is generally overlooked is that these devices will do only part of the job. They will eliminate most of the hydrocarbons, but they will no nothing about the nitrogen oxides. The truth is that in the present state of technology it is impossible to manufacture an efficient internal combustion engine that will not create smog.

137

Experimentation with various devices goes on. A fuel cell for cars, electric cars for city travel, turbine engines, all these are being tested, but none has been developed to the stage of practical use. Too little time, too little money, too little brain power has been devoted to these problems. Sen. Edmund S. Muskie (D., Me.), a leading proponent of cleaner air, has commented that we are as ignorant of the components of the air pollution problem and what to do about it as we were about water pollution 50 years ago. And we are still quite ignorant and lackadaisical about *that*.

Such are a few—and it must be emphasized *just a few*— of the new and enormous problems intrinsic to the mass urban society that our technology has created in the brief span of two decades. There are other problems, an overwhelming mass of them such as poverty in an age of affluence, slum housing, poor education, inadequate hospitalization and health facilities. All these clamor not only for the investment of our resources but the attention and dedication of our best brains and skills. Their importance cannot be overemphasized, for they were the major catalysts when hate boiled over into violence in the summer riots of 1967.

6

"A BLACK NECK IN A WHITE NOOSE"

American cities are becoming cores of black ringed with
white. Peter Maris, a British sociologist, studied American
urban renewal and characterized the central cities as an
enormous ghetto—"a black neck in a white noose." Statistics lend weight to his vivid prose. Washington, our capital city, is nearly two-thirds (61.2 percent) Colored. In
Philadelphia the white population, which was 51 percent
in 1961, declined to 43 percent in 1965. More than 50 percent of all the school children in New York City today are
Negro or Puerto Rican. In Los Angeles, Watts is a Negro
city of some 344,000 persons lost and isolated in the laby-
rinth of the freeways. In Chicago 300,000 Negroes turn
nine square miles of the West Side into total black territory,
and another 600,000 inhabit 30 square miles on the South
Side. A Federal study of population shifts shows that in a
single decade, 1950–1960, more than ten million poor,
whites and Negroes, moved from rural areas into the cities,

and it forecasts that this migration will continue into the mid-1970's.

This massive reshuffling of population has altered the face of America. If one could look down from a helicopter on American cities with zones painted to resemble the pigmentation of their residents, one would see an almost unvarying pattern of huge black bull's-eyes in the cities' cores; beyond, still within the cities' boundaries, thin rings of white signify the exclusive high-rise apartment zones to which the wealthy have repaired; and beyond these are the wider and expanding ribbons of white designating the homes of a virtually all-white suburbia.

Such a visual demonstration, if it could be staged, might be invaluable in bringing the American people and their leaders more into contact with reality. For, as a people, we live in a world of persistent and dangerous myths—the conservative myth that this is the land of opportunity for all, that the Negro is being well treated and it is his own fault if he does not make out; the liberal myth that civil rights are all important, that the great battle should be fought to achieve integration, as if integration is the only need and will really solve everything.

The inescapable fact is that the cores of our cities are black and becoming blacker. How do you "integrate" when technological and economic pressures are creating entire black communities, black cities within the cities? To ask the question is to bring an ideal into conflict with reality and to indicate that, in the context of the crucial needs of the moment, the ideal is largely irrelevant. Conservative myths fare no better, are equally divorced from reality, and indeed pack far greater potential for disaster.

140

In the predominantly white world, in a society two-thirds affluent, a Gallup poll in the summer of 1967—a poll taken even as Newark was erupting—showed that an incredible 99 percent of all white Americans believed the Negro was not being treated "badly." Even more incredibly, 75 percent subscribed to the proposition that "Negroes are treated the same as whites." But what are the facts? In July, 1967, we had the highest employment rates in American history—but not for the Negro. The Census Bureau reported that 41 percent of all nonwhites in America were living in poverty. In Cleveland the overall unemployment rate was down to 3.5 percent, but in the black slums of Hough it was 15.6 percent. Among nonwhite teen-agers the nation over, a bad situation was becoming worse. In 1961, 27.6 percent had been unemployed; in 1967, despite a still booming economy, unemployment among this non-white, teen-aged group had *risen* to 29.2 percent—and would have been higher if so many thousands had not been drafted to fight in Vietnam.

You can sit before your television set and watch Jim Dooley wave his arms and call, "C'mon down to sunny Florida." You can see a golden Yellow Bird take off into an encarmined sky. You can see the waving palms and the sunlit blue water of Hawaii or the isles of the Caribbean, and you can listen to the pitch that tells you it is a beautiful, beautiful world—and come on, don't be an old stick-in-the-mud, have yourself a wonderful vacation on your American Express credit card. Enjoy now, pay later. You see all this, you hear all this, and you live in Watts or Hough or the ghetto of Newark; you cannot get a job and, if you do get one, it pays less than relief. The world of

141

affluent America, the world of all those happy people "out there" who have it "made," swears at you and mocks you. And if it is pure inescapable hell, it is no wonder.

The 99 percent of white America that the Gallup poll showed to be living in delusion must make contact with the facts of modern life. What has happened is clear enough, but it takes a considerable amount of mental guts, a quality not noticeable in the florid rhetoric of most politicians, to face up to it and to acknowledge it. The vast migration of Negroes into our central cities has set into motion a chain of events that, until now, has been irreversible. As the cores of our cities fill up with the jobless and untrained, businesses depart, housing deteriorates, relief rolls burgeon, tax ratables fall and taxes become ever less adequate for municipal purposes; misery and hopelessness become endemic, they breed crime and addiction and violence—and so on and on it goes in cycles of ever-deepening deprivation and despair. To combat all this programs have been offered that are largely carry-overs from the depression Thirties, programs that have little relevance to an age that did not even exist when they were drafted; and we have financed even these inadequate programs in pinch-penny style while we spend billions abroad.

Probably the most vivid way to describe what has happened is to take an in-depth look at what is in the process of happening even as this is being written. The Bronx is the northernmost of the five boroughs of New York City. Not too many years ago it was a great residential borough for white of the upper and lower middle class. It was one of those outer fringes of white, with fine apartment buildings stretching along the Grand Concourse; it was not, defi-

142

nitely not, a black-core area like Harlem in Manhattan or Bedford-Stuyvesant in Brooklyn. But in recent years the tide of migration has risen and has seeped steadily northward into the Bronx, much like the ocean tide surging up a river. In a few short years the face of the Bronx has altered radically. Between 1960 and 1966 the Bronx lost 205,618 non-Puerto Rican whites, almost all of them from the middle classes with the better-paying jobs. During those same years 138,862 more Puerto Ricans moved in. So did another 89,313 Negroes. Where the borough in 1960 had a white population of 75.7 percent, this figure dropped in six short years to 60.5 percent. And Negroes and Puerto Ricans, who had constituted only 22.6 percent of the population in 1960, numbered almost 40 percent.

These sweeping changes offered an ideal opportunity to study what was happening in our cities while it was in the process of happening. A research team from Fordham University, financed by a $100,000 grant from the Federal Office of Economic Opportunity, made a detailed study of the Bronx during the early months of 1967. They found that one family out of every five in the Bronx lived in abject poverty; they found that this poverty was increasing despite rising employment elsewhere and a generally prosperous economy; and they found that the Bronx's joblessness, deprivation and poverty were largely the result of national conditions, of technological change which had dumped the burdens of the entire nation on the cities.

Dr. Joseph R. Cammarosano, who directed the research project, put it this way: "Since the end of World War II, a significant movement of middle and lower-middle income families out to the suburbs has occurred and in their place

143

have come thousands of Negro and Puerto Rican families.
. . . They live in abject poverty with little hope of the
future. The technological revolution in American agriculture which has driven these people off the land is a national
problem, and the primary responsibility for coping with it
is the Federal Government's."

The Fordham research was significant because it was
one of the few attempts that have been made to update
the 1960 census figures. Most studies and projections are
based upon those years-old figures · which, in an era of
rapid change such as this, are obviously badly outdated.
Thus one of the great values of the Fordham survey was
that it produced solid research on which to base a judgment of what is happening now. The research data was developed from interviews in 3,000 Bronx households, and it
included a survey of industry and commerce. From these
studies a clear picture emerged that tells us much about
what is happening in a time of unprecedented population
changes.

Poverty had been imported into the Bronx along with
the new immigrants from the South and Puerto Rico, Professor Cammarosano said. Of the Puerto Rican families, 27
percent had incomes below the $3,000 poverty level in
1966, and 68 percent were in deprivation, with incomes
below $5,000. The Negroes were almost as badly off.
Twenty-six percent of all Negro families existed on incomes below $3,000, and 57 percent were below $5,000.

Chronic unemployment was substantial. The Bronx unemployment rate throughout the boom of the mid-Sixties
ran steadily at 6 percent or more. Fifty-six percent of the
unemployed were Negroes or Puerto Ricans; and, of all the

unemployed in the Bronx, 38 percent had been out of work for more than six months. As the influx of Negroes and Puerto Ricans continued, family incomes steadily deteriorated, and whole sections of the Bronx began to deteriorate with them.

The industry survey showed that there had been a net loss of 216 manufacturing concerns between 1960 and 1965. Three service industry divisions—transportation and communication, construction, and retailing and wholesaling—showed an additional net loss of 357 concerns. Some of these had failed, probably as the result of a loss of buying power in the area; others had simply picked up and moved off to the suburbs. The migrating companies cited a variety of reasons for moving: lack of industrial land for plant expansion, the high cost of land compared to the much lower cost in the suburbs, lack of parking and loading facilities, the heavy burden of real estate and business taxes in New York, vandalism and the deterioration of the labor force as a result of the influx of unskilled labor.

The story of the Bronx was the story everywhere in the cities of the North and West. One of every two Negroes in these cities is a migrant, according to Herbert Bienstock, New York regional director of the U.S. Bureau of Labor Statistics. "Since 1947," he said, "there's been a net decline in farm employment of near four million jobs. In the last three years the drop was 700,000."

That year, 1947. If one can fix a time, that was when it all began. It was in March, 1947, that President Truman proclaimed the Truman Doctrine, and America's eyes turned outward, transfixed on what was soon to become the Cold War. And it was in that same year of 1947, unper-

145

ceived at the time, that the domestic economy began to be altered in radical ways. World War II shortages were behind us, and sophisticated farm machinery began to hit the countryside. Wartime chemical discoveries began to be applied to the land—and suddenly there was no place in the South for the Negro. An old Negro porter who had spent 32 years on the run of the Illinois Central Railroad connecting the Mississippi Delta country to the cities of the Midwest put it this way: "It started in 1947. This train went through the delta, and there was nothing but black faces, for years and years and years. I used to wonder, 'Where are they coming from? How can there be anybody left? My God, they must be coming right out of the ground. They got to stop sometime.' "

And Bienstock adds this comment: "The South sowed the wind, and the Northern and Western cities of greatest Negro population are reaping the whirlwind of never-ending joblessness and despair."

Ben H. Bagdikian in *The Saturday Evening Post* has personalized the mass migration, giving a vivid picture of the experiences of some of these new immigrants to the cities of the north. He told in detail the story of Walter Austin, 48, father of five children aged 6 to 17, born in Holmes County, Mississippi, a worker in the fields from the age of seven, unable to read or write, wanting only to farm in an era when the one thing he knew and could do and wanted to do was the one thing that had been taken from him.

Austin and his wife, Bessie, had been sharecroppers for 20 years on a plantation in Holmes County until they had been forced to move some ten years earlier to Merigold,

146

Mississippi. In sharecropping, the Negro is kept in perpetual poverty, in debt and in bondage to the white plantation owner. The plantation owner lets a Negro family have a shack on his property and a plot of ground to grow their own vegetables; he lets them borrow for seed and fertilizer and food, all of this to be balanced off at the end of the year by the sharecropper's half of the land's yield. Only the plantation owner keeps the books; only he decides how much the sharecropper has earned. At the end of the year, it is traditional for the Negro to find he has just come out even, if he is lucky; if his "boss man" is especially rapacious, he will be told he is still in debt for as much as $100 to $500.

The year before the Austins were forced to leave Holmes County, Walter was driving a tractor for $4.50 a day when the weather was good, and Bessie and their four children worked in the fields. Bessie and the children worked in the fields from May to October; they grew and processed 26 bales of cotton. "And all we got for that year and 26 bales of cotton was $150," Bessie said. Bagdikian figured out that, at the price cotton was selling for in 1956, the Austins' half-share on those 26 bales should have been worth $1,976, minus $480 that had been loaned them for food and their share of the feed and fertilizer. In other words they should have had $1,496 coming to them—not the $150 which was all they got under the "boss man's" accounting.

In Merigold after they moved there, the Austins were more prosperous for a time. Their "boss man" was a more decent sort, their house was better, their income slightly improved. But there came the inevitable day when the

147

"boss man" told Walter he could not guarantee him any work for the next year because his cotton acreage was being rented out to a big agricultural operator. The word that Walter Austin was in the doubtful category instantly got around. Previously, he had been able to get credit for food, for medicine, for a doctor; now everybody wanted cash. The inevitable decision was forced upon Walter. Everyone around him was moving. Ten years earlier 50 families had lived on the plantation; now there were only six. Within the past year two shacks on either side of Walter's had been vacated and torn down; now it was his turn to move.

Austin told Bagdikian what it was like. When he got up Christmas morning, he said, he cried and cried. And then he thought he should be thankful to be alive and to have his children alive and well. He comforted himself with the thought that he had been able to provide some "special Christmas food" for them—"fresh apples and oranges."

Walter Austin dreaded the move from the land into a foreign city in the North, but then he comforted himself with the thought that, in Mississippi all his life, he had been treated like a child. When he got up, his "boss man" told him what do do; when he got paid, his "boss man" took out of his pay whatever he decided Walter owed him. Walter had nothing to say about it. The "boss man" could do virtually anything he wanted, and Walter could not protest: he had to have the "boss man's" protection. In the North, this at least would be different.

When the Austins left Mississippi, they went to Springfield, Illinois, where other members of the family had preceded them. In Springfield, a city of 86,000, there were 5,000 Negroes, many of them from Holmes County, so the

148

Austins from the start had relatives and friends to give them a helping hand. Walter got a job washing dishes and mopping floors in a restaurant for $40 a week; his oldest remaining daughter went to work in a laundry, earning $5 a week more than her father. One way and another, though the start was poor and hard, the Austins began to make out.

Their story is typical of the pressures that force the Negro off the Southern land of his ancestors, the land he knows and loves. But it is by no means typical of what happens to him when he gets into the cities of the North, especially the big cities like New York or Chicago. Unless, like the Austins, he has friends and relatives who have already made contacts and can give him a helping hand, his plight rapidly becomes desperate indeed. His farming skills, the only ones he has, are useless; he can, in most instances barely read and write; he is not only untrained, he is basically so poorly educated that he is untrainable for most of the jobs available in this modern, automated civilization. In the days of World War II, well-paying factory jobs were available to the Negro, but in the 1950's automation hit the factories, assembly-line jobs disappeared, and many industrial plants moved from the central cities to the suburbs. New York City lost 200,000 factory jobs in a single decade. Though the U.S. economy developed 4,348,000 jobs in the three years 1964, 1965 and 1966, a full half of these were white-collar jobs and another 14 percent were service jobs; only 37.6 percent were blue-collar, or factory, jobs. In New York City the disparity between white-collar and blue-collar jobs was even more severe: 74 percent of the new jobs were white-collar, and only 2.6 percent were available for factory hands.

To cite such statistics is to give just the barest indication

149

of the forces that entrap the Negro in an age of ever-increasing technological sophistication. Actually there are no statistics that sum up the full dimensions of the Negro's plight, for experts acknowledge that all employment and unemployment figures, devastating as they are, miss actuality by a wide margin and really *understate* the case. The reason for this is the lost legion of the unemployed, both Negro and white, in the ghettos of every great American city. These are men who have been so long unemployed, who are so hopeless, so derelict, that they have been lost even to the census takers. They crop up at odd times; we know that they exist—but we can do little more than estimate their numbers.

Sen. Robert F. Kennedy, in a notable speech in July, 1967, tried to bring into focus the hard facts of unemployment, poverty and deprivation in the ghetto—the facts as they really are, not the surface facts at which statistics only hint. Take, he said, a typical ghetto population of 230,000 Negroes. According to census estimates, 56,000 would be adult males between 20 and 64 years of age.

"Of these neither the Census Bureau nor the Labor Department can find from one-fifth to one-third because they have no fixed address, no job—they drift about the city, separated from their families, as if they were of no greater concern to their fellow citizens than so many sparrows or spent matches."

After subtracting these "lost battalions," Kennedy was left with 41,000 "whom the labor department can find." Of these, no less than 11 percent have dropped out of the officially counted "labor force" since they have given up hope and stopped looking for work. By deducting these

150

brigades of the hopeless, Kennedy found that he was left with an active "labor force" of 36,500. And of these 10 percent were unemployed and many of the rest were holding jobs paying less than $60 a week, income below the family poverty level.

"Thus of the 56,000 men in this typical ghetto," Senator Kennedy concluded, "only 24,500, just 43.7 percent, have full-time employment which pays more than $60 a week. Only 30,600, a bare majority, have full-time work at any rate of pay. Less than three out of five have any work at all."

In a comparable effort to picture reality in the ghetto pockets of the nation, the U.S. and the New York State Labor Departments have developed what they call a sub-employment index. Unlike the straight unemployment index, this attempts to show what the situation is actually like by taking into account the legions of the lost. Some of these figures, like Senator Kennedy's, indicate that anywhere from one-third to nearly one-half of all working-age males in such depressed areas are so much useless flotsam. In East Harlem, for example, where the unemployment rate was 9 percent in the summer of 1967, the subemployment estimate of the actual situation was 33.1 percent. In New Orleans the figures were 10 percent and 45.3 percent; in Philadelphia 11 percent and 34.2 percent; in Phoenix, Arizona, 13.2 percent and 41.7 percent; in St. Louis 12.9 percent and 38.9 percent; in San Antonio 8.1 percent and 47.4 percent.

What is life like in such ghetto areas where a man is of no more use than a mangy cur? And what about children growing up in such environments? (After all, according to

151

the U.S. Labor Department, 950,000 new jobs were created for American youth between June, 1965, and June, 1966 —and of these nearly one million new jobs, just 33,000 were filled by youths from the ghettos.) What happens when the ghetto teen-ager discovers that the opportunities in this great new world of technology are not for him?

This was described to the Ribicoff committee in down-to-earth terms by two witnesses, Claude Brown, author of the best-selling *Manchild in the Promised Land,* and Arthur Dunmeyer, a boyhood friend of Brown's in the ghetto and a man who had spent almost half of his 30 years in various prisons. The testimony has to be telescoped here, but some of it went like this:

Dunmeyer: I am married; I am 30 years old. I have eight kids by various different women. . . . I might go back to jail again because this is a way of life. A lot of people don't realize this. . . . But to exist where I live and how I live, you might break the law at any time without intention. . . .

Brown: He is 30 years old and he is also a grandfather, which makes him more of a typical "manchild" than Claude Brown. . . .

Senator Ribicoff: How old were you when you had your first child?

Dunmeyer: Fifteen.

Senator Ribicoff: You were 15. And how old was your daughter when she had her first child?

Dunmeyer: Twelve.

Senator Ribicoff: And this is a common situation in your neighborhood and where you live?

Dunmeyer: Very much so. As I said before, it is

152

our way of life. We have but so many ways to express ourselves, and when you are a kid you have the expressions that want to come out, and this is the closest thing that you can get as a solvent. . . .

Brown: I would like to say something here. Our society is always condemning the high rate of illegitimacy in Negro ghettos, and it always seems so ridiculous to me to give any group of people so little means with which to cope with the dictates, the moral dictates of society, and expect them to live up to them. So sex and the Negro society and the views that the white society have on it are so completely diverse that the two will almost never get together. . . .

When I was, say, about nine years old, both of my parents had to work to make $50 a week—you know, eight hours a day. This is why at the age of six I was left out in the street to be brought up by the criminal elements, prostitutes, the hustlers, the pimps, the stickup artists, the dope dealers, the fences, and this sort of thing. . . . And so we were out on the streets learning about sex at five and six, we knew at five and six that, well, it was a nice thing. It was good. By the time we were 13 we knew it was a great anodyne, you know, before you got to heroin. . . .

Brown pointed out that his parents had come up from the South. They had come to New York as to "the promised land"; and, like millions of others, they quickly discovered that they had no talents to open the gates to that land of promise. They were caught up in poverty and frustration—and there was no hope. For, as Brown wrote in his book, "where does one run to when he's already in the promised land?" Men in this situation go to pieces.

153

They cannot provide for their families; for this reason they lose respect for themselves as men—and their women lose respect for them as men. The resulting evils are inevitable.

Brown: How can you support a family of five kids on $65 a week? So he (the father) just leaves. He ups one day and leaves; maybe becoming an alcoholic. . . .

Many of the physical reactions—they took out their frustrations on their kids—they beat the hell out of them. My father used to beat me to death every day. Still they take it out on their wives. They beat their wives. It is just frustration that they feel.

The wives lose respect for their husbands. They can't really support their families. There are many affairs, you know. . . . Like, Mama is screwing the butcher for an extra piece of meat. Pardon the term. Mama is having sexual relationships with the butcher for an extra piece of pork chop for the kids. . . .

Or maybe the number runner on the corner digs Mama or something. She has got a couple of kids. He can give her $25 a week. All her husband can make is, say, $60 at most a week, and it isn't enough, and the $25 helps because she wants her kids to have the things that TV says that they should have. . . .

Dunmeyer: In some cases this is the way you get your drug dealers and prostitutes and your numbers runners. . . . They see that these things are the only way they can compete in the society, to get some sort of status. They realize that there aren't any real doors open to them, and so, to commit crime was the only thing to do, they can't go back. There is nothing to go back to. This is understood. This is why they came.

154

Brown: It is like a war between them and us, the society which oppresses us, and us, the oppressed. When a guy goes to jail, it is OK. You are looked up to, if you are a successful hustler, you have a big Cadillac and you have always got $300 in your pocket, you are taking numbers, you are selling drugs, you are a stickup artist, you are anything, you are a prostitute, anything you may be doing. . . . As long as you were making it, as long as you were a success, that is why in Harlem people respect the guy who is always clean.

You know, he has on a $200 silk suit every day, $55 alligator shoes and this sort of thing. He drives a big Cadillac, and they know he is winning the war. He is a soldier, he is a real soldier. He is a general in the community. If he gets busted, well, he is just a prisoner of war. That is the way it is looked upon. . . .

This testimony shocked not only a number of Senators but several of the Negro civil rights leaders who reacted to it as some Italians do to a mention of the Mafia. They produced statistics intended to show that Brown and Dunmeyer had libeled their own race, that the description they had given of life in the ghetto was exaggerated and untrue. There is no question that the Negro race has its share of the honest, hard-working and law-abiding, but there can be equally little question that Brown and Dunmeyer had given the Ribicoff committee probably the most honest and forthright description it was to get of what life is really like for millions of Negroes trapped in the black ghettos' pits of despair. If anyone doubts, one has only to read Robert

155

Conot's masterpiece on the Watts riot, *Rivers of Blood,
Years of Darkness*. There, again and again, in case history
after case history, one finds life stories to match the de-
scriptions given by Brown and Dunmeyer.

The evidence is massive and undeniable that American
society is being wracked by extremes—the extremes of
affluence and special privilege and jet-set living on the one
hand, of abysmal poverty and neglect and hopelessness on
the other. In any society the tensions created by such extremes are explosive. In our own they are doubly so because, to economic inequality and injustice, there is added
the vitriol of race prejudice and race hatred. We sit, then,
on a powder keg, as the events of the summer of 1967
showed.

First, of course, there is poverty. What are we going to
do to relieve it, to ease this part of the pressure?

Today some 34–35 million Americans live in the most
abject poverty, a term defined by Federal statisticians to
represent an income of $3,000 or less for a family of four.
That $3,000 figure at first glance is misleading. When it is
broken down it means just 70 cents per person per day for
food at 1964 prices; just $1.40 a day per person for shelter,
clothing, medical care, travel—for everything else. Few in
the affluent society will be disposed to question that $2.10
a day for *everything* represents true, grinding poverty.

This poverty is concentrated in the South and in the
cities. Half of all families rated poor—and 70 percent of
all colored families in this category—live in a Southern
state. Two-thirds of the poor (67 percent) are white. We
hear less about them than we do about the Negro poor for
two basic reasons: The white poor are more dispersed, and

156

they include a larger percentage of older citizens. Of the colored poor, two out of every five are concentrated in the central city ghettos; only one out of four among the whites live in such areas. Of some 23.6 million white poor, 4.6 million are 65 or older; among the 10.6 million nonwhite poor, only 700,000 are in this old-age group. Of all those living in poverty, 10.1 million are concentrated in the central cities. And one out of every five youngsters under the age of 18—nearly 15 million in all—is growing up in a poverty-stricken family.

Statistics are dull things at times, but in such statistics one can see the mounting pressures on the whole of our society. Such statistics give us a glimpse of the herding together of millions of human beings in utter poverty in the city ghettos; they indicate the desperation of the young, caught in these inhuman traps, looking forward to a life in which there is no place for them, in which there is no hope. Sen. Robert Kennedy commented during the Ribicoff hearings that, in ghetto areas, the dropout rate in many high schools was 90 percent, and even the 10 percent who did finish did not go on to college—all this in a society in which the high school diploma represents the irreducible minimum necessary to get work in the increasingly restrictive and selective job market. At Kennedy's request Bayard Rustin, executive director of the A. Philip Randolph Institute, discussed the plight of the young.

There are 77,000 young people between 16 and 25 in New York for whom Mayor Wagner said there is no work in New York. Mayor Lindsay has not created any work for them, but I am not blaming

157

him. . . . Why should there not be dropouts when young people know for one thing that the school system giving them a general diploma is preparing them for absolutely nothing? . . . Or how can they be excited if the likelihood of the best job many young Negroes in New York can get is pushing a handtruck through the garment district, a job which has no future, a job which does not provide them with the necessary things of life, particularly in a society where the mass media tell them that they must have the things they do not need? Imagine a pimply-faced 15-year-old boy being told by television that if he doesn't use X perfume he will not get a girl.

All of this is part of it. They are told they must have, on the one hand, and on the other, they do not have.

It is significant—and this has nothing to do with Negroes in particular, but with youth in general—that of the many young boys in the Chillicothe (Ohio) Correctional Institution, who are there for stealing cars, about 75 percent of them are there for stealing a car to take a girl on a date. Now there is not only among Negroes but among all youth a feeling of "What is the use? You will not make it anyhow. There are no jobs out there anyhow."

Such is the situation that confronts us; and these are the priorities as experts see them:

• There must be a new attack on the whole question of poverty itself.

• There must be jobs for the jobless. And this means education. For without education those 15 million youths

158

now living in poverty are never going to fit themselves into this new world of technology.

• There must be decent housing, not tenements infested by rats as large as cats.

• Health and hospital care must reach the poor, who often die at twice the rate of the rest of us; who, every statistic shows, need the most care—and get the least.

Just to list the separate items in that budget of necessity gives some idea of the dimensions of our problem and of the magnitude of our blindness and failure throughout two decades of the Cold War.

Our relief-welfare system is a legacy of the depression-ridden Thirties. The Emergency Relief Act of 1933 and the Social Security Act of 1935 both were designed to deal with a world entirely different from the world of today. The image that we then had of the poor was one of the Wall Street broker who had not jumped from his window but had taken to selling apples on the street; he and his middle-class counterparts, writers, artists, teachers, professional people who had lost their footholds, needed to be helped. The Negro at the time was largely out of sight and out of mind on the plantations of the South. The people with whom we were most concerned were just like us, average, everyday Americans. Help for them would certainly be temporary until they could get back on their feet again. One class, admittedly, might be different—the aged; and the Social Security Act was designed to help them on a permanent basis.

These assumptions had some validity at the time. In 1940 almost 62 percent of all welfare recipients were on Old Age Assistance; only 36 percent were being helped

159

under the Aid to Dependent Children program, designed
to provide for children in poverty-stricken families where
there was no father to provide support. Twenty-two years
later the situation was almost reversed. The aged represented 33 percent of all welfare recipients; 57 percent were
in the Aid to Dependent Children program. This shift in
emphasis has been the basic cause of great public resentment. We could sympathize with the down-at-the-heels
out-of-work sufferer of depression times if for no other
reason than that most of us were almost in the same boat;
but this business of paying public funds to the mothers of
illegitimate children in the ghettos raises our hackles and
leads to angry shouts that we are subsidizing prostitution.
The shouters, of course, neglect the main point—the children. They are here, they will be with us a long time, and
they represent potential good or potential evil, depending
on what we do with them. The ranters also ignore the basic
fact that it is not welfare itself that is bad, but some of the
mechanics of the welfare system—the presupposition and
the methods, deriving from the very nature of its origin and
the fact that little intelligence has been applied to the
problem.

It is the built-in jokers in the system that have helped
to create new evils. One of these was the provision that
Aid to Dependent Children can be granted to a household
only if there is no father there to work and provide support.
Another is the provision that even if the mother works her
earnings are deducted *in full* from the amount of her welfare check. Such provisions (1) encourage the father to
leave his family and get lost because, with the kinds of jobs
he can get, the family can get more from welfare and are

better off without him, and (2) discourage the welfare recipient from seeking work because the poor pay from menial jobs does not permit her to get ahead and everything she earns will be deducted from the welfare allowance. So she might as well not work in the first place.

The result has been to breed generations that have existed on relief. Robert Conot in his study of the Watts riot cites instance after instance in which this short-sighted system helped to break up families and rob them of any stability they might have had. And he tells the story of how one far-sighted welfare worker, startled at the intelligence she detected in a 30-year-old mother of four living in ghetto surroundings, quietly fractured all the rules to provide extra allowances that would permit the mother to return to school and get an education. The result: With the social worker pushing and encouraging her all the way, this young and previously hopeless mother went to night school and got her high school diploma; encouraged, finding a new life with infinite possibilities, she attended junior college, got a scholarship to Stanford, obtained an M.A. degree and became a junior high school mathematics teacher.

The story, of course, is not typical, but who knows just how atypical it is? This isolated instance showed, at least, what can be accomplished in certain cases by following a route we have not tried. It is certainly a vivid example that spells out the difference between a dead-end program that offers no hope to anyone and an open-end program offering opportunity to those with the intelligence and energy to see and to take it.

In the contrast may be found the explanation of Sen.

161

Robert Kennedy's prescient explosion of May 5, 1967, when, well in advance of the summer riots, he called for "a welfare revolution" and denounced in scathing terms a whole range of services by which "in our generosity" we had sought to deal with the poor and by which we had succeeded only in robbing them of "any semblance of human dignity." Kennedy said:

> We have created a welfare system which aids only a fourth of those who are poor, which forces men to leave their families so that public assistance can be obtained, which has created a dependence on their fellow citizens that is degrading and distasteful to giver and recipient alike. . . .
>
> We have built vast, impersonal high-rise public housing projects—ghettos within ghettos—isolated from the outside world and devoid of any sense of humanity. . . .
>
> We have cleared areas of slums in the name of urban renewal, with little sense of what would become of those whose homes we leveled. . . .
>
> We have provided health services in huge, unpleasant municipal hospitals—through emergency rooms and out-patient clinics where people wait for hours to see a doctor they have never seen before and are likely never to see again.

It was as compact and comprehensive a summary as one can find of the problems confronting a 70 percent urban America in the latter twentieth century. And it raised a lot of hackles. Governor Rockefeller and Senator Javits, perhaps merely seeking political advantage, sharply rebuked

Kennedy for making sensational and irresponsible statements; and Javits, at least, was considerably shocked a few days later when he found Mayor Lindsay's Commissioner of Welfare, Mitchell I. Ginsberg, agreeing in essence with Kennedy.

Testifying before Senator Clark's subcommittee on poverty, employment and manpower, Ginsberg called the nation's welfare system "bankrupt" and said that it ought to be "thrown out." Javits said he was "disturbed" by the statement. "You better not be in too much of a hurry to talk that way, or you might get it thrown out right now," he said. He added that there were all too many in Congress who would be "delighted" to vote against almost any welfare program and who would relish quoting Kennedy and Ginsberg. In this, of course, he was unfortunately right, the composition of Congress with its rural-Southern dominance being what it is; but as Ginsberg later said, explaining that he was "sorry" if he had "upset" Congress, "It seems to me judgments have to be made on what the situation is, rather than on what somebody would like it to be."

A man to tackle situations as they are, Ginsberg got Washington and Albany to agree on a three-year demonstration of an employment-incentive plan. Under this program, child-care centers would be provided for working mothers, and mothers on welfare who got jobs would be allowed to keep the first $85 a month that they earned without any reduction of their allowance, and they would be permitted similarly to retain half of the balance of their earnings up to $4,900.

Ginsberg's plan was probably only a precursor of more sweeping programs to come. Studying the patent inade-

163

quacies of the present welfare system, many leading economists and even some industrial leaders are advocating an idea that seemed like rankest heresy only a few years ago: a guaranteed annual income for all. Under this proposal every family would be guaranteed an income of at least $3,000 annually by the Federal government with no strings attached. There would be no need for a father to abandon his family to secure for them at least a poverty-level income. Depending on the provisions of such a program if it should finally be enacted, the cost has been estimated at from $11 billion to $20 billion a year, still far less than we are spending on Vietnam.

The guaranteed annual income seems at first glance to flout ancient and sacred American traditions. As a people we have a deep-rooted prejudice against handouts, against "something for nothing," against any system of reward without work. For such reasons the guaranteed annual income was considered a radical and heretical idea when it was first proposed in an article by Robert Theobald in *The Nation* in May, 1963. But the sheer thrust of events, the undeniable force of circumstance, has won it impressive advocates in recent years. In February, 1966, it was endorsed by the Presidential blue-ribbon National Commission on Technology, Automation and Economic Progress, a 14-member body composed of some of the nation's outstanding labor, business, economic, civic and government figures. Under the commission's plan the Federal government would make up the difference between a family's income and a guaranteed national standard. More recently, leaders like Dr. Martin Luther King, John Kenneth

164

Galbraith and Daniel P. Moynihan have advocated the guaranteed income plan.

Moynihan, who wrote the controversial and temporarily suppressed Moynihan Report in 1965, detailing the collapse of Negro family life in the ghettos, was Assistant Secretary of Labor in the Kennedy administration and later became director of the Joint Center for Urban Studies at the Massachusetts Institute of Technology. Testifying before the Ribicoff committee in 1966, he bluntly said that while desegregation was a fine ideal, "it just isn't going to happen in this generation." Congress would have been much better advised, he thought, to have concentrated on direct economic action that mattered instead of wrestling with a variety of piecemeal civil rights provisions.

First in order of importance he placed "guaranteed employment for men" and "a regular program of income maintenance." The two must be combined, he reasoned, because "even full employment will no longer produce a family income in the United States at a level necessary to maintain social stability in the slums. You can't raise a family in New York on $80 a week."

Tom Wicker, summarizing the case for guaranteed income in *The New York Times*, pointed out that "the common reaction of people to increased income is to seek even more income." Wicker thought that if ghetto residents could be lifted out of their pits of hopelessness by such a plan, they could be inspired to self-betterment. He also felt that the plan "would gradually eliminate the huge administrative machinery required to administer the present programs. The complicated investigations, audits, case serv-

165

ices and record-keeping now required—and the attendant
opportunities for graft, political intervention, incompe-
tence, inefficiency and bureaucratic inertia—would be all
but eliminated." The cities and states would be relieved of
the tremendous financial burden of welfare programs and
would have more resources to devote to transportation,
housing, hospitals and other needs. And finally, surprisingly perhaps, except that in this new era in which we live
many old political labels are inapplicable, Wicker called
guaranteed income "in the oldest sense, a conservative
case." It was not, he wrote, "something for nothing" at all,
but "an idea that basically conforms to the American reluctance to put people on a dole and the American belief in
helping people to help themselves."

However, if a program such as guaranteed annual income could really combat poverty—something we have not
been able to do for nearly 40 years under the present system—we would be left with still other key problems that
clamor for solution: housing, education, health.

Underlying the summer riots of 1967 were the three
horsemen of the ghetto—poverty, joblessness, housing. One
could find reasons, considering the mass migrations of the
time and our new sophisticated technology, for the poverty
and the joblessness, but how to explain housing that would
have disgraced a caveman? The idea may come as a shock
to many Americans who have read in their newspapers
about the billions of dollars we have spent in housing programs, but the truth of the matter is that most of those
billions have gone into the pockets of as rapacious and
disgusting a crew as America has ever produced—the

166

slumlords and the real estate lobbies, with their grafting political counterparts.

Nearly ten years ago, with my reporting partner Gene Gleason, I called attention to this scandal in "The Shame of New York." This great city, harboring some of the most noisome slums in America, was being torn apart block by block in much ballyhooed "slum clearance" programs. Most of the work was being carried out under the so-called Title I of the National Housing Act of 1949. The idea behind it was that private enterprise could be stimulated to rebuild our cities with Federal "seed" money. As I wrote at the time: "The conception was this: Cities would condemn huge slum areas and would turn these over to private developers for what it was estimated the land, devoid of buildings, would probably cost. The difference between the value of the slum area complete with buildings and the same area without would be met by the taxpayers, with the Federal government paying two-thirds of the 'write-down' and the municipal taxpayers one-third. This multi-million-dollar, taxpayer-financed 'write-down' would be an inducement to private enterprise to invest additional millions to erect new and modern middle-income housing, refurbishing the faces of our cities."

Billions of dollars were spent under this give-away program with all its built-in incentives for legal larceny. All that happened was that the rich got richer and the poor got short shrift. Whole city blocks were condemned and handed over to private real estate interests for a song. In some New York projects, the real estate operators kept the tenements intact for years, collecting slumlord rentals

167

until they had recouped their entire down payments and made themselves small private fortunes. Then, and only then, did they get around to clearing the land and rebuilding. When they did, the bulldozers and the wrecking crews came in and leveled everything in sight; good buildings were pulverized with the bad, and the residents of the devastated areas were scattered to the winds. The developers were supposed to find comparable housing for the displaced and uprooted, but little attention was paid to this provision and the refugees from the bulldozers were forced to crowd in with friends or relatives, with anyone who would have them, jamming cramped apartments and laying the groundwork for the creation of new ghettos. And what went up on the land they had been compelled to vacate? Well, the New York Coliseum went up on one parcel. On others there were gleaming, tile-faced apartment houses crowned by penthouses renting for $8,000 a year. This was not even *middle-income* housing; it was flossy and expensive and highly remunerative housing; and in this creation of private windfalls for the developers, it was a common occurrence for more housing to be destroyed than was built.

New York's experience was repeated in city after city across the nation. As A. Philip Randolph later told the Ribicoff committee: "According to the report of the Council of the White House Conference on Civil Rights, during the entire postwar period *almost all of the subsidies for housing* in the United States have gone to the middle-class and the rich. The subsidy for housing which the poor has received had been quite minimal and has taken the form of high-rise segregated projects. . . . Therefore, I would argue first of all that in the postwar period we have indeed been profligate with the taxpayers' money in subsidizing the middle-class and the rich and in creating problems for our central cities. . . ." (Italics added.)

Resentment and rebellion in the ghetto were the inevitable result. Everywhere one turned in the angry summer of 1967, one found the victims of ghetto housing seething with a deep, burning sense of outrage. Though New Haven, Connecticut, had been called "a model city," though it had received Federal grants equal to $800 for every resident, it too had its disruptive riots. And when reporters sought the reasons, they found the Negro and Puerto Rican community bitter at the way it had been batted around for urban renewal projects that had benefited the businessmen, real estate developers, the upper middle-class and the wealthy—everybody but them.

Urban renewal was called "Negro removal—over and over again." One lawyer said he represented a client who had been moved eight times to make way for one renewal project after another. Time after time Negroes and Puerto Ricans complained that they had been uprooted to make way for new highways, stores, factories, middle-class co-operatives and restored town houses designed to lure back a middle-class population. As in New York, the residents of an area destined for the bulldozer had never been asked what *they* wanted, they had never been consulted; they had been shuffled around like so many tenpins at the whim of the dominant white community running the city's business and politics.

"The fault with the war on poverty in New Haven is just like the war on poverty everywhere else," one dissi-

169

dent civic leader said. "The money does not get to the poor. . . ."

The result was that New Haven, though it bragged that it was a "slumless" city, still had its slums. Negroes and Puerto Ricans, displaced in project after project, were herded together with no place to go. One Puerto Rican complained bitterly: "You pay $125 to $165 a month for a rat hole. You can get a better place for that money, but not if you're a Negro or a Puerto Rican."

This was the picture virtually everywhere, and the prospect for the future was no brighter. It was not brighter for one very good reason: The greed of local real estate interests was insatiable.

Rep. William B. Widnall of New Jersey, the ranking Republican on the House Banking Committee, not content to let Federal funds be squandered on shopping centers and luxury housing crowned by penthouses, had tried in the summer of 1966 to curb these excesses by offering an amendment to the Demonstration Cities bill. His amendment would have ordered the Department of Housing and Urban Development (HUD) to make a "substantial increase" in the construction of low-cost housing on land cleared for residential urban renewal projects. HUD, which has to deal with powerful local interests to set up its projects, evidently became panicky at the word "increase," and in conferences with Widnall and other committee members it succeeded in getting the odious term stricken out. All the bill therefore authorized when it was finally passed was the building of a "substantial number" of low-cost and moderate-cost housing units.

Since what is "substantial" to one man may be woefully

inadequate to another, this language obviously opened wide the door to all kinds of shenanigans. And shenanigans there quickly were. HUD interpreted "substantial" to mean 20 percent; then it completely subverted the intent of the Widnall amendment by ruling that this entire 20 percent could consist of "moderate" housing. Developers did not have to build even an outhouse for the poor. Widnall had no idea that he had been euchred in a bureaucratic runaround until, just before the Detroit riots, he got a letter from a lawyer working with the urban law program at the University of Detroit. The lawyer told him what had happened—that, under HUD's interpretation, not a single unit of low-cost housing need be built. Outraged, Widnall demanded that HUD mend its ways, but the prospect of his getting the kind of action the nation needs appeared dim.

Only a drastic reordering of ideals and priorities—the placing of the good of the nation ahead of the usurious demands of greedy real estate and political combines—is going to make the black ghettos livable places. If that seems like a harsh judgment, remember we have been dabbling in urban renewal for a long time, and those moneyed-political interests have had ample opportunity to see the handwriting on the wall, ample opportunity to be motivated by humane instincts. But to date this is what the record shows: Since the urban renewal program was launched in 1949, fully 40 percent of the low-income families uprooted for the projects across the nation have *not* been relocated in the rehabilitated areas; from 1949 to 1964 only 45.4 percent of all urban renewal projects were devoted to housing of any kind, all the rest was commercial adventure. And the current trend is for the worse, not the

171

better. In the last two years, in this very period of fermenting violence when slum housing had become a critical issue, *only 36.3 percent of urban renewal represented housing of any kind.*

The result, as Mayor Lindsay had told the Ribicoff committee, as other mayors and experts testified, is that housing is deteriorating at a much faster rate than it is being replaced; that, in the cores of our cities, we are creating *more* slum tenements, not less.

There are currently some signs of change; signs that the American business community at its loftiest levels where lie the money and power for achievement, has been shocked into a belated recognition of reality. In mid-September, 1967, Mayor Lindsay took some of the nation's top industrial leaders on a walking tour through the slums of the Brownsville and East New York sections of Brooklyn. Shards of shattered glass crunched under their feet as they walked past buildings with gaping holes for windows. Dogs rooted in piles of refuse, and the stench of rotting garbage, the sense of human hopelessness and decay were everywhere.

Gerald I. Phillippe, chairman of General Electric, was plainly shocked.

"Unbelievable," he said. "I have seen things like this in South America."

A remark, this, that seemed to carry with it a telling significance. Phillippe, one of the most powerful industrialists in the nation, had been aware of the incredible subhuman slums of South America—and apparently unconscious of those existing almost under his nose in our own cities. The blindness and the discovery say much

172

about what happens, even to intelligent men, when the mind is focused constantly on foreign problems to the virtual exclusion of one's own.

Other members of Mayor Lindsay's walking delegation were similarly startled by the sights they saw and the smells they smelled. "It makes you heartsick," said Gilbert W. Fitzhugh, chairman of the Metropolitan Life Insurance Company. "You don't know where to start, but you know that something has to be done." And J. Irwin Miller, chairman of the Cummins Engine Company of Columbus, Indiana, agreed with Mayor Lindsay that "the number one problem of this country is the big city—plus race."

On the same day that Mayor Lindsay was walking Brooklyn streets, bringing these powerful industrialists into direct contact with the facts of life, the nation's 348 life insurance companies were pledging to divert $1 billion from their normal $16-billion-a-year investment flow to build housing and bring jobs to the ghettos. President Johnson was ecstatic. He had been trying for two years to get Congress to implement a rent-supplement law—in other words, to appropriate funds to help pay the rents of ghetto residents so that they might secure more decent housing—and he felt that the insurance companies' $1-billion show of interest would stimulate even this reluctant, Southern-rural dominated Congress to action.

There were other hopeful signs. Senator Percy of Illinois introduced one housing-job measure; Sen. Robert Kennedy another. Kennedy's plan offered enormous incentives—features like 50-year mortgages at 2 percent interest and other advantages that would build up to an estimated annual yield of 12 to 19 percent—to get the private sector of

173

the economy really involved in the problems of the central cities. The Johnson administration fought the proposal bitterly, arguing against both its need and the fairness of such a give-away. And certainly the experience of Title I, where multi-million-dollar windfalls were pocketed in programs that only made a bad situation worse, would indicate that the even more mammoth windfall program Kennedy was proposing would have to have built into it some ironclad guarantees. Whatever might result from such proposals, the fact that they were being made and debated indicated that at long last the nation was stirring. Whether it would stir fast enough, whether it would act energetically enough, remained crucial questions of our times.

On every hand there were vital issues, twin products of long neglect and an altered world, and on their solution depended the future vitality of American society. The hard-core question of joblessness was interwoven with the issue of the education of the jobless; and this meant no mere retraining of the jobless in new techniques, but the actual, basic education of millions almost illiterate in an age that called increasingly for higher skills.

Business leaders who have made sincere efforts to give jobs to those sunk in the ghettos have been shocked at times to find that so many do not have the education required for even the simplest tasks. David Rockefeller, president and chairman of the board of the Chase Manhattan Bank, told the Ribicoff committee: "At the present time we have 600 unfilled requisitions for clerical jobs in the bank. We are interviewing many times that number of people every week, and yet we are having difficulty in find-

174

ing people with the relatively modest training required for this type of job. . . ."

One of the most significant studies of this educational gap was made by Chicago's Cook County Department of Public Aid. It included interviews and tests, and it covered 680 able-bodied persons in families with some 2,000 children in Chicago's South Side Woodlawn district. This is an almost all-Negro neighborhood of 60,000 persons, of whom 25 percent were on relief. The tests showed that 49 percent of the women and 59.8 percent of the men (50.7 percent of both sexes in the study) were functionally illiterate because they could not read well enough to do fifth-grade work. On an overall average, four out of five who had finished the seventh grade were functional illiterates—and so were three out of eight of those who had finished grammar school and, in some cases, gone higher. The study also showed that there was a marked difference between the quality of Southern and Northern education. Though 33.4 percent of those who had gone to Illinois schools remained functionally illiterate, the figure for those who had been blessed with a Mississippi education stood at an appalling 76.9 percent.

These findings showed, as Edgar May pointed out in his book *The Wasted Americans*, "that half of the relief population surveyed is unfit for almost any kind of available work because of serious educational infirmities. All the admonitions of the legislators and taxpayer groups to 'get the loafers off relief' are to no avail when confronted with this evidence. But beyond the ability to obtain a job, there may be even more serious implications. For how can society's values be taught within a family unit if the adults have not experienced those values and cannot even read about them?" The question was especially pertinent since those examined in the survey averaged 33.5 years of age, with 50 percent of them being under 32.3. As the researchers commented in their official report: "Thus, we have the appalling aspect of a whole host of persons who will themselves be long-time dependents unless something is done that will improve their employability status in our present labor market. These adults are not only dependents at a time when they should be in the full flower of economic productivity, but many are illiterate at a time when they can be expected to produce more and more children."

What emerges is a composite picture of massed populations, housing sinking to the slum level far faster than it is being replaced, education that fails to equip its recipients for life in their times.

The greatest failure of the idealistic civil rights movement is that it dealt so exclusively with desegregation and integration while the plain fact of life was that in the core areas of our cities there is literally no prospect of integration because there are no whites to integrate. As Senator Ribicoff commented at one point during his committee's hearings, the civil rights movement benefited primarily only the upper-class Negro, perhaps the 10 percent of the race that had worked their way up from poverty; it did virtually nothing for the all-important 90 percent.

Frances Fox Piven and Richard A. Cloward of the Columbia University School of Social Work have made a devastating case for the proposition that this overemphasis

176

on desegregation and integration has done more harm than good. "The myth that integrationist measures are bringing better housing to the Negro poor comforts liberals; it placates (and victimizes) the Negro masses; and it antagonizes and arouses the bulk of white Americans," they write. "The 'backlash' is part of its legacy. While turmoil rages over integration, housing conditions worsen. They worsen partly because the solution continues to be defined in terms of segregation, so that the energies and attention of reformers are diverted from attempts to ameliorate housing in the ghetto itself."

Floyd McKissick, national director of the Congress of Racial Equality (CORE) and a Black Power advocate in the sense that he believes Negroes should dominate political and economic life in their own virtually all-Negro ghettos, cited the Piven-Cloward analysis and, perhaps surprisingly to some, made the same point himself when he testified before the Ribicoff committee. "The central cities of this country are disaster areas—the debris is mounting, the walking wounded everywhere," he said. And he emphasized that CORE had "found over and over again that the great moral struggle for integration has, in fact, barely touched the lives of the people. . . . Every analysis we can find, the work of virtually every social scientist who has addressed himself to this question, leads us to the same basic conclusion—the black ghettos will not go away— they are the hard fact of our life. Any solution you may consider . . . must, in fact, accept the existence of a growing ghetto and proceed immediately to the task of restoring its physical, educational and economic integrity. . . ."

McKissick argued that in education as in all else, matters were getting worse instead of better. A recent study, he said, showed that 87 percent of all children in segregated schools in New York City were reading below grade level; by contrast, in 1954, the year of the U.S. Supreme Court's great school desegregation ruling, a similar survey of similar schools had showed just 50 percent of the children reading below level. This was progress? "At this rate," McKissick said, "by 1970 all of the children in ghetto schools will be underachievers." In such circumstances, as in housing in the ghettos, it made little sense to talk about desegregation and integration. Obviously white people were not going to move back into Harlem, and it was silly to talk about bussing white children into Negro neighborhoods to achieve integration, as if this one word would magically solve everything. A major reason for retrogression rather than progress in ghetto schools was that the newest teachers just out of college, those with little or no experience, those who were often contemptuous of the type of pupils they had to teach, were the ones who were sent to these problem districts where the highest skills were required. McKissick cited one New York school principal who said: "We have committed a horrible and horrendous crime in assigning these youngsters to classes that require an expert of experts."

To the despair and indignity of poverty, of slum housing in rat-infested tenements, of education that leaves pupils virtually illiterate, there must be added one final ingredient in the evil litany of the ghetto—bad health care. There is a reason for the statistics that show only a handful of Negroes over 65 on the welfare rolls compared to more than four million whites; and the reason is that health care in the ghetto is so bad the Negroes are killed off faster. Infant mortality rates (the number of babies who die in the first year of life) are usually considered the most accurate barometer of the state of a nation's health. In the first six months of 1967 these statistics showed, for example, that the infant mortality rate in New York's Central Harlem was 44.4 and in East Harlem 42.6—some five times the 8.2 rate in a Bronx district that had the best record in the city. Throughout the range of New York's ghettos, the infant mortality rates ran three to four times as high as they did in better-class, white districts: 44.8 percent in Brooklyn's Fort Greene area, 35.8 in Bedford-Stuyvesant and 33.6 in Brownsville.

Across the nation the story was the same. The impoverished in the ghettos had virtually no neighborhood health clinics or hospitals. It was a common circumstance to have to make an hours-long trip, including several changes of transportation, to travel from a ghetto like Watts to an overcrowded, overworked municipal hospital where, as standard procedure, one would have to wait for hours to get the cursory attention of a physician so harried he had no chance to study a case and administer adequate care. The hospital plants in central cities across the nation have been so neglected for years that it will take literally billions of dollars to modernize them and bring them abreast of medical advances in the twentieth century. In New York City *every hospital*—municipal, general voluntary and private—was woefully deficient in some respect, and the best available estimate indicated it would take $1 billion to modernize fully the hospitals of just this one city.

Professor Seymour Melman of Columbia University, an expert on industrial engineering, has attempted to place a price tag on some of the crucial needs of modern, heavily urbanized America. He has estimated that the nation needs to spend $8 billion a year for five years "to raise the level of health services to a reasonable standard." On education he has placed an even higher premium. "In order to conduct education, from the nursery school to the university at an acceptable (not gold-plated) standard," he has written, "the United States requires additional education outlays of $25 billion a year."

Such expenditures, involving programs so massive, can be made only if we decide that the time has come to stop playing the game of global policeman and get on with our long-neglected business in the changed urban world of America in the latter twentieth century.

7

HATE

"Did you see what those jungle bunnies did in Newark?" a white store proprietor in a New Jersey suburb asked. "What do they *want?*"

The speaker was a self-made man who had built a profitable business and a small fortune out of brains, hard work and ingenuity. Not a John Bircher, he had many of the Birchite prejudices, including an almost venomous attitude toward the Negro. The Negro, to him, was an ignorant, slothful, amoral creature, only one step removed from the jungle, and all the rioting and violence was a kind of pressure tactic to keep the Negro—at the white taxpayer's expense—living on better relief allowances, living without work, forever and ever.

A different view was being expressed by President Johnson. In mid-September, 1967, speaking before the International Association of Police Chiefs in Kansas City, Missouri, he launched into an impassioned denunciation of urban rioters. Though he did not mention the names of

181

such agitators as H. Rap Brown and Stokely Carmichael, the President declaimed: "These wretched, vulgar men, these poisonous propagandists, posed as spokesmen for the underprivileged and capitalized on the real grievances of the suffering people."

The police chiefs cheered when he added that "much can explain but nothing can justify the riots of 1967." Law enforcement, he said, should be swift and color-blind and effective.

The views of the shopkeeper and the President expressed on two widely disparate levels the dilemma of a society befuddled by a nationwide outbreak of unprecedented violence. Both seemed to assume an intent. The shopkeeper was convinced that the Negroes must "want" something, that they must be out to "get" something, that somewhere behind it all there must be conscious plan and purpose. The President assumed a different kind of intent. He seemed to lay the blame on a few wild agitators who had stirred up the oppressed, and his remedy, at least in part, was stern and quick law enforcement. Neither the shopkeeper nor the President seemed to have grasped the full dimensions of a truth more simple and more devastating than their theories—that there was no intent, there was no plan, there was no conscious purpose. The most horrifying aspect of the riots of 1967 lay in their very senselessness. They were spontaneous and unreasoning, the expressions of a hate so intense, so long suppressed, that when the lid blew it was like a volcano in eruption.

The real significance of the turmoil of 1967 was simply that the black man, who has endured centuries of slavery and oppression, been treated like a beast, and liberated

182

only to have his trials capped by the poverty and frustrations of the ghetto jungles, has tried nonviolence, has followed the path of civil rights—and nothing has worked. He is still the victim of white slum landlords, white politicians, white usurers and a white law that sends him to the electric chair for sins for which sometimes it only reprimands its own. The time comes when the Negro, especially the severely disadvantaged and unemployed Negro youth, can take no more; hate boils over. This long-suppressed hatred of the black man for the white is matched by a perhaps less intense but more insidious emotion among an unfortunately large percentage of the Caucasian race. The white man's hatred is compounded of contempt and fear—contempt as the white shopkeeper phrases it of the "jungle bunnies"; fear of the savagery of the erupting ghettos, fear that such ravages may be extended to the Park Avenues and suburbias of the land.

This dual hatred at times finds expression in the most trivial—and therefore the most significant—of incidents. In the ghetto the hatred focuses upon a single and ever-present symbol of the white man's rule, the cop. The policeman pounding his beat represents not the face of law and order to be respected, but the presence of the enemy. He personalizes a society that has ravaged and oppressed the helpless. It is no accident that virtually every major riot across the breadth of the land has been touched off by a "police incident," for almost every young Negro in the ghetto has felt the brutal end of a police nightstick, has seen at close hand the law's graft and corruption, and so has developed a contempt and a hatred for the double standards of white authority.

183

One could see the basic emotions fermenting in the Harlem streets more than a decade ago. To the Puerto Rican youth gangs there, the policeman was the enemy. They knew that he was taking his share of "honest graft" from the bookie and the numbers runner and even from the prostitute. But there he was, proud and untarnished in his uniform, walking his beat like the symbol of righteousness and conscience, spread-eagling them against a wall at his whim and whacking them with his nightstick for nothing at all when the mood was upon him.

There came the day when a hot car was dumped on a street in the neighborhood. It had been stolen and used in a holdup. All the wise youths of the street knew the car's history, and they watched with glee as day after day the cop walked right past it, unnoticing, unknowing, blind. It got so that members of the youth gangs clustered around, watching for the cop to goof again, snickering at him, making him play the fool. He knew that they knew something he did not know but should, and it drove him crazy. He took it out on them in his nightstick way, but to them a few bumps and bruises were a cheap price to pay for their savored triumph—this victory of their street-urchin knowledge over the law's ignorance. It was a simple incident, perhaps, and yet it told much about the widening chasm between the ghetto and the law.

Other chasms gaped visibly after the summer riots of 1967. Out in suburbia it had become almost a status symbol to decorate one's lawn with the figure of a little Negro boy, clad in racing livery, one arm outstretched holding the house number or name of the occupant. After Newark the Negro boys suddenly disappeared. The figurines re-

184

mained on the lawns, but the faces and hands, almost overnight, were painted white. A triviality, yes. But when one goes to this extent for a triviality, the action expresses perhaps better than a more significant issue the depth of an abiding sickness.

In Washington, on the highest levels of government, the white man's hate and prejudice were being exhibited in a performance whose insensitivity matched that of the House of Representatives in laughing down the rat-control measure. President Johnson had appointed Thurgood Marshall to the U.S. Supreme Court. Marshall's credentials were impeccable. In 23 years as chief counsel for the National Association for the Advancement of Colored People, he had built a national reputation as a civil rights lawyer; he had won the great victory of 1954 when the Supreme Court outlawed public school segregation; he had been appointed by President Kennedy to the U.S. Court of Appeals, and President Johnson had taken him off the bench and made him U.S. Solicitor General. But he was, of course, a Negro. And that, to the hard-core Southern bloc on the Judiciary Committee of the U.S. Senate, was all that really mattered.

As a consequence, even as the cities of the nation burst into flames of Negro protest, the public was treated to the spectacle of Thurgood Marshall being hectored by Senators as if he were a schoolboy—and all, obviously, because he was a Negro. Sen. James O. Eastland, Mississippi's relic from Civil War days, led the pack as the chairman of the Judiciary Committee. Five long hearings were held, ostensibly to determine Marshall's "legal philosophy" and his fitness to be a Supreme Court Justice. But the questions asked—"Who was the author of the Thirteenth Amendment?" and others like it—were the demeaning kind that might have been more logically put to a student in law school. Their intent to many seemed nakedly obvious—to humiliate and embarrass, to make this learned Negro feel the contempt of his white masters.

Thurgood Marshall survived the inquisition. When the Southern contingent had exhausted themselves with the baiting game, the Judiciary Committee approved his appointment by an 11-to-5 vote. The five nay-sayers were Senators Eastland, John L. McClellan (D., Ark.), Sam J. Ervin (D., N.C.), George A. Smathers (D., Fla.) and Strom Thurmond, one-time Democrat turned Republican, of South Carolina. Having run this gauntlet, Thurgood Marshall was confirmed by the Senate, the first Negro to sit on the nation's highest tribunal. But the whole performance in the Judiciary Committee seemed to many like an affront to common decency, and its timing, cast against the backdrop of the ghetto riots, seemed to emphasize the intensity of white prejudice and the extent of white intransigence.

Hate. It was everywhere.

Out in Watts during the riot of 1965, a Negro youth had shouted one short, simple sentence that summed up everything. Three square blocks of Watts were burning at the time; white firemen were trying to fight the flames; and a crowd of Negro onlookers was pelting them with everything handy. One fireman was hit by a lightbulb; another by a monkey wrench thrown at point-blank range; a third by a bottle of perfume. Cried the Negro youth with matter-of-fact venom: "This is the hate that hate produced, white man!"

186

That hate is beaten into the Negro in earliest youth at the end of a nightstick wielded indiscriminately on the ghetto streets. When Sen. Robert Kennedy questioned Floyd McKissick about the attitudes of Negro youths toward the law, McKissick put it this way: "Well, you see, we black people, two things we learn at an early age, and that is that we never trust the police, and we never trust the Government, because they have been the two forces of trial that we have always been confronted with. . . . We used to play ball a lot, and we hit a ball over into another lot and the police would come and they would literally beat us and we would just have to run, this type of thing. I have always, and I think most black people, police have always been the ones that beat them. . . ."

This is the reason, McKissick said, that most Negroes do not want to become policemen, even when efforts are made to recruit them. "They do not want to be associated with the force that beats and hurts."

In the summer of 1967, as Detroit was going up in flames, a Negro native of the city, at the time a Private First Class fighting another war in Vietnam, read the news, shook his head sadly and said: "It must be the cops that they want to get, it's gotta' be the cops. If you're colored in Detroit you just look at a cop and hate him. Like they got the badge and the uniform and they got the gun. When you're a kid and you're growing up, you know the cops just like to mess with people."

After the Detroit riots, a 23-year-old Negro on the streets, commenting about the efforts that had been made by Mayor Cavanagh's administration to change police attitudes, put it this way: "It's still the career cops who run the

187

department, and the career cop—like old 'Tobacco Chew Red' down in the 13th Precinct—hates niggers. I've been jumped by an officer, had my jaw broken in two places and had to suck food through a straw for six months. Maybe the brutality had eased off a little, but it ain't the physical abuse that hurt, anyway, as much as the verbal abuse. They come up to you on the street and say, 'Hey, boy!' Now there ain't nothin' on this driver's license that says 'boy.' They say, 'Nigger, I'd like to kill you.' The other day, after the trouble was over, this cop told one of those shopkeepers loud, so a bunch of us could hear, 'Why build your store again? Why not just put poison in the cans you got left and feed it to these niggers?' "

When hate is so reciprocated, when a mood of mutual hostility pervades a city and is polarized about two such inimical groups, riots and violence become inevitable. When all the unemployment, misery and hopelessness of the ghetto is added to this atmosphere of hate, it becomes equally inevitable that once violence starts it will not be contained, but will spread like a brush fire in a high wind as the denizens of the slums give vent to their long-suppressed emotions. The circumstances of all our urban riots indicate that they take place on two levels, a conscious level and a subconscious level. There is the initial, triggering incident. Two groups whose mutual hate guarantees ultimate collision, the ghetto Negro and the police, are brought into a direct, face-to-face confrontation; the hate of each for the other boils over, rocks are thrown, bottles hurled, nightsticks wielded. Like a rock thrown into water, ripples spread outward from this vortex; from all over the ghetto, throngs congest; the police are ringed in by hostile faces;

188

the violence mounts. Each new deed of frenzy whets the passions. Soon the entire ghetto community is erupting, throwing rocks and Molotov cocktails, burning and drinking and looting. None of this is planned. Even middle-class Negroes (for they, too, often harbor deep resentments at our double white-black standard of values) join in the orgy. It is wild, unreasoning, senseless—and, while it lasts, somehow joyously wonderful. All the repressions and bile of centuries, buried deep, smothered and suppressed, are released as if some taut, restraining spring had snapped. And in the frenzy of destruction there is the heady sensation of liberation and revenge and triumph.

All of this was foreseeable, predictable. In May, 1964, more than a year before the Watts riot, Assistant Attorney General Howard H. Jewel of California wrote a perceptive memorandum in which he predicted that exactly what did happen would happen. He had called the situation in Los Angeles "ominous" because the psychological battle lines were already drawn between the police and the Negro community. He had written: "I discussed this problem with Noren Miller [a newspaper publisher and attorney, later appointed a superior court judge] at some length. It was his opinion that violence in Los Angeles is inevitable, and that nothing can or will be done about it until after the fact." John Buggs, executive director of the Los Angeles Human Relations Commission, had read the same signs and had recognized the explosive potential in the taut, tense relationship of the minorities and the police. The minority groups expected to be treated brutally in every encounter with the police, and the police expected to meet with resistance every time they made an arrest. "The very

189

expectations of the opposing parties will create what each expects," Buggs had written at the time.

Such warnings were pigeonholed and ignored. And Watts happened.

The pattern has been repeated many times. During four days in March and April, 1966, the Massachusetts State Advisory Committee to the United States Commission on Civil Rights held hearings in the Roxbury and South End districts of Boston. It prepared a 53-page report entitled "The Voice of the Ghetto," in which it predicted violence based on deep-rooted anger and alienation. It quoted as typical the views of Charles Evans, an unemployed resident of the South End, who told the committee:

> Being a Negro in Boston is the worst thing in the world.
>
> You have no way to communicate with anybody. You can't find a decent job or a decent place to live.
>
> I have worked as a bartender and as a tailor and as a cutter, but I have nothing now. I am living in a room that isn't fit to live in. I share a bath and pay $18 a week.
>
> If nothing changes, there is going to be trouble. People are tired of talking to themselves.
>
> My grandmother said things would be better and my mother said they were going to get better, but I don't see any change.
>
> The cops keep pushing us, telling us to move on. We are in perpetual motion.

The Massachusetts committee called for prompt and vigorous action, urging major reforms in education, wel-

190

fare, employment and housing. "It is impossible to over-state the indignation and despair expressed by individuals who spoke at the meetings," it wrote. But nobody paid much attention to its report. And on the night of June 3, 1967, more than a year later, Boston had its riot. Negro youths rampaged through the ghetto setting fires, throwing rocks and bottles, looting stores. Scores of persons were injured.

Watts had shown the nation what could happen. Studies like the Massachusetts report had predicted what inevitably would happen again. Yet, in Washington, in the executive branch and in Congress, there was little appreciation of reality; all eyes were focused on Vietnam. In December, 1966, President Johnson announced he was cutting back $5.3 billion in long-term outlays and another $3 billion in immediate spending in an effort to compensate, in some small degree, for the escalating costs of the war in Vietnam —a struggle that, it was estimated, would boost Federal spending from $112.8 billion to $125–$130 billion. A few weeks later, before the public had really digested this intelligence, New York City got a New Year's Day present from Washington. It was informed that Federal officials had rejected 12 of 14 proposed antipoverty programs because there was not enough money to finance them.

On May 13, 1967, two side-by-side headlines in *The New York Times* reflected what was happening. One read: "ECONOMISTS FIND '68 WAR BUDGET $5-BILLION SHORT, Report to Business Council Sees Vietnam Costs Reaching $26.9 Billion." The second said: "HOUSE PANEL CUTS MODEL CITIES AID, Rent Supplement Fund Also Slashed Far Under Total Requested by Johnson." This story quoted Rep. Joe L. Evins (D., Tenn.), chairman of the housing subcommittee of the House Appropriations Committee, as picturing this defeat as "a great victory for the Administration." His reasoning was that the Administration was lucky the programs had not been killed outright.

In New Jersey, Sen. Clifford P. Case, a Republican who has been decidedly hawkish on Vietnam, was taking the Administration to task for its perverse set of national priorities. Case was exercised because $1 billion had been earmarked for the development of a supersonic jet transport at the expense of needed hospital construction. The supersonic airliner, he argued, would benefit "a very small part of the population," but 18 million persons were enrolled in Medicare, the hospital and nursing home situation in the nation was woefully inadequate, and "disturbingly little has been done in the last two years to close the gap." Case concluded: "Something is obviously wrong with our system of national priorities."

There was money for everything—$1 billion for the supersonic transport, billions more to land a man on the moon, perhaps as much as $30 billion a year for the war in Vietnam—but the American people, their health, their jobs, their housing, their manifold needs would have to wait. There just was not enough money for them, too. In early June, 1967, another headline capped the moral: "O.K. DEFENSE SPENDING OF $70.3 BILLION." The accompanying story explained that this probably would not be enough. The huge costs of Vietnam were such that the Administration would probably have to come back and ask for more funds later.

Then came the riots.

Newark delivered the first shock.

New Jersey's largest city was in deep and obvious trouble. Its 400,000 residents were crammed into just 23 square miles of space. Almost 25 percent of even this limited area was taken up by Newark Airport, Port Newark and uninhabitable meadowlands. Newark occupied the smallest space of all major American cities, and its population density meant that it had very few good residential neighborhoods. It had also suffered from one of the most radical shifts of population experienced by any great city in the North.

Before World War II Newark had only a small Negro population. As recently as 1950 only 17 percent of its residents were nonwhite. But then came the mass migration of Negroes and Puerto Ricans. By 1960 34 percent of the city's population was nonwhite, and in 1967 the best estimates placed the nonwhite population at around 60 percent. Newark had become a predominantly colored city. The only whites left were those who were too poor to move. The rest had fled to the Oranges and other surrounding suburbs, creating one of those typical pictures—the black core of Newark itself ringed by the white of the more affluent suburbs.

In that black core the problems of the ghetto festered. Newark had the highest crime rate, the highest tuberculosis and maternal mortality rate, the highest substandard housing rate for any city of its size in the nation. It also had the lowest per capita income. Its public schools (it has a large parochial school system attended by whites) were 80 percent colored, and the dropout rate in the ninth to twelfth grades was 32 percent. Its unemployment rate was

7.2 percent, contrasted with 3.8 percent in the rest of the country, and among the Negro youth in the ghettos unemployment ran several times higher than that. It was a background that provided a classic setting for what was about to happen.

As usual, a trivial incident triggered the mass anarchy and destruction. On Wednesday night, July 12, Newark police arrested a stocky, goateed Negro taxicab driver, John William Smith. They said that his license had been revoked and that he was driving illegally. The arrest took place in Newark's heavily Negro Fourth Precinct while a number of other taxis were cruising past. Some of these cab drivers apparently observed the arrest, and a false rumor started. Cab radios suddenly began to squall that Smith had been fatally beaten. John Buggs's observation in Watts that expectations of the worst will produce the worst was now about to be fully vindicated.

Because Newark Negroes, like the Negroes in other cities, were preconditioned to believe the worst of police, the validity of the fatal-beating report was never questioned. Soon an angry mob composed largely of unemployed Negro youths gathered outside the Fourth Precinct police station. They hurled stones and bottles at the station house. James I. Threatt, Negro executive director of the Newark Human Rights Commission, spoke to them and tried to get them to "cool" it; but someone hurled a gasoline-filled bottle against the side of the police station. That did it. Police came charging out in a phalanx, wielding their nightsticks. They tore into the mob of some 200 persons and scattered them. But as the rioters fled, looting began along the streets leading from the station house. For

194

some hours the neighborhood was in an uproar, but by about 3 o'clock the next morning the demonstration seemed to have died out; quiet had apparently been restored.

It was, however, an uneasy quiet. That same Thursday night, drawn by leaflets calling for a rally, another crowd gathered around the Fourth Precinct station house. Bottles and rocks showered against the station house once more, and a Negro woman in white slacks started breaking the basement windows with a long stick. Police Director Dominick A. Spina, a modern and intelligent police executive who had tried to improve community relations by thoroughly integrating his department and letting citizens ride in patrol cars to see for themselves what was happening, waited for 45 minutes before he again sent his police charging out into the crowd. As they had the day before, the demonstrators split up and scattered; and, as they scattered, looting broke out again, this time on an unprecedented scale. Soon Negroes were rioting and looting in all four wards of Newark, at places a mile or more away in each direction from the riot's first flashpoint.

About 12:30 A.M. Friday, some of the rioters began sniping at policemen. "We're getting bombed here," police notified headquarters over their car radios. At 1 A.M. Mayor Hugh J. Addonizio and Director Spina gave what was intended as a cautious order: "Return fire if necessary." Cheers sounded over the police radio, indicative of the mood of the force, and it was soon after this that the first alleged looter was shot to death.

The riot now spiraled on in waves of flame-streaked, shot-punctuated frenzy. The situation rapidly became so critical that at 2:20 A.M. Mayor Addonizio asked New

195

Jersey Gov. Richard J. Hughes to send in State Police and the National Guard. Hughes responded swiftly and went to Newark himself to take personal command at the scene. "If the line must be drawn between the jungle and the law," he said in a statement whose inflammatory nature was later widely criticized, "it might as well be drawn here as anywhere else in America."

The trouble, as Watts had shown two years earlier, was that the spirit of the jungle in a contest such as this quickly dominates the actions of the law; the law itself becomes lawless, and the shooting and killing become virtually indiscriminate. In Watts a Negro trying to take some of his clothes and belongings from his apartment above a burning store had been mistaken for a looter and gunned to death by police. In Watts the innocent and unarmed had been killed at least as frequently as the guilty. Newark was no different. The police, the State Troopers and the National Guardsmen, once their trigger fingers were unleashed, literally sprayed the riot areas of Newark with bullets. One woman was killed sitting in her apartment. The police fire became so intense, with bullets ricocheting off buildings and flying back at some of the law enforcers who had dispatched them, that the peace officers found themselves mistaking each other's fire for sniper fire.

Reporters who covered the riot later recalled that on Sunday night appeals like this kept coming over the police radios: "Newark police, hold your fire! . . . State Police, hold your fire! . . . You're shooting at each other! . . . National Guardsmen, you're shooting at buildings and sparks fly so we think there are snipers! . . . Be sure of your targets. . . ."

196

Snipers there certainly were in Newark, but in the post-mortems it seemed as if most of the fire that had been mistaken for sniper fire had actually come from the guns of the law enforcement contingents themselves. For six days the disorders continued. Whole blocks were burned or looted; the fronts of buildings tattooed by the spray of bullets. Twenty-six persons were killed, 1,200 injured, 1,300 arrested. Property damage exceeded $15 million. And nearly everyone agreed that an explosive situation had been made even more explosive.

Race hatred had been intensified. Some whites moved out of the city; hundreds bought guns; most spoke of the Negroes with bitter hatred. Among the Negroes, even in the law-abiding Negro community—and it should be emphasized that the great majority of Newark's Negroes took no part in the riots—hatred had become more widespread. Actions of the State Troopers and National Guardsmen were blamed for this. "The State Troopers acted like storm troopers," one Negro complained bitterly. Negro leaders charged that the troopers shot up and stormed Negro properties marked with "soul brother" signs. One Negro woman, who ran a restaurant, charged that she had seen two State Police cars shooting their way up and down West Market Street in the early hours of Sunday morning. Her restaurant and other Negro stores in the vicinity were blasted, she said, and later in the day state police drove by the wrecked store fronts and laughed. These charges by Newark Negroes were given some substantiation a few days later when the riots spread to Plainfield, New Jersey. State Troopers set out to search Negro homes for stolen guns believed to be cached in them, and television news cameras, trained on the action, showed troopers smashing down doors and overturning and smashing furniture in the homes of law-abiding Negroes. This pictorial evidence and the protests of Negro leaders led to an abandonment of the searches.

No one questioned that, critical as the situation in Newark had been before the riots, it was many times worse afterward. Businessmen along Springfield Avenue, scene of most of the rioting, said they could "smell the tension." Whatever hope there had been for better police-Negro relations seemed to have vanished. James Hooper, chairman of Newark CORE, charged that police "are stopping people on the street at night and putting empty guns to their heads and pulling the triggers. If they don't cut that out, it's going to happen again." And William Heckel, dean of the Newark Rutgers School of Law and a leader of the Committee of Concern, formed in the hope of improving human relationships in the city, acknowledged: "The riots have set Newark back 10, 15, maybe 20 years in human relations." But he found there was still "a reservoir of people of good will."

The flames had hardly died down in Newark before Detroit started to burn. It was almost like a one-two punch in a prizefight, with Newark the left-hand jolt and Detroit the right-hand haymaker. Detroit was the one city in the nation, most would have said, where it could never happen —and Detroit was to have the worst race riot of all, the worst in American history.

If Newark had provided the classic background for an outburst of violence born of poverty and despair, Detroit represented the very antithesis—a city with a long history

198

of racial integration, a city where the Negro had it "made."

Nowhere else in America is there so much Negro affluence. Of the 1.6 million persons in Detroit, some 600,000 are Negroes. In 1960 about 41 percent of the Negroes owned their own homes, and the 1970 census is expected to raise this figure to 48 percent. More than 57 percent of Detroit's Negroes owned cars, and 11.4 percent of them had reached the stage of affluence where they could afford two. The wages paid in the automobile factories gave Detroit the second highest pay scale in the nation, barely exceeded by San Francisco. In the Cadillac plant, even janitors and other unskilled help were being paid at a rate of $2.99 an hour. At the Fourth of July speedboat races on the Detroit River, at least 30 of the yachts lined up to watch the race were owned by Negroes, and from the shore one could see Negro men in yachting caps sipping cocktails while their wives and daughters sunbathed.

Detroit had no slums, no ghetto as such—nothing even remotely resembling the jungles of Bedford-Stuyvesant or Hough or Watts. Its worst housing consisted of some dilapidated one- or two-family frame houses on the East Side. But on the West Side, where the riots broke out, substantial brick buildings stood in a neighborhood that only 15 years before had been a prosperous Jewish community. Mayor Cavanagh was certainly one of the most enlightened municipal officials in the country. When he became mayor he named Ray Girardin, a former newspaperman, police commissioner. Together Cavanagh and Girardin set out to bridge "the river of hate" that had grown up between the Negro community and the police force as a result of the latter's strong-arm methods. It had been a common tactic for police to halt Negroes on the street, spread-eagle them against a wall and frisk them, all the time asking such questions as "How many white women did you rape today, nigger?" Cavanagh and Girardin put a stop to that. They instituted courses in community relations in the police department. They tried to recruit Negroes for the force, but had succeeded in getting only 217 on the 4,600-man roll when the riots broke out. In housing, as in so much else, Cavanagh had been in the forefront. He had pressed for the "model cities" program in Washington and had obtained some $200 million in Federal funds for Detroit; by far the greater part of this had been spent in the heavily Negro districts of the inner city. Detroit Negroes were unhappy because only one Negro sat on the City Council, but they had still achieved virtually unprecedented political recognition. Detroit was the only city in the nation that had sent two Negro Congressmen to Washington, and it had elected 12 Negroes to the state legislature.

Why then were the most savage riots of all in Detroit?

The answers are complicated, and they perhaps tell as much as the background of Newark about the infinite variety and the colossal scope of the racial problem.

Take 12th Street in Detroit. It is not any Bedford Avenue, but it is Detroit's version of "The Strip" or "Sin Street." It is the street where you can get almost everything, from pot and horse to the numbers and hookers and young girls and boys. Twelfth Street is at worst what might be called "a pocket slum," an area only about eight blocks long and a block or two wide set down in the heart of a prosperous, middle-class Negro neighborhood. Only a

200

block or two away on either side, mulberry and maple trees shade neatly clipped lawns and hedges around tile-roofed bungalows.

And this, indeed, was part of the trouble.

"The cat on 12th Street can look a hundred yards away and see another black cat living in an eight-room house with a 1967 Pontiac and a motorboat on Lake Michigan," a Negro school teacher explained to *The New York Times*. "For that matter, General Motors itself is only a few blocks away. . . . It's all so close and yet it's all so far away, and the frustration just eats them up."

A Negro poverty worker put the same thought this way: "Detroit has opened the Golden Door to the Negro. But only a relatively few Negroes can get through that door at any one time. That's the real trouble. In Jackson, Mississippi, no Negro can get through the door, and strangely enough that can be kind of reassuring. He can always say it's a white door, and so there's no use a black man even trying. Some call it Negro laziness or apathy, but it's the disease of the ghetto. In Detroit the door is open—at least to the prepared Negro and even to some half-prepared ones. The guy who doesn't get through no longer can find solace in saying, 'I can't make it because I'm black.' He has to face the black pain."

An important factor in the psychological trauma of Detroit is the way that golden door closes in a cat's face just when he figures he's got it made. The motor industry is subject to wide fluctuations in employment. When car sales slump, layoffs follow by the thousands. Since continued employment in such periods depends upon seniority, since the Negroes as the last to get through the door are at the bottom of the heap, they are the ones who feel the impact most severely. During 1966 and 1967 the auto industry had passed through just such a time of trial, and between May and August, 1966, some 36,000 men were laid off.

What this means to the Negro was illustrated by a Wayne University study. In October, 1966, this analysis showed, the overall Detroit unemployment rate was only 2.2 percent, but for the Negro men in the inner city it was 7.2 percent. In May, 1967, the overall rate jumped to 4 percent, and this probably meant that at least 12–14 percent of Detroit's Negroes (the percentages would be higher than that in the Negro teen-aged bracket) were unemployed. The resulting bitterness may have been more intense than in Newark, for it is one thing to be utterly hopeless and without prospects of any kind—and another to see that golden door yawning wide just a few blocks down the street and yet to know that, for all the good it does you, it might just as well be thousands of miles away.

"You're sitting on the stoop with your head down and the man comes along and lifts it up and you begin to see some sky and then—whop—he lets it fall again," Wilbert Martin, 28, a Vietnam war veteran and a laid-off auto worker, told *The New York Times*.

Such was the atmosphere in Detroit when, at 3:45 A.M. on Sunday, July 23, 1967, police raided a "blind pig" on the second floor of a building at 9125 12th Street. A "blind pig" is an after-hours speakeasy, and this one at the time of the raid happened to have a clientele of 83 persons. The police had not expected so many, and there was some confusion in herding them downstairs. Since 12th Street is

202

a street that never sleeps, a crowd of some 50 persons soon gathered, among them prostitutes, pimps, con men and numbers runners. Eyewitness accounts of what happened are, as usual, confused. One had it that police manhandled a Negro woman coming down the stairs; another spectator recalled hearing a woman scream about police brutality. All, however, agreed on one point: Suddenly a bottle arched high out of the night, glinted briefly in the light of a street lamp and crashed through the rear window of a police cruiser. That was the declaration of war. The riot was on.

As the police withdrew with their prisoners, 12th Street went wild. The store-breaking and looting began. And, as it did, the police made their big mistake. They had two choices: to get out of the area completely and let Negro community leaders try to "cool it," or to go in with full force, shooting if they had to, in the effort to quell the riot in its incipient stages before it could spread. They did neither. After the original "blind pig" raiding force had withdrawn, police cruisers were sent into the area "to show the flag" as it were, and in these circumstances a show of the flag without the application of sufficient force to back it up was only an incitement to further violence. The same mistake had been made two years earlier at a critical early stage of the Watts riots when things could have gone either way, and the result in both cities was to be the same: the creation of a holocaust.

With the rioting completely out of hand, Negro community leaders made a valiant effort on Sunday morning to talk reason to their constituents. And they quickly found that they were leaders without a following. Four of them,

203

carrying bullhorns, went out into 12th Street, and Rep. John Conyers, Jr., who has been called "the most popular Negro leader in Detroit" and a possible future choice for Mayor, climbed up on the hood of a car and tried to appeal to the rioting mob.

"No, no, no," the roar came back at him. "We don't want to hear it, Uncle Tom. Get down, Uncle Tom."

A bottle smashed against the curb behind Conyers. A rock hit a patrolman standing nearby. Conyers, visibly shaken, was helped down from the car. And, days later, he was still visibly shaken. "I don't think anybody—except maybe the late Malcolm X—could have dispersed that crowd already excited by the sight of exposed bayonets, but I have to admit I wasn't getting through to them," he said.

The incident was one of several that indicated the Detroit riots, though triggered by a typical police-Negro incident, contained overtones of broader significance. Conyers was only one of several Negro leaders to feel what might be called a black backlash. The city's one Negro Councilman sent his family out of town after receiving several threatening telephone calls. Rumors circulated through the Negro community that a number of moderate Negro leaders were "next on the list" of those to be gotten. Added to these threats against the Black Establishment was the unusual spectacle of a number of poor whites, mostly displaced Appalachians, joining lustily in the rioting and the looting. The combination carried with it a new and disturbing implication—that the Detroit riots, in part at least, *may have been motivated by a spirit of revolt against the nation's entire establishment, both black and white.*

The flames of rebellion swept through 14 square miles of Detroit and raged for days. The National Guard was called in. Gov. George Romney appealed to President Johnson for Federal troops, and after much delay and haggling about legalistic technicalities, Army paratroopers were dispatched to the stricken motor city to restore order. But, before that could be accomplished, the nightmare of chaos and looting, burning and gunfire, had registered on the television screens of the nation in scenes that seemed like vignettes torn from the hell of Vietnam.

There was some solid evidence in Detroit, far more so than in Newark, that hate-filled Negro fanatics had moved in and tried to direct the course of events once the riot started. Some snipers were planted on rooftops; some of the looting and burning seemed organized, with advance scouts in slowly moving cars spotting an attractive store to be hit, with looters moving in behind them and fire-bombers coming last after everything of worth had been taken. But the postmortems seemed to indicate that such organized forays were in a minority and generally of secondary importance. The cardinal fact seemed to be that the riot generated its own momentum and swept out of control, a gale of hate and frenzied excitement as fierce and unpredictable as some elemental force of nature. Untried for combat with such a hurricane, police and National Guardsmen, once their trigger fingers were released, literally went wild, venting their own pent-up hate and detestation for the black "enemy."

As in Newark, the number of snipers and the volume of sniper fire was wildly exaggerated. As in Newark, the law enforcement contingents sprayed return fire at their own

205

ricochets. A huge M-48 tank lumbered along one Detroit street, its guns powdering the front of a red-brick building for 25 minutes. When police moved in afterward, they found no trace of any sniper, but a family of four huddled in terror under the back porch, the two children screaming hysterically. The shooting was so wild, so indiscriminate, that a PFC in the National Guard wobbled out of 12th Street, shouting about his colleagues, "They're killing anything that moves."

They were, too. In a scene of ultimate and incredible sordidness, acted out in the Algiers Motel, white hate boiled over in deeds for which there could be no possible excuse. A sniper had been reported on the roof of the motel. Whether one was ever actually there seemed uncertain afterwards, but police peppered the building with bullets, then moved in followed by State Troopers and National Guardsmen. Once in control of the motel, the police went berserk. They rounded up all Negroes in the building, took them down to the first floor, lined them up against the wall and beat them. Then, one by one, they took some of them into separate motel rooms—and soon shotgun blasts resounded from those rooms. One of the witnesses at the subsequent Detroit hearings on charges brought against some of the officers was Warrant Officer Theodore Thomas of the National Guard. He testified that he had seen the beatings; that he saw one police officer take a Negro into a motel room, heard a shotgun roar and the thud of what could have been a falling body. One policeman, he said, handed him a shotgun and said, "You want to kill one?" Thomas said, "I got scared." He said he told the policemen "this was strictly their business" and left the motel. Afterward, three Negroes were found in the motel rooms, all killed by shotgun blasts fired at close range, all almost certainly the victims of the white cops' vindictive hate.

After the riots ended, the *Detroit Free Press* made an exhaustive study in which it questioned more than 300 persons and examined hundreds of official documents. It concluded: "Both the number of snipers active in the riot area and the danger that snipers presented were vastly overstated. *Only one sniper is among the riot victims, and only three of the victims may possibly have been killed by snipers, two of them doubtful.*" (Italics added.)

The very breakdown of the 43 dead told much about who killed whom. Only eight of the victims were white. The *Detroit Free Press* concluded that the great majority of those who died were innocent persons who were killed needlessly. The National Guard, it found, had been involved "in a total of 11 deaths in which 9 innocent people died." The "inescapable" conclusion, the *Free Press* said, was that "a majority of the riot victims need not have died. Their deaths could have been—and should have been—prevented."

The horror of Detroit in flames was matched by a second horror—the incapacity of American politics. When Governor Romney appealed to President Johnson for the dispatch of Federal troops, the nation was treated to the unedifying spectacle of the nation's leader playing politics with disaster. Quibbling over legal technicalities, Washington delayed for hours; then, after it had dispatched the troops, after they had arrived on the outskirts of Detroit, it delayed for more hours before sending the men into action. President Johnson, in a television report to the nation, referred

207

contemptuously to the inability of Governor Romney (his possible Presidential opponent in 1968) to cope with the Detroit crisis, while scarcely mentioning Mayor Cavanagh, a Democrat, who certainly had the major responsibility. In riposte, the Republican Coordinating Committee drafted a statement that matched the President in petty partisan spite. It accused him of having "totally failed to recognize the problem," though the record was clear that the Republicans themselves had led the clamor to cut back on every domestic program he had proposed; it blindly asserted that our urban decay had assumed crisis dimensions in just "the last three years" of the Johnson administration; and, in its sweeping denunciations, it managed to avoid even a mention of the cardinal issues—housing, education, jobs and health. Emmet John Hughes, a one-time Eisenhower administration aide, called the dual performance "The Great Disgrace," and wrote that the Republican declaration "could have been penned only by men serenely confident that they had nothing to fear from an American electorate too untutored to protest any insult to its intelligence."

The final result—an outcome even more fateful for America than the fact of a blazing Detroit—seemed clear. On the highest level of our politics, in the dominant power structure of both parties, there appeared to be no appreciation of the depth and seriousness of the urban-racial crisis. The two-party leaderships, out of touch with the realities of their times, had played petty political games in much the same spirit in which Nero fiddled while Rome burned.

The score across the nation in the summer of 1967 should have spelled out the lesson. Some 120 American cities were shaken by a total of some 150 riots. Everywhere there was evidence of a deepening and virulent racial hatred. The Negro was in rebellion, not just against the long-continued, unrelieved sordidness of the ghettos, but against the whole gamut of white iniquities that seemed to have chosen him as their special victim.

He was in rebellion against the necessity of paying white slumlords usurious rents for rat-infested tenements with broken-down plumbing and no heat in the coldest winter. He was in rebellion against the white shopkeeper who hiked all his prices every month just when the welfare checks came out, charging the residents of the ghetto more for inferior meat than was paid for the best grades on Park Avenues of the land. As one Detroit Negro phrased it: "All the guys who'd been sittin' on us—specially those shop-keepers who charged us 60 cents for a 49-cent half-gallon of milk—they got some dues paid."

Dues were due, too, from the white loan companies and installment salesmen who came into the ghetto selling tele-vision sets and appliances, telling the ignorant and the credulous how little they would cost—and then writing into the contract prices and carrying charges that boosted the total figure sometimes as much as 200 percent. The Negro was also in rebellion against the whole process of urban renewal; against a system that turned over whole blocks of slums to white speculators, who then brought in white contractors and white laborers to demolish the homes of the black man while the black man stood around job-less and helpless, forced out of his neighborhood and com-pelled to go hunt another slum. Again and again one heard the bitter demand that the Negro be given a piece of the pie everyone else was collecting from his own slum clearance;

209

and if demands like these were ignored, if nothing happened, no one could foretell the full dimensions of the inevitable tragedy that lay ahead.

Some of our more perceptive political leaders saw and understood the issue in its true terms. Senator Ribicoff pleaded with Congress to show a sense of responsibility and to stay in session until it had dealt in crisis fashion with the crisis in the cities. In New York State the leadershp in both parties was especially far-sighted. New York City had a brief, violent flareup in Harlem, but Mayor Lindsay in shirt-sleeves took to the streets, walking through the ghettos, talking to the people, explaining to them what he was trying to do. His presence and some wise restraint by his police force cooled the trouble quickly, and Lindsay emerged from the summer of trial as a leader with immensely increased stature. Sen. Robert Kennedy tried to get action started in Congress on his ghetto job-housing proposals and criticized the leadership of his own party in the White House and in Congress for not exhibiting the sense of urgency the moment required. Senator Javits and Governor Rockefeller sailed the same course. Rockefeller warned bluntly that unless the nation's racial and class problems could be solved, we faced the dread prospect of "an actual struggle between Negroes and whites." Rockefeller felt that we could prevent this—but only if we dealt rapidly and effectively with the root causes.

There was no sign, however, that the political power-brokers of the nation were prepared to take such action. The New York leaders were all men who occupied minority positions within their parties; theirs were not the hands that were on the levers of power. There was not a

210

trace of the perception of Lindsay and Javits and Rockefeller in the crude screed issued by the Republican Coordinating Committee blaming all the evils of our time on
Lyndon Johnson. And in the White House there was little
trace of the clear vision of Robert Kennedy. The vacuum
in political leadership was filled by the ranting cries of
Southern-rural demagogues in Congress. Reacting in blind
rage, ignoring all basic issues, these forces concentrated on
jamming through an "antiriot bill" that might help to put
H. Rap Brown and Stokely Carmichael in prison, but that
almost certainly would not stop riots. "The mood here is
poisonous and self-destructive," *Newsweek* quoted an old
Washington hand as saying.

In the White House, President Johnson was preoccupied
with Vietnam almost to the exclusion of all else. The peer-
less leader took the tack that all would have been well if a
recalcitrant Congress had only adopted his Great Society
programs. This suggested to some that he was laying the
groundwork to run in 1968, as Harry Truman had in 1948,
against a "do-nothing" conservative Congress. It was
tawdry politics that ignored the undeniable fact that none
of the Johnson programs had been vast enough to combat
a crisis situation, and that he himself had cut back on many
of even these inadequate proposals at the beginning of the
year to help meet the drain of Vietnam. The true state of
Lyndon Johnson's heart and understanding seemed illustrated by a significant contretemps involving his Vice President, Hubert Humphrey.

A compassionate and ebullient man, the Vice President
soared into action at the shock of the summer riots. He
called in glowing and urgent terms for a new "domestic

211

Marshall Plan" to salvage our cities. An aide disclosed at the time that the Vice President expected to make a dozen speeches on the theme in September and October. The image that Humphrey evoked was, of course, one of massive effort—an effort comparable to the multi-billion-dollar investment we had made in the nations of Western Europe to salvage their wrecked economies and help them regain stability after the ravages of World War II. In the White House, according to the best private sources, Humphrey's well-intentioned suggestion touched off a volcano. Never, some said, had they seen the President so furious, and since the awesome quality of even his lesser rages is well-known, this must have been fury indeed. Subsequently, there was a clear public indication of the imperial mood. Asked at a press conference about a "domestic Marshall Plan," the President remarked icily that no one in his Administration was considering such a proposal. And Vice President Humphrey, apparently chastened, dropped all mention of the idea.

The tepid, politics-as-usual mood that prevailed in Congress and the White House smothered any hope for imaginative initiatives. No heed was given to the most explicit warnings. Daniel P. Moynihan told a Senate subcommittee that detailed Federal studies of the worst-off Negro neighborhoods in Los Angeles and Cleveland showed they were "going to hell" in almost inconceivable ways, and he warned that the U.S. would suffer from riots as long as it has a "large, disorganized, frustrated, lower class." Philip M. Hauser, a University of Chicago sociologist and world authority on populations, warned that the summer riots had brought America to a crossroads: Either we could deal sensibly and effectively with the issues by providing

212

jobs and guaranteeing a livable level of income, or we could embark on a program of repression, concentration camps and ultimate genocide. "This sounds dramatic," he acknowledged, "but it is." He saw America threatened by two revolutions: the first and most visible the violent Negro protest; the second, indicated by the participation of whites in the Detroit riots, the incipient revolt of the white poor, who are far more numerous than the Negroes.

Much to the same point was the warning delivered by Julian Bond, the dynamic young Negro who had been finally seated in the Georgia legislature after having been initially barred for his opposition to the war in Vietnam. "We're going to see some real guerrilla fighting—black and white," Bond said. "There have been few if any snipers in the riots so far, just talk of them. But black nationalist groups are training snipers—I'm sure they are—and they will see themselves as protectors of rioters and looters, filling the role given to imaginary snipers in other riots."

Bond disagreed personally with the more violent Negro leadership, but he was convinced that extremists, under existing circumstances, would come increasingly to dominate the Negro rebellion. He himself had been called an "Uncle Tom" on the streets of Chicago, he said, and he assessed the Negro mood this way: "The angry Negro wants a complete reshaping of who has what in this country and the only avenue left is violence. The American way of politics and appeals to conscience have been tried, but it has not worked. Violence won't work either—the country will just get more repressive. I don't think the Student Non-Violent Coordinating Committee believes violence will work. It just sees it as the only thing left to do."

No words could paint better the despair, the desperation

213

and the overwhelming danger of the moment. When the wildest violence is contemplated not in any expectation of success but because it is "the only thing left to do," the American political dialogue stands condemned as having sunk to the nadir of the irresponsible and inconsequential.

It is clear that only national leadership of the most far-seeing kind can bring the kind of sweeping reforms and mount the dedicated national effort that is essential if we are to avoid the chasm that yawns.

The ending of the war in Vietnam, if it could be accomplished (and this is doubtful with an administration distrusted by a great percentage of its own people and even more distrusted abroad), would not miraculously and automatically solve all our problems. The mere termination of the war in Vietnam without a reexamination of our whole system of national priorities will achieve nothing. If we still intend to play the role of global policeman, if we still intend to turn over our entire income tax revenue to the Pentagon, we will still be mired in the bog of our Cold War policies that have placed the needs of the most remote sections of the world above those of our own people.

The end of the war in Vietnam would free, of course, some $30 billion annually for possible use for domestic purposes. But, given the myopia of our politics on the highest levels, there can be no certainty that we would devote such an amount, or even any considerable fraction of it, to the solution of our own domestic needs. The virtual certainty at the moment is, indeed, the opposite. We would have more billions to spend to put a man on the moon sooner, more billions to invest in supersonic transports, more billions to spend on all the accouterments of modern warfare.

With the military fixations and priorities that have ruled us for the past 20 years, all of this we would most certainly do unless, by a process of education and resolve, we can bring our minds to accept the urban realities of the twentieth century; unless, so accepting, we can radically reallocate our fiscal, physical and mental resources.

The problems of the new, massive, 70-percent urban-oriented civilization of modern America are so overwhelming that they cannot be met and solved by half measures. The assignment of some 70 percent of the nation's budget to the military and allied space pursuits has imposed an inevitable intellectual as well as fiscal drain. Senator Fulbright has pointed out that scientific talent has been siphoned steadily out of the civilian economy. "From 1954 to 1963," he has written, "the number of research and development scientists and engineers in industry increased by about 160,000, and all but 30,000 of these were drawn into government-sponsored projects. . . . At present only 25 percent of our total national research and development spending are going into industrial research for civilian purposes." Other analyses show that some two-thirds of all scientific and technical research "is now controlled by the Department of Defense and related agencies," and that probably 80 percent of the scientific and engineering talent of the nation is engaged in these militaristic pursuits. It will take a colossal effort of leadership and statesmanship to halt this avalanche of military spending, to make a sane and sensible reassignment of priorities, and so to devote the bulk of our monetary and intellectual resources to the paramount issue of our time—the solution of the urban and racial ills of modern America.

215

8

THE BASIS OF A NEW POLITICS

Lyndon Johnson has to be the most distrusted President of the twentieth century. One searches back over the men who have held that office since 1900 and fails to find a parallel. Harding was a pitiful weakling; Coolidge a non-entity who charmed the nation with his impersonation of the laconic New Englander; Hoover a curmudgeon of the old order who could only sit in a time of crisis and croak "around the corner, around the corner." Of them all, Harding presided over one of the most scandalous administrations in our history, but he was a figure more pitied than condemned. Lyndon Johnson arouses quite different feelings.

The image of the wheeler-dealer clings to him like odor to a skunk. And it will not go away. The American people have reached a point where a large percentage of them simply do not believe anything he says. They feel, to put the case most brutally, that the truth is not in him. This is a deep, intensely felt distrust. And, if one may judge by the way people act and talk, there is virtually nothing that can change it. The image of the slick and unscrupulous power-broker is fixed on Lyndon Johnson as tightly as his skin.

You can walk, as I did not so long ago, into a suburban store that is a kind of gathering place and sounding board for its community, and when the subject of the 1968 campaign comes up you find the proprietor shaking his head in honest bewilderment. "I have never seen anything like it," he says. "You know, I've run this store for nearly 30 years, and people come in here and talk, and the first thing you know the subject comes up. I don't start it. I don't ask them. They *tell* me. It just comes gushing out. They are *never* going to vote for this man again. Some of them will tell you they'll vote for George Wallace or a Communist, just to register a protest if they can't go for the man the Republicans pick."

My own pulse-taking of the public mood jibes with the impressions of other reporters. Ted Lewis, the Washington columnist of the *Daily News,* poked around the byways of six Eastern states during his 1967 summer vacation and was incredulous when he returned to Washington to find the capital, in blind euphoria, talking about how hard it would be to beat Lyndon Johnson in 1968. To Lewis it seemed as if Washington existed in a dream world, cut off from reality in the rest of the nation.

"What we have to report," he wrote, "is that every local yokel we talked to didn't like LBJ one little bit. And, what is perhaps more important, once they spotted our D.C. license plates, they spoke out bitterly and succinctly with-

217

out waiting to be asked what they thought about the President.

"There is nothing unusual about this sort of finding in grassroots tapping. It is par for the vacation courses traveled by other political observers, east, west, north or south."

Newsweek magazine did its own sampling of opinion and reported:

"In Pocatello, Idaho, a sixtyish but sprightly grandmother and good Democrat said: 'I'm beginning to hate that man.' In Portland, Oregon, Charles Snowden said: 'I've switched. I'll vote for almost anybody but Johnson.' In a modern office off New York's Fifth Avenue a young executive said: 'Johnson's too clever. He's always got something up his sleeve.' In Los Angeles, Mrs. Aljean Harmetz said: 'I don't think I like Johnson now. I don't think he's an honest man.' "

The same theme, sometimes the identical wording, runs through comment after comment and is reflected at times in the public-opinion polls. In late 1965 the Columbia Broadcasting System had the Opinion Research Corporation take a poll on one question: What the public thought about the truthfulness of U.S. statements about Vietnam. Only 15 percent of those polled believed the Government was "always" truthful. Almost as many, 13 percent, thought that it was "almost never" truthful. And all that the majority, 67 percent, could say was that they thought it was "sometimes" truthful. Such results could hardly be interpreted, even by the inveterate poll collector in the White House, as an overwhelming vote of confidence.

Everything indicates that the situation has grown worse instead of better since the CBS poll was taken in late 1965.

A group of dissident Democratic Senators held a private meeting with the President in mid-September, 1967, to discuss with him their problems in getting reelected in 1968. The President was in his most cordial and charming mood, and promised to help them all, regardless of their personal differences with him about the war. Near the end of the discussion, Sen. Frank Church of Idaho frankly told the President that he was in trouble. Church cited a poll that had been taken recently in a bellweather Idaho precinct. It showed that, of 35 persons who had voted for the President in 1964, only 3 said that they would vote for him again.

At the root of much of Lyndon Johnson's credibility gap trouble lies the festering, cancerous sore of Vietnam. Johnson's predicament bears some resemblance to Herbert Hoover's, with one vital difference. Events persist with Johnson, as they did with Hoover, in giving the lie to rosy official views of the future. Hoover kept proclaiming that prosperity was just around the corner—and events kept demonstrating that he was whistling past the graveyard of the old order. Lyndon Johnson's Administration has kept proclaiming imminent victory in Vietnam; it has kept insisting that each new escalation of the war was the thing that would bring Hanoi to the bargaining table—and events have persisted in exposing its delusion. Here, however, the analogy ends. Hoover did not cause the Great Depression; it was the result of economic forces beyond his understanding and control. But Lyndon Johnson *did* turn the Vietnam war into a disastrous American war on the mainland of Asia—and he did this after explicitly telling the American people in the campaign of 1964 that "we are not about

219

to send American boys 9,000 or 10,000 miles away from home to do what Asian boys ought to be doing for themselves. . . ."

As Professor David Frost, who had worked for Johnson in 1964 and ran against the party organization for the Democratic nomination for Senator in New Jersey in 1966, said bluntly in his campaign speeches: "I feel that I have been betrayed." A lot of Americans felt that they had been betrayed. They had voted for peace in 1964. They had voted for a President who had vowed to them that he would not do what all the available evidence indicates he had already determined to do. No betrayal could cut more deeply or more indelibly scar its author as a man not to be trusted.

The effect of this initial betrayal has been deepened by the lack of candor and plain truthfulness that has marked virtually every turn and twist of the Vietnamese debacle. The President and Secretary of State Rusk loudly proclaim that they will go anywhere and talk to anyone in the cause of peace. The American people and the people of the world simply do not believe them because their words collide with their actions; with a whole chain of actions that seem to plainly say that we will talk peace only at the end of a gun in terms of complete military victory.

Time and again we have spurned overtures and in some cases have denied that there were overtures, only to have to admit later that there were. In 1964 Hanoi, whom we keep insisting will not talk, twice proposed to talk. One suggestion, made through Secretary General Thant and carrying Hanoi's guarantee, was for a high-level meeting in Rangoon. We turned the bid down cold. When a rumor

220

about the offer got around, the State Department squashed it with what seemed like a categorical denial. But Adlai Stevenson, shortly before his death, told the whole story to Eric Sevareid; Sevareid revealed all in a magazine article; and the State Department belatedly admitted that well, yes, there had been this suggestion, but it had not meant anything really. Secretary Rusk's "sensitive antennae" had told him there was nothing of substance in Hanoi's proposal, and so the State Department had not really lied to the American people when, in response to the initial inquiries, it had said we had received no "meaningful" overtures from Hanoi.

There has been a long chain of similar double-talk and similar strangulation of peace proposals. Soviet Premier Aleksei N. Kosygin went to Hanoi to explore the prospects for peace, and he had hardly arrived when we began to rain down bombs. There was a later peace feeler through the Italian Foreign Ministry, with Hanoi making one stipulation—that it must not be embarrassed by a sudden escalation of the bombing, with special reference to the hydroelectric plants near Haiphong—and no sooner had this word reached us than we stepped up the bombing, paying special attention to those very hydroelectric plants. Time and again Secretary of State Rusk has been challenged to answer the gut question, yes or no: Will we sit down face-to-face and talk peace with the National Liberation Front (NLF)? The Secretary's favorite weasel on this one is that "this presents no problem" because the NFL can always be represented through Hanoi. This is sophistry. The National Liberation Front and Hanoi are distinct entities, as Harrison Salisbury has pointed out; their leader-

221

ship, their philosophy, their purposes are by no means identical. It is as if, in the American Revolution, the British had said: We will talk with Paris, and there will really be no problem because the Americans can have representation in the French delegation if they wish. Under those circumstances we might still be fighting the Revolution.

The blunt truth is that we do not want peace in Vietnam except on terms that can be labeled a great LBJ victory for the 1968 reelection campaign. If there had been any doubt left on this point, it was almost certainly dispelled by the Ashmore-Baggs affair. Harry S. Ashmore is a courageous, Pulitzer Prize winning journalist, and William C. Baggs is the editor of *The Miami News*. They went to North Vietnam together shortly after Harrison Salisbury's trip at the end of 1966. Like Salisbury, they saw the widespread devastation caused by our bombing, and they managed to get an interview with Ho Chi Minh. They described Ho's attitude as "conciliatory," and they returned convinced that North Vietnam wanted to talk peace. Salisbury had come away with the same strong, clear impression after a long discussion with Pham Van Dong, the active head of state. Since American journalists have a far better record than the State Department for making contact with reality in Vietnam, one might have expected that the impressions of three such distinguished practitioners of the craft, two of them Pulitzer Prize winners, would have carried some weight even in Foggy Bottom. And so it is instructive to see what happened.

Washington was decidedly miffed at the destruction of our comforting little fantasy about the antiseptic war we were running in Vietnam, and it showed no immediate dis-

222

position to react to anything. Ashmore and Baggs, however, talked to Senator Fulbright, and Fulbright tried to light a fire under the inhabitants of Foggy Bottom. With his backing, Ashmore and Baggs got to talk to high officials of state, with a silent White House representative sitting in. It was finally agreed that a conciliatory letter should be sent to Ho Chi Minh. State drafted the letter which Ashmore sent. At this delicate juncture, President Johnson injected himself into the act. He too sent Ho a letter. His was shorn of all conciliatory phrases and fostered what Ashmore later described as the harshest demands we had yet made as a precondition for talking peace. The effect was to slap Ho Chi Minh in the face; and, as Ashmore later wrote, the President's action "effectively and brutally" sabotaged this chance (perhaps a slim chance, but still a chance) for peace in Vietnam.

The entire sequence of missed chance and spurned chance makes clear the true American dilemma in South Vietnam. Behind our reluctance to talk peace, behind our unwillingness to meet with the NLF, lies the realization of the true weakness of the puppet military junta we have set up to rule South Vietnam. Some of our officials have even acknowledged privately that a compelling reason for spurning the 1964 overtures from Hanoi was the realization that the mere fact such talks were being held would undermine "our side" in South Vietnam. In essence, we have become the puppets of our puppets. And our puppets have made it clear time and time again that they will brook no participation in government by representatives of the NFL who, after all, do represent a large portion of the countryside. In May, 1966, during the negotiations for setting up a

223

national assembly in Saigon, Premier Ky made his attitude clear in an interview with Ron Nessen of CBS:

> *Nessen:* If in the election of an assembly the government seems to be neutralist or Communist and to be moving toward peace with the Vietcong, what would you and your military associates do?
> *Ky:* We will stand and fight.
> *Nessen:* You will fight the elected government?
> *Ky:* If they are Communists, I don't care if they are elected or not.
> *Nessen:* And if they are neutralists?
> *Ky:* Also.
> *Nessen:* You will fight the government and try to throw them out?
> *Ky:* But I am sure it will not happen, because I firmly believe that the majority of our people are anti-Communist and anti-neutralist.

In this dialogue was expressed the reality of the kind of "free world," the kind of "democracy," for which we were asking our soldiers to fight and die in South Vietnam. In the light of this, and added to the memory of sacked pagodas and immolated Buddhist priests and so much else, the rhetoric by which we had sought to justify the most controversial war in our history simply would not parse; it convinced only the already committed. The tissue of rationalization was so transparent that the nation instead of becoming united in belief, became disunited in disbelief. And so, having failed to sell the Vietnam war as a great crusade for the freedom and welfare of the Vietnamese, the Johnson Administration suddenly did an about-face in mid-

October, 1967, offering an entirely new rationale for our militaristic adventure on the mainland of Asia. With Dean Rusk firing the opening salvo, the justification now became that we had to contain "a billion Chinese on the mainland, armed with nuclear weapons." We were fighting in Southeast Asia, we were now told, because the security of the United States demanded it. We were making Vietnam the battleground so that we would not have to fight later in the streets of Honolulu or San Francisco.

This was quite a different story from all the stories of our past, and its major effect upon thinking men was to widen the Johnson Administration's credibility chasm. The Administration was like a naughty boy caught with his hand in the cookie jar. First he offers one justification, then hopefully another—but nothing works because his hand, after all, *was* in the cookie jar. Unfortunately, in these circumstances, as the culprit tries to defend himself, each new explanation sounds less convincing than the old.

The new Rusk-Johnson rationalization of the Vietnam war carried with it an almost bald-faced acknowledgment of big-power callousness, for it was obvious that if we were turning all of Vietnam into a war-torn hell so that those billion Chinese would not descend upon San Francisco, we were simply sacrificing the Vietnamese people and their homeland to our own selfish strategic purposes. The pretense that we were doing it all for *them* could no longer be maintained. There were other flaws in the newly promulgated policy. Just how a billion Chinese could ever invade the streets of San Francisco across a Pacific Ocean that had become an American Mare Nostrum, splattered with island fortresses and completely dominated by American air and sea power, nobody troubled to explain. And it was no more clear what conceivable purpose could be served by Asian land bases if the Chinese ever embarked on nuclear war; inevitably in that event, intercontinental ballistic missiles would be the weapons, with whole continents for their firing platforms and their targets. Land bases on the Southeast Asian peninsula could serve only as a provocation for such a war, not a deterrent. These were obvious gaps in logic, but these were not all. The new policy contained the seeds of even more bitter fruit. Under the old rationalization we had promised to get out of South Vietnam within six months after peace was declared and a stable South Vietnamese government formed. No one had quite believed us. Now no one could possibly believe us. If our object was to contain a billion Chinese on the mainland of Asia, then inescapably we would have to maintain in perpetuity all of those multi-billion-dollar ports and bases that we had established in South Vietnam and Thailand. This meant that we could never get out; that for all the foreseeable years of our future we would have to maintain garrison armies of hundreds of thousands of men upon the mainland of Asia.

This was the ultimate point of no return to which arrogant policies, initiated in trickery, their real purpose cloaked in false rhetoric, had brought a deceived and largely unwilling American people. The trauma of our involvement in Vietnam was causing a political upheaval unlike any in our history. We stood in 1968 at a crossroads of decision, and a new jet stream was beginning to sweep across the nation, wiping out old attitudes and slogans and bringing in new. This was a jet stream of public revulsion against our blithe

226

commitment to police the world, against the cost in lives and money this commitment was exacting. Under the pressure of this new and growing wave of popular sentiment, life-long hawks were turning into doves.

The first break occurred in the ranks of liberal Democrats in the Senate, among some of the most ardent supporters of the President's Great Society programs. Wayne Morse from the outset was the vocal and heroic champion of the anti-Vietnam position. He and Ernest Gruening of Alaska had stood alone in voting against the Gulf of Tonkin resolution in 1964. For months thereafter, Morse was a lonely voice vehemently opposing our deepening involvement in Vietnam, charging that the real intent of the military was war with China. Senator Fulbright came to share the same fear and moved into opposition. So did Frank Church, Vance Hartke and other Democratic Senators.

The political position of these men was difficult. The President was the leader of their party, and party loyalty normally dictates, if not outright support, at least silent acquiescence. Opposition should come from the opposition party, but one of the evils of the bipartisan foreign policy is that there has been no true opposition and debate. The foreign policy of the party in power, whether Republican or Democratic, had come to be accepted by the opposition as if it were the duty of all good Americans to rally behind the flag in all circumstances. And so the Republicans had drifted into a posture not of true and principled opposition but of outright demagoguery. Their tack from Korea to Vietnam had been to adopt the line of the harder hawk, to accuse the Democrats of "failure to win" and the lack of will to win, and to suggest that the only proper course to

227

pursue was to wage a more vigorous and more horrible war.

In this vacuum created by an opposition that did not oppose, the only real dissent had to come from the ranks of the Democrats, from those for whom the political facts of life made it most difficult. Many in the Senate who were opposed to our course in Vietnam would cheer Senator Morse in the cloakroom—and vote against him on the floor. But with the passage of time, with the deepening futility of the war and the increasing danger of its spread, many Democratic Senators became vigorous opponents of the Vietnam policy. When they did, the displeasure of the White House was unmistakable. President Johnson, returning from one of his foreign conferences, extended both hands to shake the hands of those waiting to greet him at the airport, but when he came to Senator Fulbright he gave no sign he was aware the Senator existed. Even more pointed was an anecdote, evidently spread by the White House and circulated throughout Washington. According to this story, the President upbraided Senator Church about an anti-Vietnam war speech, and Church replied: "I don't go any further than Walter Lippmann." The President's rejoinder: "Well, Frank, the next time you need money to build a dam in your state, you better go to Mr. Lippmann." Senator Church swears that the incident never happened, but the planting of the story, evidently by the White House, suggested the President "was trying to threaten the dissenters, trying to suggest the kind of punishment that *could* be taken against us."

The frustration of those Senators who felt they had to put the good of the country ahead of traditional party loyalty became deep and bitter. In March, 1966, after a futile attempt to repeal the Gulf of Tonkin resolution, a group of the dissident Democrats held a closed-door session at which criticism of the President became vitriolic. According to Drew Pearson, who had the story from some of the participants, "LBJ was called 'a desperate man,' a 'wild animal' who was taking the country into war with China." Senator George Aiken, the much-respected Republican Senator from Vermont, did not attend the Democratic conclave, but he privately told the dissident Democrats that their fears were his fears. He too thought the President was headed for nuclear war with China, the almost certain trigger of World War III.

Such was the menace of our deepening involvement in Vietnam. If there was anything to justify the risk, the Johnson Administration, in its tired analogies to Munich, had failed to demonstrate it to many of the best minds in the nation. And the result became apparent in the widening schisms of 1967. Now for the first time the old order broke, and stalwarts in Congress who in the past had backed the military in everything it wanted moved to opposition.

One of the first and most significant signs of the change came in March, 1966, when Sen. Richard B. Russell (D., Ga.), conceded to be one of the most formidable figures in the Senate Establishment, threw a roadblock against a major new Defense Department scheme. The department wanted to build a fleet of 30 "fast deployment logistic ships" at a cost of more than $2 billion. The Navy argued such ships would "act as a deterrent to hostile military adventures in any region of the globe by providing a flexible means for stationing combat equipment for land forces near any area of potential trouble for prompt use if needed."

Senator Russell, chairman of the powerful Senate Armed

229

Services Committee, got his committee to recommend unanimously against building this new deployment fleet—and then got the Senate to back him up. Russell's committee said it was "concerned about the possible creation of an impression that the United States has assumed the function of policing the world. . . ." And Russell himself on the Senate floor told his colleagues, in effect, that his opposition was based on the sound concept that if you give the military a new toy they will find some pretext for using it, dragging the rest of the nation after. He said that "there is reason to think, to put it colloquially, that if it is easy for us to go anywhere and do anything, we will always be going somewhere and doing something."

In Russell's stand there was the first significant rumble of the storms to come. The following months saw a succession of events that forced a widening split in the ranks of the old order as realities became too obvious to be denied. Most significant were three major developments. President Johnson took a first, tentative step that could have embroiled us in peace-keeping in the Congo; Under Secretary of State Katzenbach was almost contemptuous of the Senate in his testimony before the Fulbright Committee; and, with the cities rioting, President Johnson asked for a 10 percent across-the-board income tax surcharge not to meet the urban crisis, but to help cut down the enormous budget deficit (estimated at some $30 billion) resulting from the war in Vietnam.

The first of these events was the one that tipped the scales in the Senate and revived an opposition that had been virtually moribund. On Saturday, July 8, 1967, Secretary Rusk telephoned Senator Russell and told him that three

U.S. Air Force jet transports and 150 men were being dispatched to the Congo to support the Mobutu government against domestic rebels and mercenaries. Senator Russell was not enchanted. He told Rusk bluntly that he saw no reason for the United States to involve itself in Mobutu's domestic difficulties, and he argued that, should GI's be endangered or killed, the pressure would mount almost irresistibly for us to send more men in to back up "our boys." This was the way Vietnam had started; this was the way a tiny commitment, the tentative extension of a helping hand, had mushroomed step by step into a full-scale American war on the Asian mainland. Senator Russell knew that story well.

His mind went back to a scene in an Atlanta hotel room 13 years previously. Assistant Secretary of State Thruston B. Morton, as an emissary for President Eisenhower and Secretary of State John Foster Dulles, had called on Russell to tell him that the Republican Administration had decided to send some arms and a few technicians into South Vietnam. Russell's reaction at the time had been ambivalent. His astute mind warned him of the dangers, but he was evidently restrained by his adherence to the myth that all good Americans must stand together in matters of foreign policy. And so he told Morton (now a fellow U.S. Senator), "You can assure the President and the Secretary of State that I will not say a word about this publicly. But you can also tell them for me that this is the biggest mistake we have ever made."

The incident raises haunting questions. Where lies a Senator's first allegiance? Isn't it to the people of the nation whose lives and welfare are at stake? Should foreign policy

231

be so sacrosanct, so bi-partisan, that even when a powerful Senator of the opposition like Russell sees the pitfalls he must not speak? If such be the case, what good is representative government?

It was against this background that Senator Russell quickly decided he was not going to be silent again. And so on Monday, July 10, shortly after the Senate convened, he rose in his seat, cocked his head angrily to one side, and stormed up and down the aisle, thumping desks in his anger as he denounced the dispatch of planes and men to the Congo as unjustified, immoral and unwise.

The secret mood of the frustrated Senate was clearly indicated by what happened next. The Senate had been dragooned into supporting the Vietnamese war because the President had presented it with a *fait accompli,* but the Senate had not liked it. Reporters kept hearing Senators of all persuasions repeating virtually the same phrases: "Never again! There must never be another Vietnam." Now the possibility that the Congo might become another Vietnam gave them a chance to express their true feelings. Senator Russell's angry denunciation ignited the Senate. Senators of all political faiths and beliefs—Republicans and Democrats, hawks and doves—rose to echo Russell's words. Mike Mansfield, the Democratic Majority Leader, confessed himself "shocked, surprised and dismayed . . . because I do not believe we can involve ourselves in any and every part of the world." Senator Milton R. Young (R., N.D.) said the Congo foray appeared to be "a continuation of the policy which was initiated following World War II, at which time the experts in the Pentagon and the State Department determined that we were going to police the

232

whole world." And Senator Stennis (D., Miss.), that hawk of hawks, remarked that "if we have not already learned a lesson by going in alone and getting unnecessarily involved on the other side of the world, we will never learn it."

The rebellion in the Senate was so explosive that Secretary Rusk rushed up to Capitol Hill and promised the early withdrawal of our planes and men from the Congo. And the State Department shortly afterward announced that it had rejected a similar appeal for help from Nigeria's embattled government.

The Congo incident, on top of Vietnam, seemed to many to demonstrate that there was no limit to the interventions that the militarists directing our executive policy would have us undertake. It clearly showed our intent to support established governments everywhere against internal rebellions, regardless of the nature of those rebellions and regardless of the nature of the governments we were supporting. It was in this context that Senator Russell suggested to Senator Fulbright that it might be a good thing if his Foreign Relations Committee held hearings to determine just what our commitments were. And it was these hearings that led to the performance of Nicholas Katzenbach.

Senators of the United States are not accustomed to being shouted at or hectored in arrogant tones like ignorant schoolboys. Yet this was Katzenbach's tone and manner as he argued (1) that the Gulf of Tonkin resolution had had all the effect of a declaration of war; (2) that the Gulf of Tonkin resolution had not really been needed because the President had all the authority to do everything he had done, even to involving us in war with China if it came to that, and (3) that declarations of war, which the Consti-

233

tution provides shall be voted only by Congress representing the people, are outmoded in this age when wars are fought without being declared—and so the whole declaration-of-war power invested in Congress is an anachronism.

Louis XIV would have treasured Katzenbach, but it is to be doubted if the founders of the American republic would have. No one argues against the proposition that the President, in the nuclear age, must be given infinite latitude in *responding* to a missile attack which, taking into account the speed of modern weaponry, could conceivably allow only 30 minutes for decision. There is, in such circumstances, no opportunity for Congress to meet, to debate, to declare war. But this is a far cry from a situation like Vietnam that had built up slowly over the months and the years, with one small step after small step leading to an ever bigger step until in the end we found ourselves committed by executive fiat alone to waging an aggressive war 9,000 to 10,000 miles away from the American continent. If this President, or any President, can so commit his people at this whim, then the single most vital check-rein in the Constitution—the provision that only Congress, in the name of the people whom it represents, may declare war—has been abrogated for what becomes, in effect, a form of Presidential dictatorship in foreign affairs.

Into this ferment over foreign policy the President injected a third item of discord—his proposal for a 10 percent income tax surcharge. Nobody likes tax increases, but this particular suggestion was especially obnoxious to the American people for a variety of reasons. It was advocated on two grounds: It was necessary to curb inflation caused by the Vietnamese war, and it was necessary to help offset the enormous budget deficit caused by the Vietnamese war. Since nearly half of the American people thought the war was one we should never have been involved in anyway, they were not enchanted by the idea of having to reach deep into their jeans to pay for the costs of a war policy with which they disagreed. Nor were they any more delighted at realizing that they were being played for suckers by their government through a tax system that is so inequitable it is a fraud upon the conscience.

Every one of our recent tax measures has hit the wage-earner and the middle-class salaried man while protecting the old loopholes and even writing in new loopholes through which the very rich can escape paying any taxes at all. Even as late as March 9, 1967, with the Administration knowing well what the costs of Vietnam would be, with the Administration knowing well that a tax increase would be proposed for the average Joe, industries that already enjoyed bountiful special privileges had been given another bonus. The maximum investment tax credit provisions had been raised for such industries as oil and gas, airlines and railroads. This meant that while the President was asking a tax increase for the average American, the taxes paid by these giants would actually be *pared down by $400 million in the first twelve months.* This inequity was piled on top of a whole mound of other inequities. President Kennedy had tried futilely (and had intended to try again) to get some kind of justice written into our tax measures. The 27½ percent oil depletion allowance and a host of other special drilling and tax allowances have spawned so many nontaxpaying oil millionaires in Texas that we have created in this democracy a specially privileged, oligarchic class

235

that is rapidly acquiring the power to twist the entire nation by the tail. Instead of exhibiting some signs of conscience over this fraud, Congress in writing the tax bill of 1966 had opened the barn door wide to a variety of other looters and had said to them in effect: "Please come and steal the horse." It had written special depletion allowances for industries using Georgia clay and oyster and clam shells. And now Lyndon Johnson, long the faithful servitor of the oil interests of Texas, wanted to soak the average American 10 percent more for Vietnam while leaving all his former friends and backers to enjoy their special privileges.

The brazenness of the proposal touched off a storm. Deadly comparisons were made again, contrasting what the rich were not paying with what other Americans were. Former Senator Douglas recalled that in 1964 one oil tycoon had paid less income tax than did a $55-a-week charwoman. Senator Robert Kennedy pointed out that one multimillionaire *had earned more than $1 million a year for the past 14 years—and had paid no taxes at all!*

He added: "In 1965, 35 people in this country who earned over $500,000 paid no tax at all. In a recent year one man whose net worth is $1.5 billion, paid only $685 in taxes. *Another whose income was more than $20 million paid no taxes at all. . . .*"

There were other equally devastating comparisons. In 1966 Superior Oil Company of California had a net profit of $67 million. It paid not a penny in Federal income tax. In fact, it had not paid any tax since 1962. General American Oil, with an income of over $25 million in 1966, paid only $11,331 in Federal taxes. An individual making $40,000 a year would pay that much.

236

"We cannot begin to estimate how much money corporations and wealthy individuals have avoided paying their government because of tax inequities that have continued for years," said Joseph Pechman, director of economic studies for the Brookings Institute in Washington. "It is so large it would be a horror figure."

The average American was being taken for a boob; he was being clobbered—and he knew it. It was not just the proposed jump in the Federal income tax; he was being hit from all sides. New taxes were voted or old taxes raised in 21 states during the first months of 1967. Governor Romney in Michigan imposed his state's first income tax on top of a 4 percent sales tax, and Governor Ronald Reagan in California pushed through a billion-dollar tax increase, hiking the sales tax and the income tax and jumping the tariff on cigarettes from 3 to 10 cents a pack. On top of all this, virtually every municipality in the nation was raising its local taxes to meet the costs of new schools, welfare, roads and other services. A worker's pay raise was taxed away from him—and, often, more besides—before he ever got it.

There could be no question about the iniquities of our tax structure—and so no question about the callousness of a proposal for a tax hike without reform. The facts were all loaded on the side of the people, and the power in the Administration and in much of Congress was all loaded on the side of selfish interests. Tax figures for 1964, the latest year for which statistics were complete, showed what the figures had been showing for years—that taxpayers in the $10,000 to $20,000-a-year bracket were the ones who paid the heaviest share of their income in taxes. Even workers below the $10,000 level paid at heavier rates than millionaires. In 1964, 19 persons with incomes of $1 million or more paid not a cent in taxes; and, even more significant, 463 who had to struggle along on incomes of $500,000 each paid less than 30 percent to the Federal tax collector. Big businesses—the airlines, construction firms, oil companies, all the innumerable suppliers of war matériel—were making fortunes out of the Vietnam war, but it was the little man who was being asked to pay.

The iniquity was compounded by an additional iniquity —the priorities we have placed on the spending of the nation's tax revenues. With *all* of the income taxes of the nation going into the pockets of the military, an imbalance has been created in which the lower- and middle-income taxpayers, in addition to being victimized by the Federal tax system, are victimized again by onerous local tax systems struggling to raise money to combat problems that are national in their origin and scope.

New York City provides a classic example. It is a melting pot of the new national migration. Its problems and costs are colossal, and in the struggle to partially meet them, tax has been piled upon tax. In addition to the Federal income tax bite, there are these levies: a state income tax, a city income tax, a 5 percent sales tax. The compounded tax evils are such that many workers shun New York like the plague. One man I know turned down a New York City job that would have paid him double what he was getting in New Jersey. He figured out that he would be working two days a week out of every five for the various tax collectors.

238

In the suburbs, where shifting populations have brought astronomical fiscal problems, the burden falls heaviest on the homeowner, hit with real estate taxes that threaten to become confiscatory. Typical is the story of a widow in a small New Jersey town. Her husband had been a retired minister. Ministers' salaries being what they are, they never had much money. But they had acquired a five-room bungalow set on a 100 by 100 corner lot. This had been their home for years. Then he died. The local real estate taxes on the widow's home were $709 a year; with her reduced income she could not possibly pay them, and she would have had to sell her home had not her daughter and son-in-law come to her rescue. Such experiences typify on another level the hardships and tragedies that are worked by an iniquitous Federal tax system that drains off the bulk of the nation's tax resources and uses them to support a bloated military establishment. In such circumstances there was little wonder that the LBJ 10 percent surcharge tax proposal touched off a storm of popular opposition across the nation.

When the President carried his case to the people in early November, 1967, asking them to write their Congressmen pleading that they be taxed to avoid inflation, he got a response that was the exact reverse of his desires. The public wrote their Congressmen all right—a barrage of protest. Mail to individual Congressmen ran as high as 98-to-2 and 99-to-1 against the tax increase. One constituent wrote: "The honest and fair thing to do is to place the surtax on the excess war profits and not on the small taxpayers who have not made these gains." Another advised,

239

"End the war, quit giving our money to Communist countries, stop supporting the ingrates in the whole world, and we won't need an increase in taxes."

This gale of protest was typical of the hurricane that had begun to blow across the country. The first signs of a new wind became apparent in early July, 1967. Congress had recessed in late June for a ten-day summer holiday, and when it reconvened there was a complete turn-about in mood that startled Washington. It could only be explained by the fact, as some Congressmen and Senators privately acknowledged, that they had heard from their constituents in loud and angry tones. The American people were beginning to be fed up, and the more sensitive politicians recognized the grass-roots stirrings. For the first time there began to be a serious Republican opposition to the war.

This was not just a case of political opportunism. Many Senators had long harbored private doubts. Senator George McGovern (D., S.D.), one of the most outspoken foes of the Administration on the war, said in one speech that "90 out of the 100 men in the Senate believe it was a mistake for the United States to become involved" in Vietnam. But many of these men had hesitated to speak out. They were restrained by a variety of reasons. The fact remained that we were at war, that our men had been committed and were fighting; and many hesitated to take a position that, it might be charged, would give aid and comfort to the enemy. There was also a residue of the atmosphere of fear and conformity left over from the McCarthy madness, and some politicians felt it still not safe to take a stand that might later expose them to idiot shouts of "letting our boys down" and "being soft on communism." But the sheer

240

thrust of events was becoming too much for continued silence. Our latest escalations found us bombing within seven miles of the Chinese border, so close that a miscalculation of seconds at jet-air speeds might trigger World War III. And the obvious and growing public revulsion against the war changed the climate and made it possible for the once silent to speak.

Even men who had supported the war out of deep and sincere conviction began to change. Perhaps the most striking symbol of a complete reversal of attitude was Senator Thruston Morton, the Kentucky Republican who had helped to get us involved in Vietnam in the first place. Morton had always been known as a hawk. He had supported the Johnson Administration in its bombing of the North, convinced that these measures would bring Hanoi to the conference table. But by August, 1967, he had come to recognize both the futility and the infinite danger of the course we were pursuing. "I was wrong, and I'll admit it," he told the Senate. It was clear, he said, that our tactics in Vietnam "are outworn and are not working" and that we were "painting ourselves into a corner" by following a policy of escalation.

Another who made a similar principled switch was Clifford Case, the New Jersey Republican who has been called by fellow Senators "one of the most earnest and sincere members of our body." Case, a member of the Foreign Relations Committee, had supported the Administration's conduct of the war. I know, for I had considerable correspondence with him in late 1965 and early 1966, trying to persuade him to change his hawk-like stand. Case would not budge; he obviously felt it was his patriotic duty

241

to back the war effort. But then came Nicholas Katzenbach, telling Congress in effect that it was obsolete; and on
September 26, 1967, Case startled the Senate by making
what was probably the strongest, direct attack on President
Johnson that had yet been heard. He charged that the
President had "squandered his credibility" and caused a
"crisis of confidence" through his misuse and "perversion"
of the Tonkin Gulf resolution. The "people's anxiety"
about the war, he said, sprang "in greatest part from a
growing conviction that the Administration is not telling
them the truth."

This attack was followed up by Senator Morton in a
speech before a group of antiwar businessmen on September 27, 1967. He charged that President Johnson had been
"brainwashed" by the "military-industrial complex,"
against which President Eisenhower had warned, into believing that the United States could win a military victory
in Vietnam. It had become apparent, Morton said, that we
could not do this, and he added, "I am convinced that
unless we gradually and, if necessary, unilaterally reduce
the scope of our military involvement, we may well destroy
the very society we sought to save."

The reaction to this speech told much. Senator Morton's
office was deluged by a volume of congratulatory mail. The
Senator's own aides were astonished by the outpouring, and
the demonstration convinced Morton that a Republican
peace candidate could sweep the country in 1968.

On every side the evidence mounted that the political
climate of the nation was ripe for a change. The American
military, whose thinking had so long swayed our foreign
policy, had cashed in their last credibility check in Viet-

242

nam. Stewart Alsop, certainly no dove, wrote a column for *The Saturday Evening Post* (August 26, 1967) with the telling title "Almost All Generals Are Almost Always Wrong About All Wars." The American public, brainwashed in the decades of the Cold War not to question military wisdom, was questioning now.

A couple of significant newspaper polls showed the degree to which the military had been discredited. In May the Cleveland *Plain Dealer* published three articles setting forth the alternatives in Vietnam. One, written by Rep. L. Mendel Rivers (D., S.C.), a noisy hawk, was entitled "Escalate and Win," a position certainly close to that of the Johnson Administration. Senator Fulbright contributed an article headed "De-Escalate," and Howard Zinn, who had written a book on the subject, advocated "Withdraw." The *Plain Dealer* asked its readers to vote for the position closest to their own views, and it later announced these results: Zinn, 5,798; Rivers, 1,716; Fulbright, 1,648.

The *Sunday Gazette and Mail* of Charleston, West Virginia, intrigued by this performance, ran the same three articles and conducted a similar readership poll. Its results: Zinn, 888; Fulbright, 109; Rivers, 97. Such results seemed to indicate that the American people, when the issues were clearly presented and explained to them, wanted to get out of the whole Vietnam involvement in the quickest way possible.

A whole series of Harris and Gallup polls showed the swing of public sentiment. Not only was President Johnson's popularity sinking, but the American people, in various ways, expressed their resentment at the course of the war. The polls showed beyond any doubt that the great

243

majority of Americans felt the South Vietnamese should
be bearing the brunt of the war; that belief we never should
have become involved in the first place was rising, and that
the decision to send more troops to Vietnam was flatly disapproved by 61 percent of the public. One Harris poll
showed that the public, by a slim margin, wanted to
abandon the project to land a man on the moon, believing
it was not worth the $3 billion a year it was costing. An-
other indicated that most of the American people wanted
to maintain or expand the Great Society programs despite
the costs of Vietnam.

What emerged was a composite picture of an America
ready to follow new paths and awaiting new leadership.
Even one-time hawks were talking about the need for new
priorities, and the riots in the cities had brought home to
many officials and large segments of the public the simple
truth that our major crisis today is domestic; that our urban
and racial problems are the ones that can destroy our
society, and that our brains and our resources must be devoted primarily to their solution.

A decisive change in national directions and policy was
in the making. The 20-year-old dialogue of the Cold War
was outmoded and irrelevant, and the basis for a powerful
new constituency was being laid—if there was anywhere
in the nation a political leader perceptive enough to champion new causes. His following was waiting. Not only were
the older generations and their hawkish leaders breaking
away from the old patterns, but the young, in revolt against
the rigidities of their elders, formed a huge new voting bloc
of enormous potential. There were some 30 million potential votes in the under-30 age group waiting to be garnered

in 1968, and by 1972 the youth segment of the population will comprise more than half the nation's voting strength. Sen. Robert Kennedy is the only national politician who seems to have had the wit to recognize this fact of life, and he has pitched his appeal with great success to this new political constituency—young, better-educated and unwilling to be frozen in the unchanging molds of old policies.

There has always been, of course, a generational gap, but it is to be doubted if there has ever existed such a chasm between the generations as the one that obtains today. This young generation is not, of course, composed exclusively of rebels; it has its share of ultra-conservatives and followers of the accepted policy, whatever this may be. But it is quite noticeable, I think, that there are fewer sheep among the youth of the Sixties than among those of the early Fifties. Again and again they have demonstrated their willingness to dissent, their dedication to ideals, their rebellion against the accepted order.

Their disenchantment has been expressed most obviously over the Vietnamese war issue. A college-instructor friend of mine likes to challenge the youth in his classes. "Most of you are not here because you want an education," he sometimes tells them. "Most of you are here because you are draft dodgers, because you don't want to be sent to Vietnam."

Describing the reaction he gets to this blatant challenge, he chuckles and shakes his head.

"What I like about this generation," he says, "is that they're not hypocrites. They'll look you right in the eye and come right back at you. 'Sure,' they'll say, 'you're right. A

245

lot of us are here because we don't want to go to Vietnam. Can you blame us? What would *you* do in our shoes?' "

Satisfied with the result of his experiment, my instructor friend then tells them: "Sure, I don't blame you. I agree with you. I'd do the same thing."

It is safe to say that there has never been a holy war in our history that aroused such enthusiasm as this.

What is perhaps most notable about this younger generation is not the much-discussed revolt of the hippies against all facets of modern society, but the degree to which the intellectual leaders of the young—the group from which the national leadership of the future will be drawn—is alienated from the power structure of the national government as represented by the Johnson Administration. In January, 1967, 50 American Rhodes scholars sent President Johnson a letter questioning U.S. policy in Vietnam. This followed a similar letter addressed to the President by student leaders from 100 colleges and universities throughout the United States. The Rhodes scholars told the President that they found it exceedingly difficult to justify the war to themselves or to foreign students. They had found, they said, that their "feelings of conscience and national obligation counsel skepticism and concern, not active support, of the Government's Vietnam policy."

In March, 1967, in a face-to-face confrontation with U.N. Ambassador Arthur Goldberg, Gregory Craig, chairman of the Harvard Student Council, expressed the feelings of Harvard students in blunt terms. "Mr. Ambassador, we've tried everything; we've written letters signed by student leaders, we have signed petitions, we have written our

246

congressmen and to our senators, and we are frustrated.
. . . The more moderate group of students on this campus
and in universities and colleges throughout the country are
becoming increasingly disaffected.

"Six years ago the American government captured the
imagination of a whole new generation of young people.
Today, these same people, some of our country's most
talented and thoughtful citizens, regard the notion of
national purpose with cynicism, and in some cases, outright hostility. The sad thing is that our own leaders have
destroyed our idealism."

The plea of the younger generation for a responsible
leadership it can trust and follow could not be more eloquently and effectively expressed.

9

WHITHER AMERICA

By the end of 1967 more than 100,000 young Americans had been killed or wounded in Vietnam. Unless there was to be a sudden turn for peace which no one expected, the casualty list by the time of the 1968 election was almost certain to surpass the toll of Korea, the fourth worst war in our history. Granted that Lyndon Johnson inherited a difficult situation, granted that his predecessors never should have taken those first inching little-cat steps into the morass of Vietnam, still it was Lyndon Johnson who committed the entire nation, as neither Eisenhower nor Kennedy had been willing to commit it, to the disaster of a major ground war, pitting white men against yellow on the continent of Asia. And he did this in defiance of a 1964 mandate to do the very opposite. He did it without consulting Congress, without the consent of Congress, with his only justification being the trickery of the Tonkin Gulf resolution. He did it in defiance of the explicit provision of the Constitution that only Congress may declare war.

248

Now, brash and arrogant in the saddle, his minions proclaimed the un-American thesis that the President does not have to consult with Congress; that he has the power to send our troops anywhere and commit them to anything without the approval of Congress or the American people. If this concept of Presidential authority was to go unchallenged, the American people would have no more to say about where their sons and grandsons are sent to fight and die than the Germans had under Hitler.

This had to be stopped.

The quickest way to stop it was to repudiate Lyndon Johnson in 1968. Beyond that there should be a Constitutional amendment specifically reaffirming the intent of the framers of the Constitution, specifically forbidding the President to commit any American forces to foreign soil, except in response to a direct attack, without the authorization of Congress. Such an amendment would be a reaffirmation of a sacred American tradition; it would carry out the clear intent of the framers of the Constitution, men who recognized that the Presidency must be invested with tremendous powers, but men who had seen the excesses of executive power in the tyrannies of Europe and who therefore hedged the Presidential authority, or so they thought, with a tight check-rein that would prevent one man from committing his people to war.

This is an issue of paramount importance for the future peace of America and the world, regardless of what happens in Vietnam.

A second issue of transcendent importance involves a choice of directions, a selection of new priorities. Whither America? Global policeman, fighting lonely battles in de-

249

fense of the status quo throughout the world? Or a land so fortunate, a society so just and so healthy that it will be the envy of all mankind? That is the choice.

John Quincy Adam said:

> Wherever the standard of freedom and independence has been or shall be unfurled, there will be America's heart, her benedictions, and her prayers. But she goes not abroad in search of monsters to destroy. She is the well-wisher to the freedom and independence of all. She is the champion and vindicator only of her own. She will recommend the general cause by the countenance of her voice, and by the benignant sympathy of her example. She well knows that by once enlisting under other banners than her own, were they even the banners of foreign independence, she would involve herself beyond the power of extrication, in all the wars of interest and intrigue, of individual avarice, envy and ambition, which assume the colors and usurp the standards of freedom. The fundamental maxims of her policy would insensibly change from liberty to force. . . . She might become the dictatress of the world. She would no longer be the ruler of her own spirit.

Those words were spoken in an address in Washington on July 4, 1821. They read as if written by a visionary who had foreseen all the evils of Vietnam. President Johnson and the American military could have read them with profit before they involved us in the worst quagmire in our history. For the truth that John Quincy Adams saw in the simpler world of 1821 is still the truth in the nuclear age of today. The psychology of men and governments has not changed, and America, in her blind effort to impose a Pax Americana upon the world, has indeed become no longer "the ruler of her own spirit."

The true American spirit extolled by John Quincy Adams needs champions in this hour. It needs political leaders with the courage and the vision to say: "We will build here a society such as the world has never seen. We will not isolate ourselves from the affairs of the rest of mankind. That would be folly. But neither will we try to run the affairs of the whole world. We will help the poor, the disadvantaged, the distressed where our help can do some good, where our aid can get directly to the people we want to help. But we will not pour billions into the hands of corrupt rulers and fascistic dictators in the misguided belief that we are purchasing friends for the 'free world.' And the people we aid, the governments we help, must be prepared to do their share, for we cannot save them or help them unless they are prepared to help themselves. In the meantime we have enormous problems of our own to solve, and these *must* come first. We must make our urban centers livable; we must find jobs for the unemployed; we must take care of the health of our own people; we must solve the racial issue that threatens to tear our society apart."

Johnsonites will doubtless clamor that it is isolationism, a return to the discredited America First of pre-World War II days. It is neither. It is a policy of common sense. It is a policy aimed at correcting the excesses of an "internationalism" that has run riot and has saddled America with responsibility for the whole world, leading us into the cul-de-sac of Vietnam.

251

The real danger lies not in a program such as this but in the possible excesses of reaction to the policies we have pursued for 20 years. The gale of protest and revulsion sweeping the nation could indeed force us back into a disastrous isolationism unless some sane and sensible middle-of-the-road alternative is adopted. The signs abound that the danger of a reactionary excess is very real indeed. The foreign economic aid program, as distinguished from the military aid program, encountered rough sledding in the Congressional session of 1967 as pressures mounted to slash all projects that could not be eliminated. This trend, if carried to extremes, would be a national tragedy. The kind of idealism expressed in Kennedy's Peace Corps and his Alliance for Progress program of aid to Latin America must not be allowed to die if we expect to avoid more Castro-type, communistic revolutions on our doorstep; but, at the same time, such aid must not be indiscriminate, it must not be shoveled out by the carload to any mendicant who asks. The objective must always be to help the masses of the needy, not to fatten the bank accounts of greedy and debauched rulers who profess to be our allies.

Within such a framework we can fulfill the commitments that should be fulfilled. We will be helping *people*. We will not be pouring out limitless billions in the futile effort to purchase ourselves allies for our fanatically envisioned holy war against communism. We will understand that there will be ideologies in the world that we do not like. As we learned to live with them in the past, so we shall have to learn to live with them in the future. In the meantime we should and must give absolute first priority, in allocating our resources, to the solution of the thronging problems of

252

our own land—problems that, long neglected, have reduced us to only a shadow of the nation that we could and should be.

This is no visionary program. It is, on the contrary, a hard and practical program springing from the necessities of our own situation. The question of the hour is: Will the politicians of America give them a choice?

The answers are doubtful. They are because American politics today is dangerously schizoid.

The Democratic Party, hampered though it has been by its state's rights Southern wing, has been the progressive party of the nation on domestic issues. The Republicans, for the most part, have had their heads buried in the sands of the nineteenth century and have found it in their hearts, not to draft wise programs for the future, but only to make demagogic noises about the patriotism of their adversaries. This pattern would seem to indicate that the Democratic Party would be best equipped to deal with domestic crises like those that now confront us. But the party today is in a straitjacket imposed by the militarism and foreign-adventurism of Lyndon Johnson. Could it depose Johnson in favor of Robert Kennedy, it might be able to join cause with the true needs of America; it might be able to give the country the new directions and the new priorities it so desperately needs. But the harsh facts of political life make this impossible. Harry Truman is said to have remarked: "Any S.O.B. who sits in this chair can get himself nominated." Lyndon Johnson sits there—and he holds all the reins of party power.

This leaves the Republicans. Their opportunity is so self-evident that it seems incredible even Republicans could fail to see and seize it. The Democrats under Lyndon Johnson have again proven themselves "a war party," a charge that was a favorite Republican campaign slogan in 1952. The present Democratic administration has squandered billions and thrown away thousands of young American lives in an unauthorized war detested by large segments of the American people. And at home the urban problems mount, and the riots of 1967 indicated they will not wait until 1972 for solution. Instead of squandering billions on the Pentagon and casting away lives and dollars in Vietnam, we must use the great bulk of our Federal revenues to meet the new, emergent needs of our own society. We must funnel the available billions of revenue from the Federal treasury—the only resource large enough to combat massive problems national in their scope and origins—back to our overwhelmed cities and states to finance the kind of programs that will make our urban world livable.

Walter Lippmann, probably the wisest journalist of our times, has stressed this theme again and again. On repeated trips to Western Europe, talking with heads of state and feeling the pulse of the public, Lippmann has found and reported that the rest of the world looks upon us as having gone Cold War mad. England and France and Western Germany feel no compulsion to help us shoulder the white man's burden by imposing a militarily enforced peace on riotous sections of the world. The immediate postwar tensions have subsided, and these nations have found that they can live in peace with Soviet Russia without feeling unduly menaced. They believe, similarly, that they can live in peace with Communist China, especially a

Communist China torn by its own internal dissensions. If we want to go on waging a Cold War based on containment policies drafted 20 years ago, that is our business. We can go ahead and do it; we can spend our own lives and resources. But we will go it alone, without them, because they simply do not believe it. They think the whole idea is nuts.

Lippmann finds that people everywhere—and this applies to communist and noncommunist countries alike—are disenchanted with their leaderships and preoccupied primarily with the problems of living in the difficult urban age that technology has created. This mood has led much of the rest of the world, but unfortunately not America, to adopt new priorities. Power politics has become irrelevant. It cannot be played with success in the nuclear age, where the final item of force cannot be applied without blowing up the world. In addition, the domestic problems in every nation are so enormous that they dwarf all else and lead to what Lippmann calls a new kind of isolationism. This stems from the urgent need to solve one's own problems first "in the midst of the most radical revolution in the history of mankind." Lippmann adds:

> This revolution is the transformation of the human environment and of man himself by technological progress which, beginning about two centuries ago, has now acquired enormous momentum.
>
> It is changing the way men live, not only their work and their houses, their food and their communications and their pleasures, but it is changing also the structure of the human family and the chemistry of the

255

human personality. These changes are bewildering. They are frightening, and it is no wonder that the masses of mankind are much too absorbed in their own lives to care very much about what happens in some other country.

After his tour of Europe in the summer of 1967, Lippmann reported:

> We are in the early beginnings of a struggle, which will probably last for generations, to remake our civilization. It is not a good time for politicians. It is a time for prophets and leaders and explorers and inventors and pioneers, and for those who are willing to plant trees for their children to sit under.

America's conduct in this new world has left other nations both bewildered and resentful. "It is a naive illusion that 1967 is 1939, that Southeast Asia is Western Europe, that Mao Tse-tung is Hitler and that Lyndon Johnson is Churchill," Lippmann writes. It is our pursuit of these delusions, the savage war we are waging in Vietnam, that has alienated the rest of the world which feels that we have betrayed our original ideals and abandoned our primary mission—to set an example, to demonstrate for all to see, "how men can live in freedom." Lippmann sums up:

> The dislike and distrust of Johnson's America is harsh. It stems in the last analysis, I believe, from a feeling of having been let down. There is a growing belief that Johnson's America is no longer the his-

torical America, that it is a bastard empire which re-
lies on superior force to achieve its purposes, and is
no longer providing an example of the wisdom and
humanity of a free society.

All of this is grist for the Republican mill. But the deep
and disturbing issue remains: Will the Republicans offer
more than blind, demagogic opposition? The call of the
times is certainly for new and forward-looking leadership
in a world radically changed from the worlds of our past.
Can the power structure of the Republican Party recognize
this? Will it lead? This is the telling point.

The Republicans are not lacking in modern leaders, men
in touch with the realities of their day and possessed of
political charisma. They have Rockefeller, Romney, Lindsay, Percy and Hatfield, to name a few. But the trouble
consistently has been that the internal power structure of
the party has not been attuned to such men. It has chosen
in the past to ignore them and, whenever possible, to shunt
them aside.

The great heroes of the antediluvian wing of the Republican Party, the power bloc that dominated the 1964 convention and threatened to rule that of 1968, are Richard
Nixon and Ronald Reagan. Neither offers an alternative to
Johnson.

Nixon's entire political career, beginning with the demagogic "pink sheet" campaigns with which he tried to tar all
opponents with communism, has been based upon his
appeal to fanatics of the right and upon trying at the same
time to appear responsible and conservative to middle-of-
the-road America. His performance has been the imper-

sonation of a more suave and responsible Joe McCarthy. In international affairs he has a long record as a harder hawk. He belonged to the power group that would have plunged the United States into war in Vietnam in 1954 if Eisenhower had not restrained them. And throughout the present conflict his quarrel with the Johnson Administration has been that it did not fight the war hard enough. There have been reports that his advisers, sensing the growing peace sentiment in the nation, have been urging him to soften his stand, but Nixon's record is so hawkish that any shift toward a dove-wooing posture would be extremely difficult. On domestic issues Nixon has shown no passion, no commitment, no dedication to the solution of the nation's multiple ills, and it is inconceivable that he, if nominated and elected, would initiate the kind of program the nation needs.

Ronald Reagan's chief appeal lies in the fact that his is a new and handsome face and that, as a result of long years in leading-man roles in Grade B cowboy movies, he learned how to turn on charm before the cameras. He is the television-made Governor of California. When it comes to matters of substance, Reagan's appeal is to the far right. In his acting days he was known as a liberal of liberals, but then came the big switch. He went on the banquet circuit for General Electric, his message the favorite themes of the far right; and when he ran for Governor of California, there could be no question that he was the fair-haired boy of all who would repeal the Sixteenth (income tax) amendment and return to McKinley. Big money to finance his campaign poured in from all over the nation, and Republican Senators in Eastern states complained that they had difficulty financing their reelection campaigns because the party fat cats were shipping everything west to Reagan. As Governor, Reagan takes great pride in the fact that he has surpassed Georgia's Lurleen Wallace as the nation's gubernatorial champ in the number of vetoes he has written on proposed Federal antipoverty programs. He has cut back on educational and mental health funds. On the Vietnam war he has tried to out-hawk Johnson. On one occasion he suggested, much like Barry Goldwater in 1964, that the President ought to take the advice of the Joint Chiefs of Staff and do whatever they told him was necessary to win. He has blamed Johnson for not having authorized an all-out bombing blitz of North Vietnam when the bombing was started, and he has called for whatever measures are needed to "get it over with." Such a man could only be worse than what we have.

Another Republican alternative, Gov. George Romney of Michigan, has made a good record in his own state on domestic issues, but his position on the national scene has been marred by his vacillation on the Vietnam war. After failing to take any discernible stand for months, he finally made a major policy speech that, in essence, supported the Johnson Administration's war policies. Then peace sentiment began to sweep the nation and Romney switched, charging he had been "brainwashed" by the Administration and the military during a tour of Vietnam. His use of the term was disastrous. Americans hardly want a President susceptible to "brainwashing" on what is really a pretty clear-cut issue. Furthermore, though Romney's new statement seemed to align him with the doves, his real position remained obscure. He argued that we never should

259

have gotten ourselves involved in the war in the first place, but that now that we were in it we could not just get out. We would have to "see it through"—a position that was, after all, not so very different from Johnson's.

The most popular Republican Presidential prospect, according to the polls, was a man who has insisted repeatedly that he was not running—Gov. Nelson Rockefeller of New York. Rockefeller is a thoroughly modern man on domestic issues, and he has probably the most progressive record of any Governor in the nation on such problems as medical care, air and water pollution, and urban transportation. His stand on the race issue has been consistently intelligent and responsible. But on Vietnam the picture becomes cloudy. In international affairs, during his service in the Federal government under Eisenhower, he became known as a hard-liner. His hawkish tendencies were evidenced later when he supported the Johnson Administration's bombing of North Vietnam. However, when this action failed to bring Hanoi to the bargaining table, Rockefeller lapsed into a deep months-long silence. His repeated answer to questions about his stand was that he did not have "enough information" to make an intelligent judgment; that only the President and his advisers had all the facts and could tell what the real situation was. What Rockefeller's final stand on the Vietnam war might be is uncertain at this writing, but one point seems clear: There is no indication in any of his statements that he appreciates the interrelation between a global foreign policy and an impoverished domestic policy; there is no indication that he would have the vision or the desire to back an entirely new program, calling for a new assignment of priorities.

260

The one Republican who appreciated this truly gut issue and whose stand on it was clear-cut is Mayor Lindsay of New York City. Lindsay, through his service in Congress before becoming Mayor, has a clear understanding of both foreign and domestic issues, and he was probably the first major politician in the country to draw the line by saying that we could not meet the needs of our cities if we persisted in fighting a $30 billion-a-year war in Vietnam. Lindsay has all the wit, the personal charm and attractiveness of the Kennedys; he came out of the summer riots of 1967 with tremendously enhanced stature as the chief executive who had managed to "cool it" in the nation's largest city. And on the campaign trail he is indefatigable, with great vote-getting appeal. He would probably be the ideal Presidential candidate for his party in 1968, but almost certainly his party will not have him. The power structure of the Republican Party has been heavily weighted against anyone with the taint of liberalism (or common-sense modernity). The party would not have Nelson Rockefeller in 1960 though there was little doubt he could have been elected if he had wrested the nomination from Richard Nixon. The party was wrapped up in Goldwater in 1964 and failed to offer the country any reasonable alternative to Johnson. The record leaves little conviction that the party will act any more sensibly in 1968.

If it does not, the result for America could well be tragedy. It is a measure of the increasing irrelevancy of our politics to the realities and requirements of the age that the nation's best hope for salvation in 1968 lay with the Republicans—and that the Republicans were most likely to nominate Nixon or Reagan. Such men represent the kiss

261

of death, and this is a bussing for which the Republican Party has exhibited a marked fondness ever since the days of Herbert Hoover.

All one can do in the circumstances is hope—hope that the party can slake its death wish, hope that it can offer the American people a real alternative, hope that it can rally behind a leader with the intelligence and compassion to see and embrace the new tasks of a new age. The timing is imperative; the decision cannot be delayed. Either the nation will not be given a choice and the ineptitude of our politics will lead headlong to disaster or a new priority will be given to our crucial domestic needs and a new course will be charted on a compass reading that says: Let's put America first.

NOTES

Chapter 1

The opening observations are my own, and they reflect, I think, the feeling widely prevalent among those Americans whom the Vietnam war directly touches. Those whose loved ones are not involved may remain indifferent or become loudly belligerent, but among families of those who face the prospect of being drafted to fight in Vietnam, there exists a deep bitterness unmatched by anything I have seen in a reporter's lifetime. Some reflections of this may have surfaced in the polls as this is written. A Gallup poll in late July (*The New York Times,* July 31, 1967) showed that 52 percent of the American people disapproved of President Johnson's handling of the war and—even more significant—41 percent were convinced that the United States had made a mistake in sending troops to Vietnam in the first place.

Marshal Ky's expressed admiration for Hitler in July, 1965, caused a great flap in the U.S. State Department, which was trying to sell the American people on the idea that we were championing democracy and "the free world" in South Vietnam. A British reporter who had interviewed Ky quoted him as saying, "I admire Hitler." The South Vietnamese government on July 15, 1965, put out a "clarifying" statement which our State Department decided cleared up the whole incident. In this statement Marshal Ky said he had referred to Hitler only "incidentally," and that he "had in mind the idea that Vietnam needed, above all, leadership and a sense of discipline." Ky had no intention, he said, of "praising or adopting" Hitler's other "inhuman" views and methods. It seemed significant, though not to the State Department, that Ky did not deny the accuracy of the direct quote expressing his admiration, and his "clarification" seemed to add up to a considerable admiration for Hitler. (*Source:* Letter from Douglas MacArthur II, assistant secretary for Congressional Relations in the State Department, to my Congressman, Rep. James J. Howard, July 27, 1965.)

The quotes from Roosevelt's second inaugural address are taken from portions of the quoted text in *Roosevelt, the Lion and the Fox* by James MacGregor Burns, Harvest Book Edition, Harcourt, Brace & World, Inc., New York, 1956, page 292.

Statistics on current poverty trends are taken principally from the hearings "Federal Role in Urban Affairs," subcommittee on executive reorganization of the Committee on Government Operations of the U.S. Senate, U.S. Government Printing Office, 1967. See especially the testimony of A. Philip Randolph and Bayard Rustin, beginning with Part 9 of the hearings, page 1853.

For figures on the increasing number of American families earning more than $10,000 a year, see the financial page of *The New York Times,* July 28, 1967.

The description of the plight of Negroes starving in the South is based on the following: article by Gene Roberts in *The New York Times,* May 29, 1967; article by William Chapman in

264

the *New York Post,* July 10, 1967; *Newsweek,* July 24, 1967; article by Walter Rugaber in *The New York Times,* July 31, 1967; and the feature article, "It Isn't True That Nobody Starves in America," by Robert Sherrill, *The New York Times Sunday Magazine,* June 4, 1967.

Mayor Lindsay's testimony is from the hearings of the Senate committee headed by Sen. Abraham Ribicoff, previously mentioned. The quotes on conditions in New York are from Part 3, pages 552–553. Mayor Cavanagh's testimony and that of Mayor Sam Yorty are in the same volume. Cavanagh's begins at page 618; Yorty's at page 671.

For Ribicoff's estimate that one trillion dollars will be needed to rebuild the cities, see *The National Observer,* December 5, 1966.

Figures on the extent of our global commitment are from *Pax Americana* by Ronald Steel, The Viking Press, New York, 1967, pages 5–6.

The Fulbright quote on the contrast between war spending and domestic cutbacks is from *The New York Times,* October 15, 1966.

Senator Kennedy's quote on the need for a welfare "revolution" is from the *New York Post,* May 8, 1967.

For an excellent roundup of the summer riots and their causes, with special emphasis on Detroit, see "Battlefield USA" in *Newsweek,* August 7, 1967.

Rustin's quote on the attitude of Chicago Negroes toward Dr. King is from the Ribicoff committee hearings, Part 9, page 1854.

The Joseph Alsop quote is from his syndicated column of August 2, 1967.

The Rockefeller, Whitney Young quotes are from the

NBC-TV telecast of July 24, 1967; see also *The New York Times* of the following day.

The David Brinkley tax analysis is from the NBC telecast of the Huntley-Brinkley program, July 19, 1967.

Chapter 2

The views in this chapter are my own, and they hark back to a great extent to my earlier research for *The Warfare State,* Macmillan, New York, 1962. I have been encouraged, however, to trust my own thinking by two admirably reasoned books by Sen. J. William Fulbright, chairman of the Senate Foreign Relations Committee: *Old Myths and New Realities,* Random House, New York, 1964, and *The Arrogance of Power,* Random House, New York, 1966.

Virtually every knowledgeable Washington correspondent was writing in the summer of 1967 that Pentagon sources, who had so optimistically stated that we could bomb Hanoi to the conference table, were at last, privately, confessing we were in a stalemate. Especially vivid was the long reassessment of the Vietnam war and its prospects by R. W. Apple, Jr., *The New York Times,* August 7, 1967.

For an almost day-by-day account of the development of the Truman Doctrine and the onset of the cold war, see *The Cold War and Its Origins* by D. F. Fleming, Doubleday, New York, 1960. For another view of the development of the doctrine, see *The Truman Presidency* by Cabell Phillips, Macmillan, New York, 1966.

Douglas's quotes are from an interview in *Parade* Magazine, August 6, 1967; see also *The New York Times* of the same date.

266

Chapter 3

The Gallup poll conducted for the National Broadcasting Company was aired in a special NBC-TV program on the outlook for the 1968 campaign on November 10, 1967. Some accounts of the poll's findings appeared in *The New York Times* and other newspapers the following day. One statistic that was not mentioned in the press reports, however, was the one that showed seven out of every ten Americans now had no faith in the honesty of the political dialogue—this despite the fact that NBC had emphasized this was a question that had never been asked before and the finding was, therefore, new.

Drew Pearson's roll-call on our so-called friends who sided with Russia is from his syndicated column that appeared in the *New York Post,* July 11, 1967.

For background and much material on the course of the war in Vietnam, I am indebted to the following books: *Vietnam: Between Two Truces* by Jean Lacouture, Vintage Books, New York, 1966; *The Lost Revolution* by Robert Shaplen, Harper Colophon Books, New York, 1966; *Behind the Lines—Hanoi* by Harrison E. Salisbury, Bantam Books, New York, 1967; *The United States in Vietnam* by George McT. Kahin and John W. Lewis, The Dial Press, New York; *The Making of a Quagmire* by David Halberstam, Random House, Inc., 1965; *The New Face of War* by Malcolm W. Browne, Bobbs-Merrill, Indianapolis, 1965.

The Lacouture quote is from page 9, *Vietnam: Between Two Truces.*

The previously mentioned book by Salisbury gives an excellent, brief account of the career of Ho Chi Minh; Ho's quote from our own Declaration of Independence appears on page 49.

Lansdale's account of Diem's arrival in Saigon is to be found in Shaplen's book, page 103; Shaplen's quotes on the beginning of the war are from pages 138–141.

Lacouture's quote on the Diem witch-hunting is from page 52.

For the quote on the military's proposed solution in Laos, see *Kennedy* by Theodore C. Sorensen, Harper & Row, New York, 1965, page 645.

For an account of Lyndon Johnson's trip to Southeast Asia and the subsequent Taylor-Rostow mission, see *A Thousand Days* by Arthur M. Schlesinger, Jr., Houghton Mifflin, Boston, pages 540–550.

James Reston's account of his interview with Kennedy and the background for the Vietnam war came in an interview on the National Educational Television Network. An account of it may be found in *The New York Times,* January 18, 1966.

Both Browne and Halberstam in their books give vivid accounts of the Diem regime's police-state tactics and the attack on the Buddhists. The quotes on our perpetual optimism are from Schlesinger.

Kennedy's important quote laying down the guideline that it was "their war" was carried live on nationwide television; it is also found in Schlesinger, page 992.

For brief backgrounding on President Johnson's military ties, see Drew Pearson's column of July 7, 1966, in the *New York Post.*

An account of Bill Moyers's speech revealing the details of LBJ's first briefing on Vietnam appeared in Ted Lewis's column in the New York *Daily News,* May 31, 1967.

A thorough recapitulation of Johnson's dove-like 1964 campaign quotes appeared in an article by David Wise in the New York *Herald Tribune,* March 20, 1966.

The account of the Tonkin Gulf incident indicating that LBJ had drafted his sweeping authorization of power in advance of the event is from *The Accidental President* by Robert Sherrill, Grossman, New York, 1967, pages 253–255.

Katzenbach's testimony contending that the Tonkin Gulf Resolution was tantamount to a declaration of war may be found in *The New York Times,* August 18, 1967.

The American bombing of North Vietnam, one of the most controversial elements of the war, was also an important factor in the creation of the so-called "credibility gap," a polite way of saying that our government is lying to us. Our propaganda had pictured us as conducting the most antiseptic of wars. We had perfected pinpoint bombing control, we insisted, and only military targets—those specifically designated by President Johnson himself—were being hit. The truth was the very opposite. We had bombed whole cities out of existence. We had even bombed rural villages, far removed from any visible strategic targets. Harrison Salisbury's eyewitness dispatches from North Vietnam at the end of 1966 and the beginning of 1967 produced a national shock of comprehension for the first time, and brought down upon him the most vicious counterattack of which the Pentagon was capable. He was criticized on the one hand for having used North Vietnamese casualty figures without having specifically identified them, though it was inconceivable any other figures could have been available; and then the figures he used on civilian casualties, because they seemed low for the scale of destruction he described, were held up to ridicule, the plain implication being that they showed our bombing had not been so bad as Salisbury had said. To believe all this, one would have to believe that the North Vietnamese had phonied their own casualty figures to disprove that they were being bombed. What was even more significant—a point that, so far as I know, has not been appreciated to this day—was that nothing in Salisbury's dispatches could have been really news to Washington and the Pentagon.

269

Contrary to Salisbury's own belief and the universal assumption of the American press, he was *not* the first American newsman to visit Hanoi and report on the bombings. On Saturday, December 17, 1966, while Salisbury was walking the streets of New York preparing for his trip to Vietnam, I was in Chicago for an appearance on Irv Kupcinet's marathon Saturday night television show. The major portion of that program was devoted to a vivid description by David Dellinger, an editor of *Liberation,* of the widespread and virtually indiscriminate American bombing of North Vietnam. Dellinger had been there and returned; he had seen the bombed-out cities that Salisbury was soon to see; he had taken pictures, as Salisbury was soon to take them, of wrecked schools and hospitals. Not only was his description detailed and vivid, carried to hundreds of thousands of viewers of Kup's Show in the Chicago area, but a representative of the American State Department was present and participated in the discussion. In view of all this, Washington could hardly have been unaware that the truth was out. Yet, when Salisbury's dispatches broke in *The Times* a couple of weeks later, the Pentagon and Washington insisted on treating them as brand new revelations—and as the exaggerated disclosures of an irresponsible journalist.

I have made several references here to the reporting of R. W. Apple, Jr., from Saigon for *The New York Times.* The quotes I have used are from a long roundup article he wrote, "Vietnam: The Signs of Stalemate," *The New York Times,* August 7, 1967. The figures on the loyalty of the countryside are from this same issue of *The Times.*

Taylor's hard-line views on Vietnam and the world are clearly expressed in *Responsibility and Response,* Harper & Row, New York, 1967.

For an account of the CBS poll in South Vietnam, see column by Murray Kempton, the *New York Post,* May 5, 1967.

270

Stewart Alsop's interview with Saigon student leaders appeared in his column "Vietnam: Whose War?" in *The Saturday Evening Post.*

For a discussion of the Johnson Asian Doctrine, see *The Arrogance of Power* by Sen. J. William Fulbright, Vintage Books, New York, 1967, pages 52–53, 108–111. Dean Rusk's assertion we will fight aggression with or without a commitment is taken from his testimony before the Senate Preparedness Investigating Committee, *The New York Times,* August 26, 1966.

For article on Johnson's toasts as commitments, see the Associated Press dispatch from Washington in the *New York Post,* August 18, 1967.

Schultze's breakdown of our military and domestic spending was detailed in an article by Hobart Brown, the *New York Post,* August 16, 1967.

Chapter 4

The opening quote is from "The Shame of New York," which I wrote with Gene Gleason, *The Nation,* October 31, 1959.

The rat-control debate in Congress provoked a spate of articles. See especially the column by James A. Wechsler in the *New York Post,* July 25, 1967; article in the *Daily News* by Anthony Burton, July 22, 1967; Associated Press article on rat damage, *Daily News,* July 29, 1967; *The New York Times* of the same date; articles in the *New York Post* and *The New York Times,* August 5, 1967.

My discussion of the archaic structure of Congress is derived largely from *The Senate Establishment,* American Century Series, Hill & Wang, Inc., New York, 1963, by Senator Joseph Clark and others. This paperback book is essentially a verbatim transcript from the *Congressional Record* of the four-day debate (February 19, 20, 21 and 25, 1963) provoked by Senator Clark's attack on the Establishment. It has a foreword by James MacGregor Burns and a preface by Senator Clark.

Senator Johnston's quote is from Clark's preface, page 16.

Kennedy's inaugural quote is from *A Thousand Days* by Arthur M. Schlesinger, Jr., Houghton Mifflin, Boston, 1965, page 4.

The figures used here on the youthfulness of the American population are from an analysis by Peter Drucker in *The Public Interest,* Summer, 1966.

The quotes summarizing Senator Clark's feeling about the antidemocratic influence of the Establishment are taken from the preface to his book, pages 10, 15 and 16.

The cloture and noncloture breakdown is in Clark, pages 100–101; the Southern overrepresentation on committees is detailed on page 105.

The Douglas quotes, from which I have here used selected excerpts, appear in Clark, pages 122–129.

For articles on the coalition's domination of Congressional committees in 1967 see column by Clayton Fritchey, the *New York Post,* March 22, 1967; column by Drew Pearson, the *New York Post,* July 27, 1967; two columns by John Herbers in *The New York Times,* August 10 and 24, 1967.

For an account on Congressional weed-killing appropriations see Drew Pearson's syndicated column of August 23, 1967, in the *New York Post.*

272

Chapter 5

The first part of this chapter is personal reminiscence. The incident of the introduction of cotton-picking machinery in the South and the figures on its ultimate impact on the Mississippi Delta country are taken from an article by William Rugaber, *The New York Times,* July 31, 1967.

For further details on the impact of machinery on agriculture and other aspects of automation, see *The Wasted Americans* by Pulitzer Prize winning reporter Edgar May, New American Library, New York, 1965, pages 70–73.

For statistics and information on air and water pollution problems, including those relating to our population concentration, I have relied heavily on two 1967 studies by Justine Farr Rodriguez and Joan Mahfouz of the economic research division of the Chase Manhattan Bank in New York.

For other discussions of the pollution problem, see *Moment in the Sun* by Robert Reinow and Leona Train Reinow, Dial Press, New York, 1967, and *Crisis in Our Cities* by Lewis Herber, Prentice-Hall, Englewood Cliffs, N.J., 1965. I have benefited from the research of both in this account.

Staten Island pollution and its differing cancer rates was discussed in an article by Peter Kihss, *The New York Times,* January 12, 1967.

For articles on the seriousness of pollution and official warnings about it see *The New York Times,* May 10 and August 4 and 18, 1967; the New York *Daily News,* June 14, 1967; the *World Journal Tribune,* April 19, 1967; the *New York Post,* March 30 and 31, 1967.

Some figures on the overall cost of cleaning up pollution and other details are taken from a roundup in *Newsweek*, May 22, 1967.

For a description of a ride on the New Tokaido Line see an article by Charles N. Barnard in *True*, July, 1967.

For accounts of the new Pennsylvania streamliner see articles in *The New York Times* and the New York *Daily News*, May 25, 1967.

The estimates of urban growth and urban rapid transit needs are taken from the report *State and Local Public Facility Needs and Financing* by the Joint Economic Committee of Congress, U.S. Government Printing Office, 1966, Volume I, pages 306–307.

Chapter 6

The Peter Maris quote is from "A Report on Urban Renewal in the United States" in *The Urban Condition,* edited by Leonard J. Duhl, Basic Books, New York, 1963, page 117. For details on Negro concentrations in our cities, see Floyd McKissick's testimony before the Ribicoff committee, Part 11 of the Senate hearings, pages 2283–2336. See also "The Black Immigrants" by Ben H. Bagdikian, *The Saturday Evening Post,* July 15, 1967. For details on the Federal study of population shift, see Will Lissner in *The New York Times,* August 13, 1967.

For a succinct roundup of the Gallup poll results as contrasted with unemployment statistics, see "Look Homeward, America" in *The Progressive,* September, 1967.

A full account of the Bronx study was given in an article by Will Lissner, *The New York Times,* September 3, 1967.

274

Bienstock's quote and details on Negro migration are from *The New York Times,* July 28, 1967. The story of the Austins is from the Bagdikian article previously mentioned.

For details on lost jobs in New York City and the changing nature of employment, see the article by Homer Bigart in *The New York Times,* July 30, 1967.

A full account of Senator Kennedy's speech showing how official statistics understate Negro unemployment was given by Joseph Alsop in his syndicated column, August 2, 1967. A table showing results of the Federal subemployment index was carried in *The New York Times,* July 28, 1967.

The Brown-Dunmeyer testimony is from the Ribicoff hearings, Part 5, pages 1086–1115.

For details on groups living in poverty and what this means, and for Senator Kennedy's comments, see the testimony of A. Philip Randolph and Bayard Rustin before the Ribicoff committee, Part 9 of the Senate hearings, pages 1853–2013.

Excellent discussions of the breakdown of our outmoded welfare system are to be found in Edgar May's book, previously mentioned, and in Robert Conot's *Rivers of Blood, Years of Darkness,* Bantam Books, New York, 1967. The incident of the ghetto mother who became a high school teacher is from Conot, pages 127–128. The quotes on Senator Kennedy's attack on the welfare system are from *The New York Times,* May 9, 1967. For Ginsberg's attack on the welfare system, see *The New York Times,* May 10, 1967.

For material on the guaranteed national income idea, see *The New York Times* and the New York *Herald Tribune* of February 4, 1966, for details on the report of the Presidential commission. Moynihan's testimony was carried in *The New York Times,* December 14, 1966. Tom Wicker's column, quoted here, appeared in *The New York Times,* December 22, 1966. See also the editorial in *Look,* June 13, 1967.

My earlier discussion of urban renewal appeared in "The Shame of New York" in *The Nation,* October 31, 1959.

The New Haven urban renewal problem was discussed in an article in *The New York Times,* August 22, 1967.

Widnall's struggle with HUD was described in the syndicated column of Rowland Evans and Robert Novak, August 7, 1967.

For accounts of Mayor Lindsay's tour of the ghettos and the insurance industry's housing plan see *The New York Times* of September 14, 1967. Accounts of Senator Kennedy's proposed legislation and reactions to it may be found in *The New York Times,* July 13 and 14 and September 15, 1967; the *Daily News,* July 19, 1967; the *New York Post,* August 5 and September 13, 1967.

David Rockefeller's quote may be found in Part 7 of the Ribicoff committee hearings, page 1453.

The Cook County functional illiterate study is described in May's book, pages 79–80.

The Piven-Cloward article on housing desegregation in the *New Republic* is reproduced in full in Part 11 of the Ribicoff hearing transcript, pages 2301–2307. McKissick's quotes are from the same volume of testimony, pages 2285–2286.

For a discussion of ghetto health problems, see my own previous book, *The Plot Against the Patient,* Prentice-Hall, Englewood Cliffs, N.J., 1967. For updated figures on New York ghettos which I have used here, see an article by Joseph Kahn in the *New York Post,* September 1, 1967.

Professor Seymour Melman's estimate of our national needs domestically may be found in an article he wrote, "American Needs and Limits on Resources: The Priorities Problem" in a special issue of *New University Thought,* 1967, Vol. 5, No. 1 and No. 2.

276

Chapter 7

An account of President Johnson's speech to the police chiefs was carried in *The New York Times,* September 15, 1967.

The vote of the Senate committee on Thurgood Marshall, including some background on the hearings, was described in *The New York Times,* August 4, 1967.

The Watts hate quote is from Conot, page 260.

McKissick's quote on ingrained hatred may be found in his testimony before the Ribicoff committee, Part 11 of the hearings, page 2323.

The quotes of the Detroit soldier in South Vietnam are from an article in *The New York Times,* July 30, 1967. The quote from the young Detroit Negro on the streets is from the article "Postscript on Detroit: 'Whitey Hasn't Got the Message,'" by J. Anthony Lukas, *The New York Times Sunday Magazine,* August 27, 1967.

Jewel's report and the indifference with which it was received are described by Conot, pages 97–98.

For an account of the similar indifference to the warnings from Boston, see *The New York Times,* July 30, 1967.

For articles on the indifference in Washington and cutbacks of domestic programs for Vietnam, see the *New York Post,* December 14, 1966; *The New York Times,* January 2 and May 13, 1967; the Chicago *Tribune,* June 10, 1967.

The description of the Newark and Detroit riots is based on a day-by-day file of *The New York Times* and other newspapers during July and August, 1967. The comparisons with Watts come from Conot's book. On the Newark riots I here mention only the principal items of reference: column by Mary McGrory in the *New York Post,* July 18, 1967; article by Robert Terrell in the *New York Post,* August 15, 1967; article by Peter Kihss in *The New York Times,* July 20, 1967; article by Richard Reeves in *The New York Times,* July 22, 1967.

Similarly, on the Detroit riots my principal sources were the Lukas article in the *Sunday Times Magazine,* previously mentioned; *Newsweek,* August 7, 1967; articles on the Algiers motel slayings in *The New York Times,* August 15 and 16, 1967; article by George Larnder, Jr., in *The New York Post,* August 23, 1967; the *Daily News,* September 5, 1967.

For the mood of the nation politically after the riots. I again cite only the principal sources: *Newsweek,* July 31, 1967; the *New York Post,* July 27, 28 and 31, August 1, 11, 12, 14, 18 and 28, and September 12, 1967; *The New York Times* of July 24 and August 28, 1967; the *Daily News,* September 25, 1967; editorial in *The Saturday Evening Post,* August 26, 1967.

Senator Fulbright's quote is from his book *Old Myths and New Realities,* Random House, New York, 1964. See especially chapter IV, "The Cold War in American Life," in which he emphasizes that the Cold War has been at times a pleasant distraction, diverting our minds from more serious and more controversial problems at home. The direct quote on the resulting drain of brain power from the domestic economy to war-like pursuits may be found on page 126. For an additional discussion of this problem see the special issue of *New University Thought* (1967), especially the article "Humanizing Modern Technology" by Prof. Stephen Unger and the following discussion, pages 66–83.

Chapter 8

For the public antipathy to Lyndon Johnson see Ted Lewis's column in the *Daily News,* August 29, 1967; *Newsweek,* September 4, 1967; Pete Hamill in the *New York Post,* March 8, 1967; Mary McGrory in the *New York Post,* September 28, 1967; the Harris poll in the *New York Post,* August 12, 1967; *Newsweek,* August 21, 1967.

There can no longer be any reasonable doubt about the fact of the betrayal of the American people. Roger Hilsman, an intelligence specialist in the Kennedy administration and so privy to much inside information, has revealed in *To Move a Nation* (Doubleday & Co., Inc., New York, 1967) that the Johnson Administration's decision to seek a military solution in Vietnam was almost certainly made within a month of Johnson's taking office. Hilsman himself quit government service on January 20, 1964, "sure that the United States . . . was obviously going to take the military path—even though it climbed the ladder of escalation slowly and deliberately." Theodore Draper in his *Abuse of Power* (Viking Press, New York, 1967) has put together a devastating critique of the American position by an analysis of official American statements. He shows that Secretary Rusk's many-times repeated apologia that our hand was forced by the infiltration of the entire 325th North Vietnamese division into South Vietnam between November, 1964, and January, 1965, simply is not true. Former Secretary of Defense McNamara, who was in the best position to know, has revealed that it was not until the end of March, 1965—four weeks after we began our systematic bombing of the North, three weeks after our first combat troops had landed in Vietnam—that our intelligence confirmed the presence of North Vietnamese troops in the South. And then all we could find was a single unit, some 400 to 500 troops of the 325th Division, not the entire division.

Even at the end of 1965, when we had some 200,000 troops in Vietnam, the North Vietnamese had only some 14,000 troops in the South. The figures themselves tell much about who was the real aggressor. Draper shows that as early as March, 1964, a detailed plan for bombing North Vietnam and for large-scale ground action was on the President's desk. By July there were secret negotiations with the Saigon government for carrying the war to the North. And the President himself subsequently told Charles Roberts of *Newsweek,* as reported by Roberts in his book, *LBJ's Inner Circle,* that his decision to bomb North Vietnam was reached in October, 1964. That was the same month in which he was telling the American people in speech after speech that American boys were not going to be sent to fight an Asian war; that we would not go south and we would not go north; that we sought "no wider war."

My description here of the long chain of frustrated peace negotiation efforts is a condensation of a voluminous file on the subject. The final episode, the Ashmore-Baggs fiasco, is described in detail in *The New York Times,* September 18 and 19, 1967.

The direct quotes of the Nessen-Ky interview may be found in the *New York Post,* May 12, 1967.

The Frank Church-Walter Lippmann episode has been recounted many times in the press. Church's denial that it ever happened may be found in Sherrill's *The Accidental President,* page 267.

The Drew Pearson column detailing the frustration of anti-war Democratic Senators appeared in the *New York Post,* March 10, 1966.

For a succinct account of Senator Russell's opposition to the new deployment fleet idea, see *The New Republic,* April 1, 1967.

The account of Senator Russell's opposition to the Congo

involvement and his earlier silence despite his appreciation of the Vietnam danger is based on Don Oberdorfer's excellent portrait of the mood of key Senators, including Russell and Thruston Morton, in *The New York Times Sunday Magazine,* September 17, 1967.

The built-in frauds in our income tax system have been exposed many times, most fully by Philip M. Stern in *The Great Treasury Raid,* Random House, New York, 1964. For the newer details used here, see the following: column by Jerry Greene in the *Daily News,* August 15, 1967; column by Rowland Evans and Robert Novak in the *New York Post,* August 24, 1967; syndicated Washington columns of Andrew Tully, July 18 and August 17, 1967; columns by Drew Pearson, October 25, 1966 and August 12 and September 5, 1967 in the *New York Post;* T.R.B.'s column in *The New Republic,* December 17, 1966; and accounts in *The New York Times* and the *New York Post* of September 8, 1967, detailing Sen. Robert Kennedy's attack.

Senator McGovern's speech in which he estimated 90 Senators privately opposed the war was quoted in the *New York Post,* February 15, 1966. See also Ted Lewis' column in the *Daily News,* July 12, 1967, in which he described the suddenly altered mood of Congress in response to what its members had heard from the people back home.

Senator Morton's views are covered fully in the Oberdorfer article previously mentioned. See also editorial in *The Nation,* August 28, 1967, and the account of Morton's "brainwashing" speech in *The New York Times,* September 28, 1967.

Senator Case's surprise attack on the President was detailed in *The New York Times,* September 27, 1967.

For an account of the Cleveland and Charleston, W. Va., newspaper polls, see editorial in *The Nation,* August 28, 1967.

For the various polls mentioned here, see the *New York*

281

Post of April 3, July 31, and August 28, 1967; also, the New York *World Journal Tribune,* December 11, 1966.

For material on the youth revolution see "Don't Trust Anyone Over 30" by C. D. B. Bryan in *The New York Times Sunday Magazine,* July 2, 1967; article by George Getze in the *New York Post,* August 29, 1967. The protest by the Rhodes scholars was carried by *The New York Times,* January 27, 1967, and the Craig quotes are from a column by Joseph Kraft in the New York *World Journal Tribune,* March 25, 1967.

For a full discussion of the Administration's changed rationale for the Vietnam war see the lead article in the issue of *Newsweek,* October 23, 1967.

For further articles on the tax increase debate see the columns of Drew Pearson for October 30 and November 1, 1967, in the *New York Post;* for the backfire on LBJ's plea for support of his tax policies see the Associated Press article from Washington in the *New York Post,* November 8, 1967.

Chapter 9

The John Quincy Adams quote is used as a kind of foreword in Ronald Steel's *Pax Americana,* The Viking Press, New York, 1967.

Walter Lippmann has written repeatedly on the domestic versus global-policeman theme. See especially his columns in the New York *World Journal Tribune* of November 15, 1966; the *New York Post,* September 30, 1967, from which some of these quotes are taken; and *Newsweek,* October 9, 1967, from which additional quotes are taken.